# *Swimming Upstream*

To Sylvia
with love
& best wishes
from
Scarlett

*In memory of Bill,*
*whose support helped me to*
*continue swimming upstream*

# *Swimming Upstream*

## *A Jewish Refugee from Vienna*

T. Scarlett Epstein

VALLENTINE MITCHELL
LONDON • PORTLAND, OR

First published in 2005 in Great Britain by
VALLENTINE MITCHELL
Suite 314, Premier House, 112–114 Station Road,
Edgware, Middlesex HA8 7BJ
*and in the United States of America by*
VALLENTINE MITCHELL
c/o ISBS, 920 NE 58th Avenue, 300
Portland, OR, 97213-3786

*Website:* http://www.vmbooks.com



British Library Cataloguing in Publication Data

A catalogue record has been applied for

ISBN 0-85303-606-3 (cloth)
ISBN 0-85303-607-1 (paper)

Library of Congress Cataloging-in-Publication Data

A catalog record has been applied for



Typeset in 11/13pt Palatino by FiSH Books, London WC1
Printed in Great Britain by
MPG Books Ltd, Victoria Square, Bodmin, Cornwall.

# Contents

# Plates

# *Foreword*

As a young girl in Nazi-occupied Vienna T. Scarlett Epstein learned to think quickly and assess what had to be done to save herself and her family from the Holocaust. She carried out her plan, and her life has been shaped by the same quick thinking and determination ever since.

A refugee in England during the second world war, and with an iron will not unlike that of Scarlett O'Hara herself, she mastered the new language and went on to a take degrees in both economics and anthropology. Severely burned in an accident and in excruciating pain, she completed her university exams from her hospital bed.

In 1954 she visited India as a postgraduate student. This not only marked the start of a brilliant academic career, but was also to change her life. It was here that she saw and began to understand the roots of grinding poverty and the economic and social conditions of rural farming families. Henceforth she was to struggle to find a balance between the necessary distance required for empirical research and observation and her need to be a member of the human environment she studied so intimately.

Dr Epstein's research in two southern Indian villages resulted in a study that would become a standard for students of both economics and anthropology the world over. Twelve other books followed.

Dr Epstein's many professional achievements, often as the only woman in her academic circles, are charted, as is her family life. Her difficulties in having children and her enduring love for her husband, Bill, are movingly described.

Her autobiography is the story of a woman who, with her quick mind and sheer force of will, has overcome setbacks that would stop most of us in our tracks. Dr Epstein has spent all her life swimming upstream, seeking answers to the fundamental questions of human, social and economic survival.

**Richard Wasserman, Film Producer**
**Stockholm, Spring 2004**

# Acknowledgements

This book is the result of a tripartite effort, involving not only myself as author but also my two daughters. First and foremost I must thank my daughter Debbie, who spent a lot of time and effort on helping to get this book into its present shape. She acted not only as my consultant but even as ghost-writer for those parts of my story where deep emotions prevented me from stating what had happened or how I had felt. Michelle, my elder daughter, also offered a lot of helpful advice and guidance, which I much appreciated.

My thanks are also due to my brother Otto, to whom I feel I owe my survival. Without his help and guidance I guess I would have perished, like so many other Austrian Jews, in one or other of the German concentration camps.

Finally, I want to express my heartfelt gratitude to Frank Cass, whose generous offer of a publishing contract on the basis of only two draft chapters provided the encouragement I needed to make me settle down to write my autobiography.

# 1 • *Ordinary Beginnings*

I never thought that I would ever describe my life as swimming upstream. Like every other child I strongly believed that my dreams would come true and my life would unfold, as in the fairy-tales we all grew up on. I would go as far as to say that I had the precociousness to believe in my divine right to the future on my terms. From the outset I did not envisage that gender, religion or race could impede my rightful path, nor could I imagine the twists and turns my life would take.

However, I should first introduce myself. My name is Trude Grünwald and I was born into an ordinary family, on an ordinary day in July 1922, in an equally ordinary part of Vienna. I lived with my parents, Siegfried and Rosa, and my two elder brothers, Otto and Kurt, in a small flat on the second floor of an apartment house in the Brigittenau, a working-class district, where the poorer Jews lived. Our building was fairly nondescript with a depressing grey exterior, gloomy, airless corridors and a narrow, winding staircase. There was always a strange rubbery smell lingering in the hallway outside the concierge's flat. I always imagined it was a witch's brew, but later I learned that the concierge and her daughter carried out illegal abortions and burned the foetuses to dispose of any evidence.

Our apartment was small like all the others in the building; it consisted of two rooms and a kitchen. One room was the bedroom of my parents and the other served as our living-room, playroom and also my brothers' bedroom. This room had two large windows protected by iron railings, and I loved to sit and watch the world go by. Life outside always seemed to hold much greater fascination than the daily drudgery of my existence. Before Papa began working as a salesman in Yugoslavia I also slept in our multipurpose living-room but afterwards I was promoted to sharing the double bed with Mama in the other small bedroom. I treasured this time together, and it made us extremely close from a very early age. However, when Papa came home on visits a camp bed was put up for me in the living-room to allow my parents to have the bedroom to themselves. Our bedroom had only one small window which looked out on to the backyard, shared by a restaurant on the ground floor. How I longed for that restaurant to close down in the warm summer months, as they always deposited their rubbish in the open bins below our window and we had to suffer the smell of rotting meat and vegetables wafting in through our flat. Our kitchen was small and unfriendly, with enough room only for a large wood-burning stove and some shelves along the walls. We had no bathroom, but shared a lavatory on the landing with our neighbours, who were fortunately my grandfather David Löbl and my Aunt Thea.

Although our apartment was small, Mama filled it with love and tried to provide a happy home for us. We had lots of friends in our building as we all went to the same schools and led very much the same lives. Mama would often visit one or other of her friends in the afternoon and leave Otto in charge of the group of youngsters assembled in our apartment. All that she asked of him was to ensure that no one got hurt; otherwise she was fairly relaxed about our antics. We often played war-games using Papa's thick walking-stick as a canon, or Otto carved armies of soldiers out of large horse chestnuts that we had collected from the streets. Mama always returned to a flat that had been turned upside down, our furniture fortresses completely destroyed and our chestnut armies lying defeated on the floor. She was the tireless type: she rarely complained, but quietly returned the room to order.

Nearby there was a large park and, weather permitting, I often went there with Otto and Kurt, my two brothers, and a group of our young friends. As a little girl I had been given a doll's pram which I insisted on taking along on these outings. However, my brothers and the other boys were not interested in playing with dolls and used the pram for other purposes. Sometimes it was an ambulance in which they rushed me to hospital; at other times it was a fire engine or a racing car. I was always made to be the passenger in these various vehicles, and I was always terrified of being flung out to an early death, but never would I admit my fear in case of being ridiculed by the boys. Even at the age of five I was not prepared to exhibit any sign of weakness.

The Brigittenau was just like a Jewish ghetto as almost all our friends were Jewish and all the local shops and facilities were run by Jews. Some of them came from an Orthodox background, whilst others like ourselves were completely assimilated. Our routine did not include weekly trips to the synagogue, nor did we keep the Sabbath or any of the High Holy Days and we had no Jewish education. My Jewishness was never an issue as we were surrounded by people like us and therefore we never stood out as anything different.

I was the youngest of three children. Otto was born in 1912 and being a full ten years older than me I elevated him to godlike status and looked to him as my role-model from a very early age. I regarded him as my knight in shining armour as he was so brave and so daring and made me feel secure. Once a Catholic procession was stopped right in front of our apartment and a number of rounds of bullets were fired into the air by participating soldiers. Otto immediately rushed to the window to watch what was going on. I followed him, whilst Kurt and Mama hid, shaking, in the bedroom. Otto thus became the father-figure in my early life, particularly since Papa was away so much of the time. I had a very different relationship with Kurt, who was only four years my senior. I always viewed him with a degree of contempt, as he was a sickly child whom my mother was always fussing over, whereas I was an independent little girl, strong and tall for her age. I was often taken to be the older sister, which infuriated Kurt. We had an ambivalent relationship from an early age. I thought Kurt was sly and manipulative, whereas I was impulsive and hot-headed. At mealtimes he used to pinch me underneath the table, whereupon I would openly hit him back over the head. Mama, who was always so worried about his health and unaware that he had started the fight, always took his side and reprimanded me. She was never prepared to listen when I told her that he had started it all and that I was sore from where he had pinched me. During these exchanges between Mama and myself Kurt would put on an angelic expression as if butter wouldn't melt in his mouth. This of course only reinforced Mama's anger against me and my rage against him. Bitter experience finally made me realize that there was nothing I could do to persuade Mama that she was blaming the wrong person or to change Kurt's behaviour.

As the baby girl of the family I held the position of favourite in Papa's eyes and could twist him round my little finger. However, in the same vein I was teased mercilessly by my elder brothers who found various ways to torment their little sister. They often claimed that I was not really the child of our parents because I was not at their wedding. This obviously distressed me greatly and although I knew their argument was flawed I could not figure out the missing logic. Not only did my brothers seem to have the upper hand when it came to brains but they were also good looking – whereas I was cross-eyed, wore glasses and had lots of freckles. Mama admitted to me that she was also concerned about my looks, but tried to console me that even the most attractive people lose their good looks with age. She kept stressing: 'Looks disappear, but what you accumulate in your brain stays with you for ever.' Judging by photographs of Mama as a young woman she herself was not particularly attractive and must have been only too familiar with my angst and even called me '*Muttinko*' (little mother) as she must have seen in me a replica of herself, at least in appearance. Much as I knew she meant well, it didn't stop me from feeling like the ugly duckling of the family. Thus I grew up feeling at a great disadvantage with regard to my brothers, as I believed that I could not compete with them in looks, age or knowledge. Instead of being able to accept this I became a surly and moody child. To Mama's greatest embarrassment I often refused to greet her many female friends when we encountered them in the street. When she tried to understand my behaviour I explained that I couldn't see why I should have to pretend to be a happy little girl just to please her. Mama was a wise woman and simply uttered one of her many idioms: 'A smile and a kind word do not cost you anything, but they can get you a long way in life.' At the time, of course, I did not appreciate the wisdom of what she was telling me.

When I was a little girl I loved listening to Mama recounting tales of the days when Papa was courting her. She first met Papa when she was serving in a kosher delicatessen and he came to buy sausages for his lunch. His visits became daily events and Mama was flattered that this handsome young man took the time to stop and chat with her. He told her that he spent his evenings dancing and that he loved Viennese waltzes. He even recounted how many starched collars he had sweated through the night before, which greatly amused her. Mama had never been to a dance; instead she spent her evenings attending lectures offered free in the community hall and trying to read some of the books the various lecturers recommended. It appeared that Papa had the looks while Mama had the brains. Then one day Papa asked her to spend one of her days off with him at a place in the Vienna woods. At first she was too shy to accept, but having gained her father's permission decided to venture out. They finally arranged to go out on a day in the middle of Passover, which meant when they stopped at one of the little restaurants where they served the normal fare of frankfurters on rye bread Mama had to refuse lunch. Mama came from an Orthodox Jewish home and therefore could not eat the bread during Passover nor the non-kosher pork sausages. Papa, who came from an assimilated background, tried to convince her to tuck in, but she remained adamant for, she admitted to me later, she was sure that God would punish her if she ate such forbidden food. However, Papa continued to insist that she should eat something. He finally wore her down and she agreed to taste the sandwich, fully expecting that God would strike her down. The fact that there was no such disapproving sign from God was the beginning of her detachment from Jewish Orthodoxy.

Papa was less forthcoming with his tales than Mama, but he would sometimes sit me on his knee and relate his war stories from when he was called up and served as an NCO orderly in the Austrian army medical corps during World War I. At first he served at the Eastern Front in Poland and later in the Alps against the Italians. I well remember the box Papa seemed to treasure and kept stored away; it contained pictures of horribly mutilated war casualties. Otto, Kurt and I were fascinated by these gruesome images and often tried to get hold of Papa's box. It must have been Papa's war experience in the medical corps that turned him into a lifelong pacifist and a devoted supporter of the Austrian socialist party, as he later became one of a group of leading socialists who were involved in bringing about the abolition of the Austrian monarchy. I had never realized how integral to the movement he was until when I was at primary school one day the Minister of Education visited our school and my class. He spotted my surname in the register and asked me if I was the daughter of Siegfried Grünwald. When I answered 'yes' he asked me to convey his fondest greetings to my father. Being singled out in this way made me feel very proud of Papa.

Papa was also a member of the 'Free-Thinkers' Association' (Freidenkerbund) which made him a staunch atheist, so as a child we never celebrated any of the Jewish festivals, nor of course did we celebrate any of the Christian ones. Mama never seemed happy with her husband's atheism and denial of his Jewish identity, but she did not argue about it with him – at least not in front of us. It always seemed to me that Mama constantly had to exercise a huge degree of self-control. For in contrast to our Mama's quiet ways Papa was very excitable; when something upset him he quickly lost his temper and would throw a tantrum, although he never became physically violent. Papa never imposed any sense of a paternal regime on our household, but left most of the parenting to Mama. She was gentle but firm, and always tried to put the onus on us for any of our wrongdoings. If, for instance, she asked me to go and get something for her from a shop and I did not feel like carrying out her request she would always get her way by saying in a quiet and resigned voice: 'You are right in treating your mother like this; I obviously deserve this from you,' which made me feel deeply guilty and I would immediately do whatever she had asked me. In her gentle but manipulative way she got us to conform and carry out her demands. For instance, when friends of our parents volunteered to take us on an outing to the Prater, the famous Vienna fair-ground, Mama told us: 'Whatever they offer you, and even if you would very much like to accept, just say politely "No thank you".' So when Mr and Mrs Schwarz, a childless couple, took me to the Prater and generously offered me rides on the glittering Big Wheel or the prancing horses on the brightly painted roundabout, I simply said quietly 'No, thank you'. Having refused all their entreaties to let them buy me something they gave up, convinced that I felt uncomfortable in their company. On delivering me home they pronounced to Mama that 'Your little girl was not happy to be with us; whatever we offered her she declined by saying politely: "No thank you".' After they had departed Mama took me in her arms and said 'I am so proud of you.' I deemed her praise sufficient compensation for what I had forgone because I had followed her instructions.

Mama's role as head of the household was to increase further once Papa worked abroad. After the First World War Papa found it increasingly difficult to find work. He tried numerous different jobs, but times were hard and he did not do very well. Eventually, Mama's brother, our rich Uncle Bill, who had started the first textile factory in Yugoslavia, at Mama's request offered Papa the job of a salesman. Not only did this change Mama's role but it also changed our relationship with Papa. He was no longer an integral part of our family. He returned to Vienna only for the holidays, and we began to regard him more as a visitor than our own father. Mama always tried to revive our attachment to him by insisting that we wrote to him regularly, telling him the details of our lives, but this did not bridge the gap that now existed between us. Not only did the emotional framework of our family change but its financial stability was affected. Papa was paid in Yugoslavia, where there were currency restrictions, so it was always difficult to transfer his income to Austria. Thus at the beginning of each month it always took about seven to ten days before Mama received her spending money. She had to struggle to make ends meet, and by the end of the month she was usually out of housekeeping money and desperately waiting for the next salary payment to come through. We knew that during those lean days Mama would serve us meals that she could prepare by spending very little money; we usually had *Gulash Suppe* (potato soup with sausages) for dinner, which I loathed. It didn't make it any easier for Mama that I was a very fussy eater. Otto always said when I left plates untouched or took only very little, 'Eat up now or we shall get what is left over tomorrow in some other shape or form!' Not even this warning encouraged me to eat more. I criticized almost every meal that Mama put in front of me. This infuriated everyone, and my brothers threatened that they would reciprocate when they came to have a meal with me after I was grown up and married. They would embarrass me by turning their noses up at everything I offered them, just as I did to Mama. However, I simply replied that I would get a take-away so that they would never be able to complain about my cooking.

Fortunately for us we had a Jewish grocer, Mr Reis, who had become a friend of our family and who kindly allowed Mama to run up a bill which she would repay as soon as she received her monthly money transfers. I loved accompanying Mama when she went to that grocer, for he always took me behind the counter and let me pick a small quantity of whatever I fancied. He used to tell me when I was about 5 years old that he wanted to marry me when I was grown up, to which I would reply: 'But you are far too old for me.' He responded reassuringly: 'I shall stop growing older so that you can catch up with me.' I was not quite sure that he would be able to this, but at the time I was in no position to argue with him.

Life had been fairly routine up until now; school reinforced my relations with the boys and girls of my age who lived in our neighbourhood and whom I had already befriended. However, in 1930 my life was to change dramatically. The progressive postwar Austrian government pioneered council flats to ease the shortage of housing in Vienna, and Papa, as a staunch supporter of the socialist party, had no difficulty in securing a flat for us. Although I was upset about having to leave my friends behind, I was thrilled to find that the flat was brand-new with white doors and window-frames. It was also much bigger, with a living-room, two bedrooms, a hall, a kitchen equipped with a water-tap and sink, a toilet and a large balcony. There was still no bathroom or shower, but there was a central laundry where each tenant was allocated laundry-days and had access to the most up-to-date laundry and drying equipment. The same building housed baths and showers and we made use of these facilities at least once a week. (In between we used a bowl of water in the kitchen for our daily ablutions.)

The Karl Marx Hof in Döbling, the 19th District of Vienna, was in fact an experiment in community living. It was a huge oblong block, about 1 km in length and comprised over 1,000 apartments. It attracted world-wide attention, and many foreign dignitaries were taken on conducted tours round it. The then Prince of Wales (the future King Edward VIII) was one of these visitors. He turned up on a day when I was helping Mama in the laundry. We felt very proud to have seen an English prince in person.

When we moved to the Karl Marx Hof in 1930 I was in the second year of primary school, which meant that I had to transfer to a different school in the 19th district. I was extremely upset about being taken out of my familiar school environment and having to leave my close circle of friends. When Mama took me along to the primary school on the Grinzinger Strasse, which was within easy walking distance from our new flat, I was obstinate and refused to respond to the friendly approaches of my new form teacher. To Mama's great distress, I replied to all of the teachers questions in monosyllables, which gave the impression that I was stupid. It must have been very difficult for Mama not to lose her temper with her stubborn daughter, but I insisted on displaying my bitter resentment at our move about which of course I had not been consulted. Mama herself was ambivalent about our move: on the one hand she was happy about having a new and bigger apartment; on the other she felt uprooted from an area where she had spent most of her life. After we had been in our new place for a few days and she needed to do some shopping, she said to me '*Muttinko*, you come with me back to the Brigittenau so that we can do our shopping at our grocer and meet our many friends there.' Neither she nor I ever really felt fully at home in the Karl Marx Hof, and we went back to the Brittenau as often as possible.

I grew up in a large extended family: my parents each had several brothers and sisters, and most of them had children of their own, so I had many uncles, aunts and cousins. Papa's parents, Theresa and Leopold Grünwald, still lived in Boskovice in Moravia, which when Papa was born (in 1885) was part of the Austro-Hungarian empire. My grandmother Theresa was a tall, impressive-looking woman who dominated her husband both physically and by her personality. I never knew if or how he managed to support his large family, but he always struck me as a man ruled by and dependent on his wife. By the time I got to know him he was a small, elderly man who spent most of his days in the local coffee house smoking a pipe and playing cards with his friends.

During the summer holidays we usually went to stay with them in Boskovice, where the people all knew each other. Grandmother told me that their street had formerly been part of the ghetto where Jews had lived to segregate them from the Gentiles, though at the time I did not grasp the significance of what I was being told. When we reached the railway station at the bottom of their hill, the news of our arrival reached them long before we did. I can still see my tall, beautiful grandmother rushing to greet us with outstretched arms ready to clutch each one of us children to her large bosom and cover our faces with sloppy, wet kisses that we disliked intensely.

Once we had arrived, Otto and Kurt had numerous friends they were eager to see again, having already spent a number of holidays in Boskovice before I was included on these trips. As far as I remember I was only 4 years old when I first visited my grandparents. I did not know any other children there and clung to Mama like a limpet. We often spent time browsing through the clothes shops in the market-square to look for things for us, as it was a lot cheaper there than in Vienna. On my fourth birthday she took me with her to one of these shops where Leo, a young and goodlooking shop assistant, tried to distract me while Mama made her purchases. He chatted with me and when I told him that it was my birthday he went behind the counter and presented me with a lovely little doll. I fell in love with him instantly and treasured the doll for years. On subsequent trips to the market-square I always tried to get Mama to revisit that shop so that I could meet Leo again.

One summer Mama sent Kurt and me on our own to Boskovice. She put us on the train in Vienna with instructions that we would have to change trains at the Austrian–Czech border and be met by Papa's sister in Brno; she would then take us on to Boskovice. It all seemed straightforward. When we arrived at the border station we disembarked as instructed and followed the other passengers to what we assumed was the train to Brno. As we saw big notices outside each carriage which said not 'Brno' but '*Necuszarsi*' we assumed that this meant these carriages were going not to Brno but to a place called Necuszarsi. We walked several times up and down the platform looking for a carriage that would indicate it was going to Brno without finding one. We became very worried, particularly when we saw the guards preparing for departure. Fortunately, one of them noticed us youngsters looking lost and asked where we wanted to go. When we told him our destination he opened a door for us and quickly shoved us onto the train, shouting 'this carriage does go to Brno,' while the train began its journey. We were puzzled and settling in one of the compartments we asked a lady sitting there whether this train was going to Brno or to Nekuszarsi, whereupon she laughed and told us '*Nekuszarsi* does not indicate the destination but means no-smoking,' which made us feel really ignorant.

All of Papa's kin except for Leo, one of his younger brothers, lived in Moravia. This meant that I never really formed close relationships with any of them. However, I considered Uncle Leo as part of my immediate family, as living in Vienna he was a frequent visitor. I loved him dearly because he always played with me and often brought me presents. He seemed to know what made a little girl happy and gave me my first umbrella and swimsuit, which made me feel so grown up. Thus I was not only Papa's favourite child but was also spoilt by my uncle. Leo married Lintschy, a Gentile of lower social status, which not only upset my mother, but also the rest of the Grünwald extended family.

Grandfather Grünwald died a natural death in December 1936 at a time when Papa was home with us in Vienna. He took me with him to Brno for the funeral and we stayed with one of my aunts throughout the mourning period. During that period I met almost all my father's kin, but did not manage to get to know any of them very well. Armin, the youngest of Papa's brothers, is the only one of whom I have a distinct memory. He had his mother's impressive stature and her good looks. He was the most successful of all the siblings.

I presume Uncle Armin realized how lonely I felt among all these many relatives because he spent a great deal of time with me telling me about his experiences during World War I, which I found fascinating. Having been drafted into the Austro-Hungarian army he was taken prisoner by the Russians and invited to join a newly formed Czech legion which would fight against the German–Austrian alliance. As soon as the Bolsheviks had come to power in Russia and had made peace with the

Germans, the legion joined the White Russians and others engaged in fighting the Red Army. As that army enjoyed enormous popular support throughout Russia the legion was forced to retreat to the east through Siberia until they ended up in Vladivostok. From there, they were evacuated by the US navy, and finally in 1921 Armin was able to return to his family who were thrilled to see him. As they had not heard from him for many years they had resigned themselves to the fact that he was dead. Members of the Czech legion formed the nucleus of the army of the new state. Uncle Armin became a high-ranking reserve officer in the Czechoslovak army, which enabled him to enjoy a number of privileges.

Armin became my favourite uncle once Leo married and became estranged from the family. It seemed the affection was mutual. Whenever I met him he treated me more like a friend than a young niece, which of course I enjoyed immensely and felt all of a sudden grown up. He confided in me about his marriage: how much he loved his wife and the many problems her personality and preferred lifestyle caused him. I felt very close to him and told him some of my most treasured secrets, such as the hopeless love I felt for Hans Jaray, one of the young and good-looking Viennese actors whom I adored from afar. I kept his photograph hidden under my pillow and looked at it with longing every night before I went to sleep, knowing that I had no chance of ever meeting him in person, let alone getting close to him. Uncle Armin never thought my behaviour childish and always took me seriously. It was this that I admired about him.

My mother's maiden name was Löbl and she too had many relatives, but except for her father and Aunt Thea most of them did not live anywhere near us. Though Mama told me a lot about them, to me they seemed almost like strangers. As a little girl I adored my grandfather and loved to sit on his knee, listening to his tales of days gone by. I never knew my grandmother because she had died shortly before I was born. Unlike Papa who came from a completely assimilated background, my maternal grandparents were Orthodox Jews who kept a kosher home. When I was about 6 years old Mama took me to Stupova, a village near Bratislava in Slovakia, to show me the place where she was born and to visit her mother's brother called Leopold Kugler who still lived there with his family. He walked on crutches as he had lost a leg during World War I. He seemed a very kind and gentle old man to me. He and Mama reminisced about how her mother gave birth during nearly every one of her childbearing years. Being almost continually pregnant undermined her health, which made it extremely difficult for her to fulfil her family duties. As a result, my mother was taken out of school when she was only 9 years old to help in the house, as they could not afford to employ a servant. At that tender age she was expected to take charge of everything. Many of my grandmother's babies were stillborn or died very young. Mama became like a mother to her younger siblings. She established a particularly close relationship with Willie the youngest of her five surviving siblings, who was 14 years her junior. When in later life Willie became a successful and rich entrepreneur he never forgot the close bond that had existed between him and his eldest sister when he was a small child. She knew until her dying day that she could always count on his help and support when she needed it.

As a child I used to love sitting with Mama often late into the night listening to her accounts of what her life was like when she was a young girl. Her father was then a salesman for agricultural machinery. Being a pious Jew he realized his obligation to provide a new set of clothes for every member of his family every year for Passover which commemorates the exodus of the Israelites from Egypt. Each year shortly before Passover, a Jewish festival that always occurs round about Easter in early spring, Grandfather Löbl walked across the countryside visiting farmers who were his potential customers in the hope that they would purchase some of the machinery he was trying to sell. While trotting wearily across field after field he would raise his head to the heavens and reason with the Almighty: 'Why do you make life so difficult for me? For a change can you please make the farmers buy sufficient machinery from me so that I will have enough money to celebrate Passover in the way you want me to do. Is this too much to ask from you?' As spring is the time when farmers are prepared to invest in new equipment Grandfather usually made just enough money to meet his commitments. He would then turn once more to the Almighty saying 'thank you for having listened to me and helped me out of a tight spot! I only hope you will do this again next year!'

Grandfather Löbl died at the age of 65, when I was just about 4 years old. I seem to have a clear recollection of the day he died, or maybe I have been told the story so often that it has become ingrained in my mind so that I am convinced that I remember it. At lunchtime on the day that Grandfather died Mama had sent me with a plate of coconut biscuits we called '*busserl*' (kisses) next door to him. When I tried to get him to eat at least one he said 'I don't want coconut kisses but I would love a kiss from you!' whereupon I climbed on his lap and we hugged and kissed. He was always a very loving grandfather and I liked his cuddles, though his beard always tickled me. After lunch Mama took me with her when she went to visit a friend, while Otto and Kurt stayed behind. Shortly after we had arrived Otto came running after us. He told Mama that Grandfather had been taken very ill and that we should return home immediately. Mama picked me up and we ran home. However, by the time we got there her father was already dead. I remember Mama bursting into tears. This made a huge impression on me for I had never before seen her cry. Though at the time I was obviously too young to understand what death meant I deduced from all the ongoing commotion that something terrible had happened. Strange bearded men appeared and began to busy themselves around our place. This made me feel scared and I tried to keep close to Mama, but she absentmindedly lifted me up and put me gently on the seat which I had always been told was reserved for my brother Kurt and which I had never dared to use for myself. The fact that Mama had allowed me to sit there made me feel very happy and in my childish ways I did not care any more about what was happening around me. Only when I was older and recollected the happenings when my grandfather died did I realize the full implications of what had happened on that day and what a silly little girl I had been at the time.

Aunt Thea I remember as a reasonably attractive-looking but heavily built woman who seemed to have only one topic of discussion: how to find a husband. I often heard her talk to Mama how much she would love to marry. She lived with my grandparents and looked after Grandfather once Grandmother had died; she then stayed on in their flat after he too died. Before grandfather died he made Willie, his youngest and wealthiest offspring, promise always to look after Thea. Accordingly, Willie arranged to send Thea a monthly allowance which sufficed to keep her going.

Uncle Willie was too young to be called up during World War I, but not too young to go into business. He established the first cotton mill in Marburg (Maribor), a small town in Slovenia. He became quite a rich man. Being devoted to Mama, who had effectively been his mother during his childhood, he would give money to her from time to time to make sure that she was all right. He never had a very high opinion of Papa, whom he regarded as a poor provider, though in response to Mama's pleas he took Papa on as a salesman. Willie married a very beautiful 17-year-old school leaver, Aunt Grete, who bore him two sons, Hans and Paul, with whom we were also very friendly.

Thus my early childhood was fairly uneventful and the pattern of my life revolved, like most people's, around the large network of kin. Our neighbourhood in the Brigittenau was close-knit with a strong sense of community; my parents were known and respected and my brothers were popular. My life already seemed to have a map and I was navigating my route with apparent ease.

# 2 • *Storms Brewing*

Our move to the Karl Marx Hof heralded a new phase. Suddenly I became aware of something I knew nothing about. I was never aware of the concept of anti-Semitism in my early years in the Brigittenau. However, it was not long after moving to the more diverse Karl Marx Hof that I realized that from now on I was to be considered different: an outsider and an outcast.

I was 8 when it happened. Mama had just enrolled me into the local primary school and I was then eager to enjoy my last moments of freedom and explore the new play area. I noticed a number of children whom I had seen earlier, while enrolling. They were engrossed in a ball game, but appeared to recognize me. When I tried to join them they stuck their tongues out at me and shouted in chorus: 'Saujüdin, Saujüdin!' (Jewish pig). I was completely taken aback, and, deeply wounded, ran upstairs with the dreadful words still echoing in my ears. When Mama opened the door I threw myself into her arms and sobbed uncontrollably. Finally, I calmed down enough to explain to her what had happened. Choking back my tears, I kept asking why these children treated me the way they did: what was wrong with being Jewish? Why did it make me any different? In her wisdom, she tried to explain to me that these youngsters disliked me simply because they believed I differed from them. She also told me that she was sorry for not overruling Papa and never instilling in us a sense of Jewish pride so that we would be able to stand up for ourselves. It was so hard for me to comprehend why all my new schoolmates had taunted me.

Once school began I tried hard to hide my upbringing to try to make myself acceptable to them. In truth, I never did understand what was so different from their childhood and my assimilated one. Yet, as the school years passed it became increasingly obvious to me that even to my few non-Jewish friends I remained a stranger. The alienation in my own class was just about bearable, but since I was the only Jewish child in the whole school

I quickly developed a hard shell and concentrated on activities I could enjoy on my own. I became an avid reader and loved solving mathematical problems. Thus I became a studious young girl and was regularly top of my class. This of course did not endear me to my classmates, but I had ceased to care.

The only real friend I had during this period was Lizzy Mekler, the daughter of the Jewish family who had moved into the apartment above ours. Lizzy was two years older than myself and therefore already went to a girl's high school; she had a younger brother, Hansi, who was too young to go to school. Lizzy and I often confided to each other about the deep hurt we felt because we considered that our mothers preferred their sons and discriminated against us girls. Lizzy's father had an engineering degree but having failed to get a job in his profession he became a glorified bank clerk. Yet to preserve his self-respect he insisted that everyone address him as 'Herr Ingeneur' (Mr Engineer), which I found very amusing. Lizzy's mother was a sickly woman who had had an operation for cancer on her leg and was bedridden for days on end. This meant that Lizzy had to take over many of the domestic chores in her home, which left her little time to play with me; yet since neither she nor I were able to join other local youngsters of our age we stuck together as much as possible.

I had taken it for granted that I would join the high school to which both my brothers had been sent once I finished my primary education. However, Mama had different ideas on the subject. Though in most respects she was progressive and broadminded, she was convinced that it was a waste of money and effort to put a girl through higher education. She argued that since girls were destined to get married and have children their education was of little use. I was enraged and openly accused her of discrimination against me while favouring my brothers. That finally made her allow me to sit for the high school entrance examination. I guess she never expected me to pass. I was therefore delighted when I came top of the list of candidates.

The Glasergasse high school was located in the 9th District of Vienna, where a number of middle-class Jewish families resided. It was quite a distance from the Karl Marx Hof and I had to travel to school by tram. I joined a class of about 40 girls of whom about a third were Jewish. Finally, I could join in the games and discussions and my long days of enforced segregation were over, or so I thought. It did not take me long to make a number of close friends in my new school environment and we became inseparable. I told them about the isolation I had felt in the primary school which spurred us on to try to discover the roots of anti-Semitism. At other times we debated the merits of the evolutionary theories versus what we were taught in religious studies; we argued endlessly whether present-day society was descended from Adam and Eve or whether it was the result of natural selection and evolution. I was happy in this group of intelligent youngsters who enjoyed challenging each others' intellects: so happy indeed that I would often let a number of tramcars go by before running to get on one, suddenly remembering that Mama would be anxiously awaiting my return home.

During my first year at high school I worked hard to prove to Mama that I was at least as clever as my brothers. This got me a distinction in my school report. When I proudly brought my report home, Otto, who by then was a student at Vienna's technical university, praised me and, in a somewhat stilted fashion, kissed my forehead. I was so thrilled with this formal recognition that I silently vowed to work even harder the following year. I didn't realize at the time that to Otto this was no more than a joke – he was already then a budding amateur actor and in his own mind was simply playing the part of a father when he ceremonially kissed me. While I looked up to him with true adoration he was merely acting out the paternal role.

I did not agree with Otto all of the time. Once, when I was only 11 years old, I decided to read Sigmund Freud's *Introduction to Psychoanalysis* having been told about it by one of my high school friends. When Otto found me reading it he tore the book out of my hands shouting: 'You are far too young to understand what you are reading and if you do continue you will suffer for it in later years!' Finding his objection lacking in logic I retaliated: 'You can't have it both ways: either I do not understand what I am reading in which case it cannot do me any harm, or it may harm me, in which case I must be able to understand what I am reading.' He obviously resented his little sister questioning the logic of his argument and after a few more heated exchanges he threw the book back at me saying: 'You are welcome to it, if you insist!' I then sat up till late at night to finish reading the book. I often rebelled against Otto the way most youngsters rebel against their parents.

Although my schooldays were now happy and settled, the political scene in Austria was becoming increasingly turbulent. On 12 February 1934 the Austrian Social Democratic Party declared a general strike and the Schutzbund, their paramilitary wing, took up arms against the recently elected extreme right-wing government. A branch of this protective guard barricaded itself in the southern end of the Karl Marx Hof (we lived in the northern section). Overnight the atmosphere changed: people were tense and nervous. Nobody knew what was happening and there were people panic-buying, expecting the worst. Otto had joined the socialist Academic Legion, a branch of the Schutzbund which meant that he had to report for duty. Being responsible for his family he gained permission to check on us and return later. We were so happy when we heard his key in the lock, and so frightened when he subsequently left us some hours later.

As darkness fell Otto had to return to his assigned post. After he had left we sat motionless round the table. There was a deadly silence in our flat, all we could hear was the ticking of the clock. Suddenly we heard loud bangs. We looked at each other in shock, knowing that they were gunshots. We were all convinced that these shots must have been aimed at Otto and that by now he must be lying somewhere, injured or even dead. We sat petrified for what seemed an eternity to us at the time but in fact could not have been more than a few minutes. Then the doorbell rang and I ran to open the door, expecting bad news but thrilled when I saw Otto – alive and unhurt. He burst in on us telling us excitedly: 'The gunfire stopped me and I turned back as it was too risky to go on.' The release of our tension was so sudden that each of us coped with it in different ways: Mama busied herself with preparing a meal; Kurt withdrew to his books; while I kept hugging Otto, who seemed to feel very guilty for having let his comrades down.

The next few days were difficult for us all. The noise of the continuing exchange of gunfire was terrifying. Periodically the militia's armoured cars would tour outside and whenever they saw a face at a window they fired. We had no way of contacting Papa, who was on his travels in Yugoslavia, as the telephone connections in the Karl Marx Hof had been cut. We feared he would be very worried about us, hearing the disturbing news without being able to get in touch. Mama and Otto discussed what we should do and decided that it would be best if we tried to take refuge with the family of a colleague and close friend of Papa's. They lived in a Jewish quarter of Vienna, far away from any of the ongoing fighting. We expected that Papa would phone them to get news about us. Accordingly, we each took a small bag and packed a few necessities, put on our coats and sat waiting for the firing to stop. Otto instructed us that he would lead the way and indicate to us when and where it was safe for us to walk to get out of the building. When all was quiet we walked out of our flat. Mama locked the door and we followed Otto downstairs. None of us said a word. Otto carefully opened the front door, stepped outside while motioning for us to wait behind. Once he had established that it was reasonably safe for us to leave he waved us on, and we quietly walked across the deserted playground to one of the exits. In doing so, we passed the bodies of two young men lying at the entrance to another house. Blood was gushing on to the pavement. It was the first time that I had seen anyone dead, let alone lying in a pool of blood. I wanted to stop and take a closer look, but Mama took me firmly by the hand, pulling me after my brothers. Once we had managed to get away from the danger area Otto explained to me that the right-wing militia left the bodies lying there on purpose, to frighten other freedom-fighters from continuing the battle.

Without any more problems we managed to get to our friends' apartment, where we received a hero's welcome. They told us that Papa had been frantically phoning them to find out how we were coping. A few minutes later Papa phoned again and was reassured that we had all survived the fighting. I was still thinking of the men I had seen shot dead and told Papa about my frightening experience over the phone. His reply was: 'Please, my darling, stop thinking about these things – you are far too young to think of death', which did nothing to erase the vivid images from my mind. We decided to stay with our friends, hoping the situation would improve. However, the political situation worsened and everyday we sat glued to the radio waiting for news. We heard that the right-wing Dollfuss regime was overpowering the resistance, which was what we all feared would happen. Otto paced nervously up and down, expressing his concern for his friends involved in the fighting. Then it was announced that the Schutzbund had been defeated and that the Dollfuss government was again in full control. To set an example and prevent any more uprisings the government ordered the immediate execution of some of the commanders of the Schutzbund whom they had managed to capture. Two were colleagues of Otto, and he had told me all about them. So when we heard the news of their execution it was a great shock not only to Otto but also to me. It made a great impression on me as I started to realize that we were not always in control of our own destiny.

*

The success of fascist forces that had been unleashed by Chancellor Dollfuss in his effort to overpower all resistance meant that I had to face increased anti-Semitism not only from the Gentile girls in my class but more importantly from our high school teachers. I had thought that my definition of what was 'fair' or 'unfair' was fairly universal. However, I became appalled by the 'unfair' treatment our Gentile teachers were handing out to Jewish students in general and myself in particular. Mama tried her best to explain to me that it was necessary to accept the fact that as a Jewish student I had to behave and perform at least twice as well as my non-Jewish peers to warrant the same marks. To my young and rebellious mind this was the height of unfairness, but there was simply nothing I could do to combat the prevailing anti-Semitic attitudes. It was then that I began to resent that I was being persecuted for something of which I had never experienced any positive aspects. All I knew was that I was discriminated against because I differed from my non-Jewish fellow students, yet I had no positive identity of my own and I felt I did not belong anywhere.

These events coincided with the onset of puberty: a difficult time even in the most favourable circumstances. During this period I established an even closer bond with Mama, who simply encouraged me to study harder and read more widely. Much as I understood her rationale, it spoiled my chances of fun and pleasure that most girls experience during early adolescence when they start to have boyfriends. When I was beginning to experience the first intimations of womanhood I was so convinced of my unattractiveness that I could not imagine that any boy would ever want to woo me, let alone love me. As a result I was not interested in boys and feigned a tomboy personality. I was thus completely taken by surprise when at the age of 14, after I had stopped having to wear glasses and was no longer cross-eyed, during a summer holiday I was pursued by numerous boys one or two years older than myself. I guessed that a large part of their attraction was precisely the independence of mind I displayed, in contrast to most other girls of my age who were still giggling incessantly and acting foolishly when boys were around. While several boys began to profess their admiration for me I at first was convinced that they were just trying to make fun of me. It took me some time before I came to realize that my appearance was no longer as ungainly as I had thought. Once I had adjusted my self-image I became much more light-hearted and started to enjoy myself much more.

In the summer of 1937, on a trip with a youth group to visit the Paris World Exhibition, I met my first real boyfriend, Willie. He was three years my senior, also Jewish, bright and goodlooking. During the 1934 political upheavals when he had been at high school he acted as one of the leaders of the socialist student movement. After the defeat of the socialist rebellion he was imprisoned for one month and thrown out of school. When I met him he worked as an apprentice in a small engineering firm that was near the high school I attended. I fell head-over-heels in love with him. Almost every day I ran after school to meet him during his lunch-hour, and we met again in the evenings. It was with him that I shared the thrill of a first kiss. During the next few months I seemed to float on air, enjoying the emotions of young love. It made it easier for me to accept my teachers' anti-Semitism and their unfair discrimination against the Jewish students. I had my young love to keep me buoyant. Life was exciting. Willie and I went to concerts, plays, exhibitions, parties and spent every spare moment together. We got on so well that we even began to contemplate marriage in the future.

I would have to cast aside ideas of my future for the moment as my brief period of happy girlhood came abruptly to an end on 11 March 1938 when the German troops crossed the Austrian border and Austria became part of Hitler's Germany.

# 3 • *Instant Adulthood*

My well-laid plans began to go horribly wrong as my dreams of being a doctor and marrying Willie evaporated overnight. The morning after Hitler's Germany annexed Austria I tried to call Willie. Normally he rushed to answer the telephone, so I was surprised to hear his mother's voice at the other end of the phone. She gasped as she in turn heard that it was me, and in stilted tones – almost as if she was being strangled – she told me that Willie had been picked up by a group of Hitler's storm-troopers. He was seen by a group of his friends who had watched helplessly as he struggled, but he was restrained and bundled brutally into the back of a car and driven away. I felt as if I was on the roller-coaster at the Prater, careering to the bottom whilst my stomach stayed in mid-air. I wanted to be sick, but couldn't. I wanted to offer some consolation, but couldn't. Most of all I wanted to wake up from this terrible nightmare, but couldn't. I tried to regain composure as Willie's mother's resolve shattered and she collapsed in tears. She begged me to try to help her find her son. Hearing her sobs was more than I could bear and I tearfully assured her that I would do all that I could. I waited anxiously all day for Otto to return and as soon as I heard his key turn in the lock I ran to him. I was distraught and it took some time for Otto to understand my garbled words. When he realized what had happened, he put his arms round me and hugged me close. He then told me that there was nothing anyone could do to find Willie. Otto added that it was going to be a hard lesson for me to learn, how often life can play nasty tricks, over which one has no control. I hated Otto then for being the bearer of such news and could not imagine life without Willie. I so wanted to grieve for Willie, for our dreams and for myself. However, I was not allowed the time to spend reading and rereading Willie's letters and gazing at his photograph, as I was thrust into a whirlwind of even more life-threatening events.

Fortunately, we had stopped Papa from returning home from Yugoslavia to participate in the referendum. The irony was that this was the poll to determine whether the Austrian people wanted to retain their independence or become part of Germany. The voting had been scheduled to take place on Sunday, 13 March 1938. However, Hitler had managed to forestall the referendum by annexing Austria two days prior to that date. Thus Papa never personally experienced what it was like to live under Hitler's rule. Mama was shocked and debilitated by the turn of events. Kurt was similarly affected, but Otto immediately rallied and began plotting and planning how to save his family.

On the second day after the Anschluss Mama, Kurt and I sat huddled together wondering what would happen next. Suddenly, the doorbell rang. Having already heard that a number of our Jewish friends had been taken away, we cowered in the bedroom hoping that whoever was at the door would simply go away. Suddenly, we heard a voice through the letterbox pleading with us to be let in. We recognized the voice as being the non-Jewish assistant of Camilla, Mama's friend, the one and only Jewish shopkeeper in the Karl Marx Hof, so we immediately rushed to let her in. Tearfully she told us that when she saw that the Nazi hooligans were making their way over to the shop she quickly emptied the till, took all the cash and fled out of the back door. She told us that she made sure that no one was following her. She had decided to come to us as we were the only friends of Camilla's that she knew in the neighbourhood. She left the money with us and quickly returned to the shop. On the one hand we were impressed by her presence of mind and courage, but on the other we were immediately worried that someone might have seen her come up to our flat. Mama and Kurt looked petrified, but I knew we needed to act. I took the bundle of money and found a safe hiding-place for it. About an hour later Camilla herself hammered on the door. As we slowly opened it she collapsed in a heap. She had been beaten black and blue and had blood pouring from several deep gashes on her face. Mama was so shocked when she saw her friend that she started to tremble violently and was incapable of doing anything. I was also horrified by Camilla's treatment at the hands of the Nazis but I reacted very differently. I became very calm and immediately took control, cleaning and bandaging the wounds and trying to reassure everyone. Maybe I was imagining being the doctor I had always dreamed of becoming, or was it simply that I needed to remove myself from the reality as it was too frightening to comprehend?

Some hours later I took Camilla home and returned the money her assistant had deposited with us. As the days passed I heard that more and more of our Jewish friends had been whisked away or terrorized by young uniformed Nazis. We spent our days at home, waiting for the imminent knock at the door, and we were all so jittery that we jumped every time someone spoke to break the silence that had descended on us. We huddled around the radio, hoping for some news that would restore our safety, or read the increasingly censored newspapers that told of the evil deeds Jews had committed. During the day I managed to put on a brave face, but at night I let down my guard and lay in bed sobbing, pondering the eternal question of why Jews were subjected to all these atrocities. I usually fell asleep wishing that I would not have to wake up again the next morning.

Soon after, on the day of Hitler's triumphant entry into Vienna, Otto ventured out to see some friends of his. He phoned and gave me instructions to dress up in the uniform of the association of fascist girls: white blouse, navy skirt, white knee-length socks and black shoes. Once I had done this I was to take our four passports to the Yugoslavian embassy where I was to ask to see Mr Maidanatz from whom I should request visas for our passports. Naïvely, I thought it all sounded very easy and straightforward. Otto gave me the address of the Yugoslavian embassy and directions on how to get there. Mama was terrified and kept murmuring quietly to herself that I should not be going out alone into the inner city. I kept reassuring her that Otto would never have sent me on a dangerous mission. He had sounded so matter of fact on the telephone that there could be nothing to worry about. I felt nervous but excited at being asked by Otto to undertake this mission. I took the underground where I joined the throngs of people travelling to the inner city to welcome Hitler, the Führer. Public transport was free that day to encourage as many people as possible to turn up for his speech. I hadn't realized that the Yugoslavian embassy was near the Schwarzenberg Platz, a big square where the official welcome for Hitler was being staged. This meant that I had to walk along the Ringstrasse, the circular road that surrounds Vienna's inner city, just at the very moment when Hitler's cavalcade was passing. Crowds of people had gathered there and on seeing Hitler they raised their right arms in unison in the Hitler salute, shouting 'Heil Hitler! Heil Hitler!' It was as if a spell had been cast over them as they behaved as if one. It was frightening as I found myself carried away by this mass hypnosis and joined in the shouting and also gave the salute. Once Hitler and his entourage had passed and the crowds began to disperse I felt amazed at myself for having joined so enthusiastically in welcoming Hitler. While walking along to the Yugoslavian embassy I kept asking how could I have shouted 'Heil Hitler' when the last thing I had wanted to happen was for Hitler's Germany to annex Austria? I would have been terribly ashamed had any of my Jewish friends been able to observe me welcoming Hitler to Vienna. Then I told myself that had I been the only one in this large pro-Hitler crowd who had failed to salute, the people standing next to me would probably have lynched me. Perhaps my spontaneous and unintended participation saved my life.

Arriving at the embassy I encountered a long queue of people who were obviously Jewish and who presumably had also come to enquire about visas. They looked at me, in my Nazi Youth disguise, with contempt and hatred, seeing a fascist girl. I was at a total loss as to how to handle the situation, so I tried to shrug it off and get on with the task in hand. I made my way through the queue to a fair-haired young official who was trying to keep the crowd in order, and asked him where I could find Mr Maidanatz. He must have assumed I was a family friend as he immediately took me into the inner courtyard of the embassy building. I still remember the impressive staircase as I looked about me in awe. We came to a door marked 'Ambassador's Private Quarters'. The official tapped lightly at the door, and when a tall man opened it my guide pushed me inside and said 'Mr Maidanatz, this young lady asked to see you personally.' Having thus introduced me he closed the door behind me and disappeared.

To my greatest surprise Mr Maidanatz, this tall, good-looking man, turned out to be the Yugoslavian ambassador to Austria. Otto had not told me who exactly Mr Maidanatz was, and foolishly I had forgotten to ask him. It had simply never occurred to me that Otto would send me to the ambassador without warning me first or briefing me on how I was supposed to behave. I couldn't quite believe the situation he had put me in and for a few moments stood dumbfounded, facing the ambassador. To calm myself down and in a vain attempt to try to hide my acute embarrassment, I started to look around the room. It was typical of the old inner-city houses, with ornate, high ceilings and windows from floor to ceiling. The rich colours in the brocade curtains complemented the numerous pieces of beautifully carved baroque furniture. It was a lovely room, but I noticed that it was very untidy: papers were piled on the floor and the furniture was strewn with files. In the middle of the room was a large semi-filled trunk and numerous empty boxes. Mr Maidenatz was obviously packing in a hurry. However, he had stopped, waiting for me to speak.

For some time we stood facing each other silently until he asked: 'What can I do for you, young lady?' I replied (as instructed by Otto) that I was there to collect visas for my family. With this I removed the passports from my handbag and tried to hand them to him. He looked at the passports. I was sure that seeing the surname Grünwald he would realize that we were Jewish, but he never alluded to it throughout our encounter. He seemed bemused by the cheek of this young girl and, smiling, asked me who had recommended me to approach him personally. I quickly realized that it would sound foolish if I replied that it was my elder brother Otto. So, on the spur of the moment, I said it was my uncle, who I knew was a big industrialist in Yugoslavia and whose name and that of his large business it occurred to me might possibly be familiar to Mr Maidanatz. This answer seemed to satisfy him, though I never found out whether he had ever really heard of my uncle or of his business. Anyway, he proceeded to explain to me that he, the ex-ambassador, was about to return to Yugoslavia, and that since Austria had ceased to be an independent country, diplomatic matters would now be handled by a consul. He therefore had no power to issue any visas.

On hearing this, my heart sank. I had got this far and I couldn't believe that now I would have to return home empty-handed. Otto would be so disappointed in me. I felt tears coming to my eyes, but I knew that I had to maintain my composure and think on my feet. I doubt whether Mr Maidanatz, who was watching me closely, realized that I was undergoing a dramatic change in front of his eyes. I suddenly realized the implications of not getting the visas. Initially it had been about letting Otto down, but it was now a question of survival. I was not going to leave without our passports stamped and dated. I was scared of outstaying my welcome, but I had to secure the visas. I quietly but firmly told him that I was sure that there must be something that he could do. To which he replied charmingly that if I believed he could help then he had better see what could be done. Whereupon he bent down and, gently putting his arm round my shoulder, ushered me through the door that connected his private residence with the consular offices where he introduced me to the consul, his successor. Referring to me as his 'young Viennese girlfriend', he urged his colleague to help me obtain our Yugoslavian visas as soon as possible. Having said this he shook my hand wished me good luck and left. I have neither seen nor heard from him since, but I have always remembered him with affection. Not only was he instrumental in ensuring that we got our visas but he also helped me find strength and determination when I needed it most.

It took a few months before we actually managed to get the visas; in the meantime I always had free access through the back door to the Yugoslavian consular offices. When I finally collected our visas the consul could not resist enquiring how I had come to be a personal friend of the former ambassador. I simply answered with a mysterious smile and left it at that. Little did he realize that it had all been due to Otto's ingenuity. On my return from the embassy I triumphantly related my encounter with Mr Maidanatz and quizzed Otto as to how he had known to ask for him. He replied with a broad grin that he had checked the previous year's Yugoslavian visa. It was signed by a 'Maidanatz', and so he had reasoned that this must be the man responsible for the issue of visas. Since that day, whenever I have needed anything from an agency or organization I have always tried to find out the name of the person who heads it and contact them personally.

All the schools in Austria were closed for two weeks after the Anschluss. When they reopened and I met again my small group of Jewish girlfriends we were all very depressed and exchanged experiences and tales of anti-Semitic atrocities. As we entered our classroom we were immediately segregated from our non-Jewish classmates and ordered to go to the back of the room. Our headteacher made a speech telling us that there were now new and welcome rules which separated Aryan from Jewish pupils. We were ordered out of the school and had to change to an all-Jewish high school in the Albertgasse, which had become the coeducational school for the local Jewish children. We couldn't believe it: the teachers were all newly appointed young Nazis with no teacher-training or experience, and they treated us like subhumans. To top it all, a group of Nazi storm-troopers had established a meeting-place for themselves round the corner from our new school. This meant that not only were we subject to Nazi taunts and ridiculing in school but also on the way to and from school. The young Nazi storm-troopers of course knew that we were all Jewish, and every morning they would round up a number of us to polish their boots or clean out their cupboards or mop up the dirty floors in their quarters. I felt so angry at the injustice. I had done nothing to deserve this, but here I was polishing boots and cleaning toilets. I very much wanted to hurt these young Nazis, but of course realized that we were powerless; they had guns and batons and we knew all too well that they would not hesitate to use them. I learned to pretend that I readily accepted these indignities, but inside I was seething. Where were my happy schooldays, the friendships, the long debates, the outings? I had always needed answers and all of a sudden there weren't any.

School attendance was still compulsory even for Jewish children, though there was little formal education in these Jewish-catchment schools. Only two of the girls from my high school had gone on to the Albertgasse school with me; the others had either managed to leave Austria or their parents still had enough money to send them to private schools. So not only had I been forcibly removed from my school but I had also lost contact with my close circle of friends. I established a new set of friends and we tried hard to create a semblance of normality by having all-night parties in different homes where we would snuggle up to our boyfriends and try to bury our constant injustices in young love. I started seeing Freddy, the son of a rich Jewish family, and though I was still dreaming that Willie would return, I quite liked him. We began to go out with each other as much as possible under the constraints imposed on us. He then still lived in what seemed to me like a mansion and bestowed gifts upon me which made me feel like a queen. Mama was worried when I stayed out some nights, but I insisted that it was safer for me to walk home during the day than during the night. Since I had taken a dominant position in our household Mama had no other option but to accept this rather unruly behaviour for a girl not yet 16 years old.

On the last day of the school year our young Nazi teacher turned up in his storm-trooper's uniform. While handing out our school reports he said, with some degree of malice: 'I sincerely hope that very few of you will be able to get out of Austria. If any of you do manage to leave it doesn't really matter as you'll all end up in the gutter where you belong.' As I listened to his parting speech I vowed that I was going to prove him wrong. After that last school session in Vienna I gladly accepted Freddy's invitation to join him at his home for the afternoon. We sat close together and after kissing me he whispered in my ear: 'I shall love you even in the gutter!' which made both of us burst out laughing and helped to relieve the tension that had built up.

Life had changed dramatically at home: since the Anschluss Mama had been a different person and a role-reversal had taken place in our relationship. I no longer tried to unburden my worries by confiding in her, for I realized she had lost the emotional strength to accept additional worries on top of her own. I couldn't even tell her about the awful last session at school, though I desperately wanted her to put her arms round me and make it better. I tried to look to Otto for emotional support, but he was too busy organizing our lives and trying to arrange our escape. As a result, I had to become emotionally self-sufficient, which meant that I acquired an increasingly hard outer shell while remaining frightened and vulnerable inside.

It was now extremely dangerous to move about Vienna without the Nazi uniform, or at least a swastika badge, and we were increasingly concerned about Otto's constant errands. Soon after the Anschluss Otto received a letter from a Mr Simon, a London Jewish car-dealer, asking how he could help. They had met and become friends the previous summer when Otto and Kurt were hitchhiking in Austria and had been given a lift by Mr and Mrs Simon. Otto ingeniously managed to produce fake backdated business correspondence, with Mr Simon's conivance that enabled him to obtain a visa and travel to England. Though of course we were happy that he was able to leave, when we said our farewells we felt like individuals condemned to an indefinite prison sentence while watching one of the inmates being released. Otto of course kept reassuring us that he would move heaven and earth to get us out too. I was devastated. I was 16 years old and now in charge of the family with no support. Where had my childhood gone?

After Otto's departure in May 1938 Mama fell into even deeper despair. The isolated Nazi atrocities that had been happening around us escalated and rumours started circulating about unmentionable incidents on a much larger scale. Mama became scared to venture out of our apartment and seemed to withdraw into herself. Kurt also considered it extremely hazardous to go about Vienna, scared of what might happen to him. This left me to make not only most of the errands but also most of the decisions. Mama was petrified whenever I left our flat, but we needed food and I still had to run to the embassy to check on the status of our visas. I was also curious to see how Vienna was responding to Hitler's regime. Once I dressed in the uniform of the Nazi youth to hide my true identity and made my way to the Jewish area where I had heard that the Nazis had been demonstrating their new-found powers.

I saw with my own eyes how old Orthodox Jews dressed in their long robes were rounded up and ordered by young stormtroopers to take off their hats and replace them with buckets full of water. Then they were told to run round in circles and not to spill a drop of water. As they ran, the water spilled and they were whipped mercilessly. Finally they collapsed one after another and drenched with water and sweat they lay on the ground exhausted. Their young tormentors were so amused by the scene that they were doubled up with laughter. I observed all of this motionless, for to display disgust at their treatment would have given me away. I was deeply shocked by the inhumanity of these young hooligans and disappointed that the old men hadn't tried to resist, although I knew that it would have been in vain. Then I saw it – a glimmer in their eyes. I then realized that none of them had been touched by the ridiculous spectacle of them running around; they had all retained their self-respect and dignity. They all had this serene expression on their faces as if they pitied their tormentors and forgave them because they were the chosen people and it would take a great deal more to break their spirit.

As I walked on I saw another group of Jewish men, this time some of the more assimilated, subjected to similar indignities, and I was struck by the difference in their response. They looked completely defeated and even after their tormentors had disappeared from the scene they just lay there seemingly unable to rally themselves. It was the first time I had an inkling of what it meant to be Jewish and I swore that if I managed to get out alive I would try my best to instil in my children a positive Jewish identity.

While we remained in Vienna we received regular letters from Papa, who repeatedly told us how worried he was about us, and from Otto who kept us informed of what he was doing to enable us to join him. It made us feel much better to know that we hadn't been forgotten and that we had contacts in the outside world who cared, but it didn't help our immediate problems. Shortly after Otto got to London he informed us that he had heard from one of his friends living in Milan that one could get into Italy by plane even if travelling with a passport that had a big red 'J' on its front page indicating that the holders were Jewish. The Italian government had not worked out that airports were also border stations just as railway stations were. This meant that refugees arriving by train were not allowed to enter Italy, but those arriving by plane at some inland airport were regarded as having already entered the country, and were allowed to stay in the country without restriction. This was the chance we needed to get Kurt out. In response to Papa's request Mama and I stayed on in Vienna waiting until we would get our Yugoslav visas and join him.

Once again I put on my Nazi Youth outfit and made my way to the CIT Italian travel agency to try to get Kurt a plane ticket. I soon found out that other people must have had similar ideas, for the first available flight was 29 June 1938, more than three weeks away. Without thinking twice I handed over the money. Pleased with myself for having once more successfully completed my mission I presented the ticket to Kurt who merely demanded why he would have to wait so long? I was furious, no one appreciated me or acknowledged my doings. Instead of receiving thanks and congratulations I was faced with his selfish concern for himself. Finally the day of his departure dawned and Mama was distraught and in tears. Much as she didn't want to favour any one of us over the other, she had admitted to me that Kurt always held a special place in her heart. She explained that this was so because he was born not long after the end of World War I, when she had been without news from Papa for many months and while carrying his child she did not know whether he was alive or dead. Then, without any prior notice, Papa turned up just in time for Kurt's birth. (Under the disarray of a lost war when he found himself in Italy he had left the army and walked home to be reunited with his wife as quickly as possible.) This made Mama feel as if Kurt had helped to bring her husband back to her and so made him special to her.

I knew that it would be traumatic for Mama to watch Kurt leave, not knowing if she would ever see him again. I had planned to accompany Kurt to the airport and wanted Mama to stay home, but she insisted on coming. The three of us took a taxi to the airport bus station. However, when we got there we learned that only people with flight tickets were entitled to use the bus. It seemed as if nothing would ever be straightforward again. I suggested we say our farewells at the bus stop but Mama insisted that we should see Kurt off at the airport. Seeing how upset she was, and not wanting to make things worse for her, I hailed a taxi and we tried to follow the bus on which Kurt was travelling. This was not so easy as there were many delays on the road. I sat with Mama in the back of the taxi, holding her hand and trying to calm her down. When we finally reached the airport we were just in time to watch Kurt walk from the terminal building to the plane and wave to him. We then made our long journey home, hardly saying a word. I knew that Mama was shattered and on arrival home she sat anxiously waiting for his phone call informing us of his safe arrival. It was a great relief when it finally came.

Now I only had to worry about Mama and myself. I increased my visits to the Yugoslavian consulate and each time was told dismissively that our visas would be available shortly. I finally collected our visas two weeks after Kurt's departure. I rushed to tell Freddy the good news. He was obviously thrilled, but it made him all the more worried at being left behind and apart from me. His parents were trying to get them all to England; I never found out if they succeeded.

I raced home from Freddy's with the good news. Mama simply shrugged and returned to her morose state. I had hoped that this would help to lift her from her depression, but it seemed to have no effect. Her only response was that we would have to pack all of our belongings, all the many things she had accumulated over the years. I had thought that we would just pack our clothes and a few other things in suitcases and leave. This meant we had to arrange for a removal company to pack our furniture and goods into a large container, whilst Mama and I packed the smaller boxes. As we were sorting out what to pack and what to throw away I came across a little parcel containing Willie's love letters as well as a few of his photographs. Since he had been taken away I had never heard from him or found out where he was. Though I could never say it, inside I had come to accept that he must have been killed. I stopped, transfixed, as I saw a flash of what my life was supposed to have been. I started to sob, knowing that they had no part in this new life. I threw them out, one by one, and I felt a little part of me go with each letter. At least the Nazis would never get hold of them now. As Mama sorted she found the three medals Papa had been awarded for his service in World War I. It seemed ironic that we were being forced to flee. She decided to place the medals under the lid of one of the big cases to indicate to any Nazi who might open our boxes that Papa had been a recognized Austrian citizen even though he was now being denied the basic human right of citizenship.

Mama also found three gold crowns. I remembered her sometimes showing them to us, explaining that there would be one for each of us when we were grown up. They meant so much to her that she could not possibly leave them behind. We knew that they would be confiscated if they were found so we decided to hide them under the filling in the bread rolls that we had prepared for our train journey. We thought that if a guard became suspicious and they asked to inspect the rolls we would quickly swallow the coins.

We left the Karl Marx Hof on 23 July 1938. Neither of us shed a tear or even looked back at the home we were leaving behind. For it had ceased to be a home during the past few months; rather it had become a prison from which both of us were pleased to be released. Freddy came to the railway station with a big bunch of red roses and a card on which he had stuck his photo, so that I would always remember him and his love for me. A last kiss and embrace from him and I boarded the train with Mama. We sat silently next to each other, afraid to utter a single word, as the train passed through the Austrian countryside. We had put our precious food-parcel safely between us, nervous that we would be discovered concealing our coins. Fortunately, we were sitting at the front of the train whilst the border guards mounted it at the rear.

At the first station after the frontier with Yugoslavia, before we had encountered any of the guards, we disembarked, clutching our parcel, and fell into the arms of Papa and Uncle Willie. In our relief, the tears flowed freely and we could not stop hugging. We could hardly believe that we had escaped. Uncle Willie shepherded us to his large chauffeur-driven car and we were taken to his home in the nearby town of Maribor.

We arrived late at night, so we were quickly ushered to our different rooms. Suddenly I was alone. I tried to sleep, but was so exhausted from the months of carrying the family burden that I hardly knew what to do with myself. I think I had expected a hero's welcome after all my efforts to get us out of Vienna. I so desperately wanted Papa to congratulate me and treat me like the adult I had now become. However, in their joy of reunion my parents were oblivious to my needs. In the days that followed I began to suspect that Papa, as a true authoritarian, resented his temporary loss of control and it was impossible for him to believe that his *Puppinko* (little doll), had orchestrated the great escape without him. Looking back, I realize it must have been hard for him to have left his little girl and be reunited with an apparently confident and self-sufficient young woman.

As I lay in bed, tossing and turning, wishing I had someone to turn to, I saw Freddy's flowers in the moonlight. They were already beginning to wilt. I started to cry – long hot tears that drenched the pillow. I had had to leave behind my only solace and once again I had no one. I had lost my brothers, my home, my friends, my school, my future. I finally fell asleep in the early hours of the day, drained and depressed, wondering where my life would take me.

# 4 • *Asylum Seeking*

I awoke the next morning dazed and confused. I met a new Mama at breakfast: she seemed to have regained her composure overnight, while I seemed to have regressed and now swung from temper tantrums to periods of silent withdrawal. My parents tried to understand what I was going through and assumed that my behaviour was the result of what I had seen and experienced in Vienna, as I screamed every time I heard Hitler's voice or news from Austria. I tried to understand it myself, but had no control over my behaviour. I seemed to be grieving for Vienna and had some perverse longing to be back under Hitler's regime of anti-Semitism and persecution. I so resented the fact that no one asked for my opinion or help any more. I was no longer the decision-maker and I was being treated like the child that I felt I no longer was. I was once more Papa's beloved little girl rather than the adviser and confidante I considered I should be. Mama tried to reason gently with me while Papa lost his temper and shouted. Neither approach had any effect.

The honeymoon of our escape from Nazi Austria lasted no more than a few weeks. After a brief stay with Uncle Willie, Papa continued his travels selling textiles, while Mama and I moved to Zagreb, where we settled with my Aunt Julla, my mother's sister. There we were leading a fairly normal life as part of my aunt's family, and I became a close ally of my cousin Gert and his network of friends. Papa had by then been a commercial traveller for many years, representing a Yugoslavian firm that had bought out Uncle Willie's company. To conform with Yugoslavian labour laws his bosses had issued him with a certificate showing that he was working for a Czechoslovak business, and as long as he could periodically leave the country and return to Austria he had no problems. However, with the Nazi annexation of Austria he could no longer return to Austria safely and we had to start offering the Yugoslavian police officials ever larger bribes not to report Papa. Finally, he was arrested for working illegally in Yugoslavia and was threatened with repatriation to Austria. We received a phone call advising us of his arrest and were told that the Jewish community in the town where Papa had been taken had put up bail for him so that he could stay in the local hotel under police guard. At the same time our tourist visas had expired and we were also staying illegally in Zagreb, hiding every time the doorbell rang in fear that it would be the police coming to take us away. So when Mama heard this she burst into tears, muttering 'This is the end, this is the end.' We knew now that Papa was imprisoned that it would only be a matter of days before the police would find us too and threaten to return us to Austria. By then the rumours of the concentration camps had been substantiated and we were certain that for us to return to Austria would mean instant deportation.

Unfortunately, there are too many people in this world who prey on the needs of others, and Yugoslavia had become full of crooks and con-men who took advantage of the plight of the many Jewish refugees. Some made their living by pretending they could obtain permit extensions or false passports, while others faked their ability to forge documents. There were so many crooks that it was impossible to know whom to trust. Through some business connection of my uncle's in Zagreb we met Vladimir, a tall handsome man in his early forties who claimed to be an ex-police official with connections in high places. He proposed that he should take me to a small town in Dalmatia to stay with him there for one week, during which time he would secure an extension to our visas. We struggled to raise the money for the increasing number of bribes we had to pay, but realized we had little choice. Mama was horrified at the thought of letting her little girl go on her own with Vladimir, but I assured her that I could look after myself. I did not really think about what Vladimir might have in mind for me; I was just excited to be involved again, facing the prospect of further challenges. Mama kept insisting that she should come with me, while Vladimir produced numerous arguments to persuade her to let me go alone with him.

As Mama once again became depressed and debilitated I took charge of the situation, surprising my uncle and aunt at how their seemingly neurotic niece was transformed into a calm and capable negotiator. I threw no more tantrums. Instead I discussed our problem with Vladimir, who of course realized that his earlier suggestion had been overtaken by more recent events. In return for allowing him to kiss me I got him to arrange Papa's transfer to

Zagreb, so that at least we would be together and could discuss our options before the police sent us back to the Austrian border. I never told anyone of the deal I had made with Vladimir.

Mama had become dependent on me again and expected me to take whatever decision I considered to be in our best interests. I had never thought that she would delegate control so readily, and it was hard to accept that my mother was again much weaker than I had come to believe her to be. However, I had little time to dwell on our shifting relationship. When we heard the details of Papa's arrival at Zagreb's railway station (accompanied by a detective) I persuaded Vladimir to come with me to meet the train, so that we could immediately arrange bail at the local police station and enable Papa to return home with us.

I was deeply shocked when I saw Papa on the platform: my once handsome and debonair father now looked dishevelled and defeated. In the middle of the crowded station he went on his knees in front of me and cried out: 'This is what your father has come to, a prisoner!' I tried gently to calm him down, but I actually felt like saying to him: 'Now at least you know what it is like to be hunted and persecuted. You should now appreciate what an achievement it was to ensure Mama's, Kurt's and my own escape from Nazi Austria.' Even then, however, he refused to acknowledge all we had been through. That day heralded the start of a new relationship with my father. I knew I loved him dearly and admired him greatly, but I also realized that I hated and despised him. He was no longer my all-powerful Papa and I was no longer his doting daughter. This ambivalence proved to be mutual, as Papa openly rebuked my tough persona and unemotional outlook.

As soon as bail had been arranged for Papa and we were reunited with Mama in Aunt Julla's flat, we started exploring the various options open to us. Papa kept insisting that he should try to pull strings, pay more bribes just to ensure an extension of our stay in Yugoslavia. I argued, however, that this was pointless as it was only putting off the inevitable. In the meantime our relatives in Yugoslavia and their Jewish friends were also trying to find a way out. Vladimir had managed to get the police to agree to allow us one week's grace, after which they insisted we would be deported to the Austrian border. Papa had to report to the police daily, which seemed to destroy the last remnants of his self-confidence. I hated seeing him like this and my heart reached out to him, but I kept thinking if only he had seen the suffering in

Vienna: Camilla beaten up; his daughter cleaning toilets and polishing boots; the Jews whipped and beaten in the streets; the shops ransacked and the homes destroyed.

One week gave us little time to find a way out of our dilemma. I queued at all the consulates in Zagreb, but once they had noted the big red 'J' on our passports, none was prepared to offer us any assistance. Then three days before our time was up, my uncle burst in shouting excitedly: 'There is an escape for you, you can go to Albania.' I listened eagerly when he explained that he had discovered from a Jewish business friend of his, who happened to be the Albanian commercial consul in Zagreb, that King Zog of Albania was celebrating his jubilee in 1938. Because of this, anyone could visit the country on a tourist card, which was freely issued even for passports with a red 'J'. We knew nothing about Albania, but that did not matter. I vaguely recollected that I had learned in my geography lessons that Albania was a wild country situated along the Adriatic coast between Yugoslavia and Greece, but that was all I could remember. I began to get very excited at the prospect of an escape route. However, Papa argued that it was unwise for us to venture into the unknown, while Mama said nothing and simply sat motionless with a pained expression on her face. I tried to convince Papa that anywhere was better than Austria and anything was preferable to being sent to a concentration camp. My aunts and uncles supported my pleas. I finally won my parents round by pointing out to them that our chances of being reunited again with Otto and Kurt were much better if we went to Albania than if we remained illegally in Yugoslavia. They had also ignored the fact that whoever harboured us would, as an accomplice, also be in grave danger.

The only good news we had during these difficult days was that Otto had managed to get a permit for Kurt to join him in England. This meant that at least two of our immediate family were in a reasonably safe place. After spending a short time with Otto in London, Kurt heard that jobs were easier to get in Manchester and he moved there where he got employment as a weaver in one of the Lancashire textile mills. I was so confused: I wanted to be happy for them and their relative safety, but I wondered at the injustice that, I the youngest, was having to take charge of the situation with my parents and that we seemed to be moving from one dangerous and unknown situation to another. I could not see where it would all end. I just knew that I had to keep on going.

*

Once Papa had agreed to our going to Albania I set about planning our departure as speedily as possible. I arranged with Vladimir for a police detective to travel with us by train to Spalato (Split) and carry our passports until we had boarded the ship for Albania. We had to pay handsomely for this privilege, but we all agreed it was worth it. Before our departure I negotiated Vladimir's payment for services rendered. It was extortionate, but I managed to reduce his asking price by 25 per cent. I felt a sense of freedom as we left Vladimir behind us, as he symbolized the seedier side of life that I so much wanted to be rid of. As we stood on the platform at Zagreb station we were surrounded by the many relatives, friends and sympathizers who had come to see us off. I had come to enjoy the sense of family once again and was reminded of our community in the Brigittenau, so I was sad when it came to our final farewells. Little did we realize that we would never see any of them again. Our perilous escape via Albania proved to be our salvation, as those that we left behind us perished under the subsequent German occupation of Croatia.

Yugoslavian currency restrictions prohibited travellers from taking more than a small amount of dinars out of the country. So my parents were very worried what we would do on arrival in Albania without enough money to pay a porter let alone a hotel. With the help of one of Aunt Julla's Jewish friends Papa managed to change a sum of money into sterling so that we would be able to survive for a week. The question then arose how we could possibly take this money with us, as we were going to be accompanied to the border by a police guard. Mama and I then remembered how we had taken our gold coins out of Austria and devised a similar strategy. We were given numerous bags and boxes of chocolates as parting gifts. We took the sweets out of one of these bags and put the carefully folded sterling notes at the bottom, covering them up before refilling the bag. Mama put the precious bag with chocolates into her large handbag.

On the long train journey to the port of Spalato I began to chat with our police escort while standing in the corridor outside the compartment where my parents were silently sitting facing each other. He introduced himself as Yaroslav and I told him my name. To cement our relationship I opened the door and asked Mama to let me have the bag of chocolates so that I could offer some to our police guard. At first Mama looked horrified at the suggestion, but I motioned to her that it would be all right. I thought that this was the safest way to ensure our hidden money would not be discovered. I was right. Yaroslav remained oblivious of the fact that he was choosing a sweet out of a bag which contained our hidden money. He was unaware why he had to accompany us to the border and when I subsequently explained our circumstances he seemed to feel guilty. During the long train journey we talked a lot and we even joked together, but I could see that he was anxious as he constantly quizzed me about the likelihood of ensuring our safety; he really seemed very concerned. Shortly before our train was due to arrive at its destination, while we were still standing in the corridor, he suddenly turned to me saying: 'Let's get married, then you and your parents will be free to stay in Yugoslavia. I'll talk to your father and we can make the necessary arrangements as soon as we get to Spalato, then you will never have to board the ship for Albania.' While he made this sudden marriage proposal he looked deep into my eyes trying to convey not only his feelings for me and my family but also for the general human suffering that was taking place all around us. We both knew that his gallant offer was not the answer, but it was a ray of light in an otherwise gloomy world. I thanked him and hugged him closely until the moment came when we had to take leave of each other. I never told my parents the experience I had had with our police escort, but by then I had stopped confiding in them about most things.

We boarded the Adriatic coastal steamer on 20 November 1938, which happened to be Otto's 26th birthday; we even managed to send him a card from Spalato. As I watched the shores of Yugoslavia retreat into the distance, I felt that I had become completely rootless. I no longer cared where I lived as long as I had my immediate family with me and my basic needs were met. In stark contrast, Papa's departure from Yugoslavia meant giving up his livelihood and venturing into the unknown, which obviously worried him greatly. Yet to me it was just another move further away from my native country, which I had grown to hate.

On board ship we met a young German Jewish couple with a small baby. This was the eighth time they had travelled along the coast between Yugoslavia and Greece. They had heard that if they bought tickets for this Adriatic steamer they could escape Germany and hopefully be allowed to stay in one of the countries in which the ship was due to dock. Alas, their hopes did not materialize, and they were forbidden to go ashore anywhere. The captain and the crew of the ship were obviously reluctant to be responsible for having this young family deported back to

Germany and therefore allowed them to stay on board. In return, the young couple helped out in the kitchen and tried to make themselves useful. They had no idea how long they could continue like this, and I frequently saw the young mother crying as she watched her baby boy crawling happily about the deck, oblivious of the tragedy of which he was part. We told them about the Albanian tourist cards for the jubilee, but they had established that to obtain these cards one had to apply in person to an Albanian consulate, and this was impossible for them since they were not allowed to disembark anywhere. I never found out what ultimately happened to them; like so many of these brief encounters they just left a deep and lasting impression on my young mind.

We docked in Durres, Albania's port, on a grey and rainy morning. The weather was in tune with our mood. It looked a pretty grim place, but we knew we had to get off and that this was going to be the place where we would have to stay until we found a better alternative. On board ship Papa had changed some of our sterling currency into Albanian money, so that we would have some money to get settled. As we were walking ashore we were pleasantly surprised to be met by two German Jews who welcomed us and told us that there was already a small refugee community of about 55 individuals in Durres. This cheered me up no end as I had expected that we would be the first refugees to get to Albania. I reasoned that if others had managed to survive here for some months already then it could not possibly be as bad a place as my parents had tried to make me believe. We were advised that near the port was the Hotel Metropole, where we could rent a room cheaply. We arranged for our luggage, which now represented our entire worldly belongings, to be transported to the hotel and ventured there ourselves accompanied by our Jewish guides.

The Hotel Metropole brought me back down to earth with a bang. It was the filthiest place I had ever seen. The wallpaper was peeling off the walls and there was an overpowering smell of damp that permeated the whole building. We were shown to a room where we silently noted the worn, stained sheets, the cracked basin, the rickety furniture and the rotting window-frames. Even I, young and adventurous as I was, could not muster up any enthusiasm nor make any attempt to be positive. Meanwhile, Mama and Papa had turned white with horror, and looked as if they were about to faint. Realising what we were going through, our new Jewish friends reminded us that although the Hotel Metropole was certainly not the Ritz, it was still a lot better than any concentration camp. This remark helped to put the place into perspective for me and I tried hard to rally around and make the best of the dreadful situation.

Durres was a small town, typical of many in Albania. It was poor and dilapidated and had numerous shanty-towns where people lived under conditions I had never imagined possible. The majority of the population were Greek Orthodox and those that were not were Muslims. Neither religion allows women to walk freely in the streets or be uncovered in public. The only young women seen openly were the few prostitutes who, I learned later, lived in a brothel. I was only 16 years old, still wearing ankle socks and school dresses, and could see no reason why I should not explore the town. My parents did not attempt to stop me as they were overwhelmed by their change in status and had withdrawn into themselves. As I roamed the streets I soon began to attract the attention of some of the local young men. When they realized that I was not a new member of the brothel but came from Vienna and was here with my parents, they began to treat me with great respect. My knowledge of colloquial French was sufficient to hold a simple conversation with them. My parents and I ate our evening meals at the only restaurant in Durres and soon a band of young men began to join us and we would spend the long evenings chatting. The owner, who was also the chef and waiter, was delighted with his new clientele and told us proudly that he had learned to cook in Vienna. Whilst the food was edible his standard of cleanliness was well below what we would normally expect, but I was beginning to become immune to the filth. He seemed to take a liking to Mama and myself and often invited us down to the cellar where he prepared the food so that we could pick a choice piece of fish or of meat. Knowing how fussy Mama was about cleanliness I always insisted that it was too dangerous for her to climb down to the cellar and went on my own. She would have been horrified and would have refused to eat another morsel had she seen the conditions under which the food was prepared.

We stayed at the Hotel Metropole for a few weeks during which time we visited the compound where the other refugees were staying. It was a strange mix of people, professions and nationalities, but we were pleased to meet any kind of kindred spirits. They lived together in a sort of commune, which was run by an elected committee. Each family or group had a room and each member was allocated a certain task. Women took turns to prepare the food while men did the shopping and cleaning. One day the committee invited us for lunch and offered us a room in their commune. We must have passed our initiation test finally, but I was still rather annoyed with them for having let us stay for so long at the dreadful Hotel Metropole before offering us a place. Papa's immediate question when he heard the offer was how much would we be expected to pay? He was obviously worried that we would soon run out of money. His fears were allayed when we found out that the commune was funded by an International Jewish Aid Committee from America who sent a certain amount per refugee per day.

It was a relief to leave the Metropole, and while our room in the compound was no palace at least it was ours. Papa managed to rally round and even began to make furniture out of orange boxes. Soon we had a room furnished with beds, chairs, a table and even a cupboard. Our daily allowance was meagre and required careful budgeting. We figured that between the 55 refugees living in the commune we could afford one pound of fat per day. We survived mainly on bread, cheese and vegetables. Meat and fish were rare treats, while fruit was a luxury we were never able to afford. I grew used to the sounds of my hollow stomach, and while I hate to admit it, was occasionally driven to stealing bread from the communal food store. Papa and Mama were deeply upset when I was once caught stealing and hauled before the committee. They had mixed emotions: horror at their daughter, the thief, but also guilt at their inability to provide their child with the most basic of things. I did not take it at all seriously at the time, but considered my 'trial' as part of my everyday refugee life.

Life fell into a somewhat dull routine. I had explored most of Durres; there was no school and few books to read, so I was thrilled when I was asked to teach two local girls German and French. They were the daughters of an Albanian cabinet minister who had recently died and their mother did not want them to return to their boarding school which they had attended in Italy. The girls' brother was one of the local young men I had befriended and it was he who had made the suggestion. For the first time in my life I was earning money and thoroughly enjoyed my new elevated status. I was the only refugee in Albania who could work and be paid for it, because I was the only one with friends among the local population. It was a strange time for me as I had no experience ot teaching and my two pupils were only a few years younger than me. We had no common language: they spoke Italian and Albanian while I spoke German and a smattering of French. I began to teach them German and French with the aid of sign-language and a lot of pointing and gesticulating. In the process I also picked up some Italian and even a little Albanian. To my surprise the girls enjoyed their lessons so much that I was asked to extend them to include mathematics.

Life had a purpose and I enjoyed my mornings teaching. Sometimes I had to laugh, as my young students would often ask me questions I couldn't answer and I would have to swot up that evening to provide them with the right answer the following day. The mornings sped by and in the afternoons I usually went for walks along the seashore accompanied by a crowd of young men most of whom were Albanians, though a few were refugees. Being the only young refugee girl made me the centre of attention and I hate to admit that I enjoyed every moment of it. Sometimes I was invited back to my students' house after the morning sessions to spend time in the women's quarters, which were reserved solely for the use of the females in the family: no male was allowed to enter, not even a family member. The rooms were ornately furnished with large, comfortable chairs swathed in wonderfully colourful fabrics, and there were beautiful glass cabinets in which the family jewels and trinkets were displayed. I was treated as one of their female guests and always proudly shown the accumulated treasures of each of the women. I was always pleased to be invited, for even though we had no way of conversing and we sat most of our time together in silence, simply exchanging smiles, I was always offered cups of very strong sweet coffee with sugary cakes. I never left as hungry as when I had arrived.

One morning while I was teaching my pupils in one of the upstairs rooms we suddenly heard screaming and shouting downstairs. Among the voices I recognised Papa's so we rushed to see what was happening. We found him surrounded by a number of the family women who were shouting and trying to push him out of the door. My students explained to me that the women were upset because my father was the first man who had ever dared to enter their quarters. Poor Papa had no idea what was happening. I quickly rescued him from the wrath of these women and shoved him outside, explaining how he had trespassed into what was literally no man's land. He was panting after running to find me and had difficulty in telling me why he had come. From what he said I gathered that he had been summoned by the police prefect of Durres to report to his office. Since French was the official language and Papa did not know any French he desperately needed me as his interpreter.

I immediately requested permission to leave early and proceeded with Papa to the town hall. I knew the police prefect by sight, having passed him frequently in the streets when I was walking along with my numerous young male friends. As soon as we asked to see him we were ushered into his office. He sat behind a huge desk which dwarfed him completely: he looked ridiculous and immediately lost any sense of menace. He invited us to sit down opposite him and then asked me why I had come along since he had asked only for my father. I explained that I was there solely in the role of interpreter, whereupon he fingered in an embarrassed fashion the papers lying in front of him and remained silent for some time. I was puzzled by his behaviour. Papa, anxious about us being expelled from Albania, kept asking me what was going on. The prefect then kept repeating over and over again that my presence made things very difficult for him. I told him once again that my father needed me as an interpreter. Finally, he requested me to ask my father whether he had a permit for me. Since I could not understand what sort of permit Papa might need for me I asked the prefect to be more specific. After another long silence, the prefect, turning crimson, said, 'In Albania there is a law which states that men who control prostitutes have to obtain a permit for them and that the prostitutes have to be regularly examined by the local doctor.' I then realized that my free and easy behaviour with the young local men must have led the police to assume that I was a professional prostitute and that my father was collecting money from my immoral doings.

Papa kept urging me to explain why the prefect had summoned him. I knew that if I told him the truth he would be furious and would have regarded this accusation as yet another indignity he had to suffer. I therefore whispered that he had nothing to worry about and that I would explain it all to him as soon as we were out of the office. I then calmly told the prefect that I had never prostituted myself, that I was still a virgin, prepared to be medically examined in evidence, and that my father would consider it an unforgivable insult if I interpreted truthfully the question he had wanted me to ask him. I proceeded to tell the prefect, who had never been outside Albania, that different countries had different customs. In Vienna, where I came from, young men and women were accustomed to join in group activities and outings without being interested in or having sexual relations. He became so interested in learning about life in other parts of the world that he kept asking all sorts of questions which I tried to answer as best I could. Meanwhile Papa was fidgeting beside me, anxiously wanting to know what we were talking about. Finally, when the prefect dismissed us he apologized for having levelled against me what he now realized was such a preposterous accusation, and we agreed that the whole thing would remain a secret between the two of us. As Papa and I walked out of the office I quickly made up a story that the prefect had asked to see him to find out whether he was a true refugee since he had not been in Vienna either during or since the *Anschluss*. The fact that we had parted on such amicable terms from the prefect reassured Papa that the issue was resolved, and I never ever told him or Mama the real reason for the police summons.

Subsequently, the prefect joined the group of young men who accompanied me on my walks from time to time. I began to feel like the Pied Piper of Durres, as the number of young men who followed me on my walks grew almost daily. I naturally enjoyed my popularity, and for the men it seemed a novel experience to hear about life in central Europe and to have a platonic relationship with a young girl. Whilst I had tried to make a life for myself in Albania, the more I adjusted to my new surroundings, the more unhappy my parents seemed to become. They were in denial of our new way of life, still in shock that our lives could have changed so dramatically and frustrated by their dependence on me and the support from Jewish charities.

Commune life was dull and there was little to occupy oneself with other than the daily menial tasks. Since our funds and food was shared equally by all members it should have been an egalitarian existence. However, soon the bickering started as some wanted to be more equal than others. Mrs Greenberg, whose husband used to be a senior engineer in a large German car factory, insisted on being addressed as 'Frau Ober-Ingeneur' (Mrs Senior Engineer) and frequently got upset when a fellow refugee either forgot or purposely called her simply 'Mrs Greenberg' without giving her her rightful title. The atmosphere in the commune was often tense as there were constant clashes between different families whose paths would probably have never crossed had we not all had to flee for our lives. One of the most obvious and contentious differences was the degree of religious upbringing, which ranged from the truly Orthodox to the completely assimilated Jews. The Orthodox faction insisted that we keep a kosher kitchen, whereas the assimilated Jews among us kept arguing that this was an unnecessary luxury given the conditions of extreme deprivation under which we were forced to live. While this was a daily debate, everyone agreed to celebrate the Jewish festivals. For the first time in my life I learnt about Hanukah and thoroughly enjoyed the ritual of lighting the candles and the warm, festive atmosphere. Mama seemed to blossom when participating in these Jewish rituals which had been so much a part of her childhood.

Hanukah offered a much-needed unifying distraction, but as soon as it was over we slipped back into a deeper depression, aware that our days in Albania were numbered. Each family stepped up its desperate attempts to get visas and permits to any of the few countries that were still prepared to admit Jews. Many applied for visas to America, but for this one not only needed an affidavit, which was hard to obtain, but also a quota number. To get to England one needed a permit from the British Home Office, and this was extremely difficult to secure, particularly for men. Otto was trying his best to obtain our British permits and managed to get some of his English friends to apply for a domestic permit for Mama, and a hairdresser to agree to employ me as an apprentice. In January 1939 he cabled us advising us that our entry permits had been granted and that we should make plans to travel to England as quickly as possible. He obviously did not realize the depth of depression from which Papa was suffering. Papa was also nonplussed and did not appreciate just how much Otto must have gone through to obtain our visas. I was just about to berate him for being so ungrateful when he burst into tears and said despairingly, 'You two go and leave me. I am no good to anyone or anything any more. I might as well die here as anywhere else!' Mama tried her best to console him and I decided that we should delay our departure for as long as possible in the hope that Papa might also get a visa in the meantime. Understandably, Otto was not pleased about delaying our arrival in England as this meant that he had to apply for an extension to our entry permits; he had battled hard enough to secure them in the first place. He later informed us that our permits would expire on 30 April 1939, by which date Mama and I would have to have arrived in England or we would lose our chance of entry and it would be impossible for him to arrange new visas. He kept reassuring us that he was trying everything possible to get a permit for Papa, but it was much more difficult to get them for men than for women. Mama and I remained in Durres throughout February and March 1939.

The fact that we had permits to go to England aroused considerable envy among our fellow refugees as they could not understand why anyone who had the opportunity to leave would stay on in Albania. Their jealousy became so all-consuming that the committee threatened to expel Mama and myself on the basis that the Jewish aid was only meant for those in dire need and we no longer qualified. They finally allowed us to remain in the commune due to Papa's increasingly suicidal tirades, which they knew all about as Papa often ranted late into the night.

One day in February 1939 a young Italian who was a regular member of my 'entourage' told me that the Italian consul was keen to meet me with a view to exploring the possibility of my teaching him German. After my morning's lesson I called on the consul. I warmed to him immediately and agreed that I would teach him three hours per week, for which he offered me a small remuneration, which I gratefully accepted. Little did I know that this chance encounter would become so instrumental to our plans.

# 5 • *The Great Escape*

Shortly before Easter 1939 Mussolini occupied Albania. The country's military defence was pitifully weak: its army had no more than about half a dozen machine guns and its navy consisted of the personal yacht belonging to King Zog. My Albanian friends told me how important their independence was to them, but there was little they could do with so few weapons and a handful of soldiers as their army.

As soon as the large Italian warships were visible on the horizon Durres became chaotic. The wealthier residents all left hurriedly and moved inland. People were raiding the shops to stockpile provisions, windows were being boarded up and the bus station was teeming with people trying to board buses to carry them as far away as possible. The residents of our commune were all advised to evacuate the house since it was situated next to the police station which housed the only two machine guns in Durres and would therefore be an obvious target for the Italians.

The Italian invasion was expected to begin on Good Friday. The previous evening the town was deserted: except for a few Albanian soldiers there was not a soul to be seen. We sat in our commune at the emergency committee meeting, discussing our options. After much heated debate it became obvious that there was little we could do but remain in Durres and see how the Italians would treat us. We decided that as soon as any fighting broke out we would shelter in the cellar of one of the nearby homes whose owners had fled. None of us slept that night; we sat around fully dressed, waiting anxiously for the inevitable. I tried hard to remain calm but again I found myself wondering why? I had spent so much time and energy trying to establish a safe haven in Albania and yet here I was again worried for our lives. I had no idea if the Italians were as anti-Semitic as the Germans and whether they, like Hitler, would want to be rid of us. We had given up our chance of getting to England because of Papa. Who would want us now? The questions swam round and round my head until I became dizzy.

Just as dawn was breaking and the first light of day glimmered through the shutters we heard the first round of gunfire. A policeman rushed in and told us to get out. At this we raced round in blind panic. Having been waiting for this all night, now it was suddenly upon us we realized how little prepared we were. Questions flashed up in our minds: Would we ever return to this surrogate home? What would happen to all our worldly possessions? Should we pack? In our haste we agreed to take only what could be easily carried. I grabbed my favourite book, *Der Schüler Gerber hat absolviert* (The Student Gerber has Finished), by Torberg, and ran through the door without looking back.

We ran across the open fields at the back of our house as shots were being fired over our heads. The older members of our group struggled to keep up with the rest of us as we ran for shelter. We had to help them climb over fences and literally had to carry some of them. Finally we reached the large house we had identified as being a suitable shelter and hammered on the door. The servants who had been left behind to look after the house opened the door gingerly, wondering at the noise. As soon as we heard the bolts slide across the door we surged forward. They tried to prevent us from entering, but we easily outnumbered them and quickly overpowered them. We made straight for the cellar and crouched, motionless, waiting for the gunfire to stop. We sat like this for some hours until I could no longer stand the tension. I decided, as a distraction, to find out what was the one item that each of us had taken as we left the commune. One man had snatched up his razor, as if shaving would give him a semblance of normality in this otherwise crazy life. While so much had been taken out of his control he refused to let his personal standards slip. Most of the others had simply taken their wallets containing their passports and other documents. Some had certificates of degrees or medals awarded for bravery during the First World War, as if to show that they had been of some value in their past life.

The exchange of gunfire between Italian and Albanian forces lasted no more than a couple of hours. A deathly hush fell on the town and I imagined the streets strewn with dead bodies, just as I had seen at the Karl Marx Hof. With my usual curiosity I crept upstairs to peep out of the windows. I saw a number of Albanian soldiers in tattered uniforms running down the hill away from the coast. I immediately reported this to the throng huddled in the cellar and we again debated what course of action we should take. We voted on staying in the cellar and waiting for the Italians to find us or returning to our house and surrendering from there. The latter option won. Since I was the only one among us who could speak any Italian, I was asked to lead our procession waving a walking-stick to which we had tied a white handkerchief. In deathly silence we climbed the steps and walked out into the open street, afraid of what we might face. My parents tried to dissuade me from leading our group, fearing that I was likely to be among the first to be shot should we encounter any soldiers. They also begged the others not to ask such a young girl to head the procession, but everyone agreed that we needed our one and only Italian-speaking member at the front.

We set off in the direction of our house, aware that we were the only people on the streets. From time to time we caught sight of Albanian soldiers crawling along the sides of houses, trying to hide from their Italian pursuers. As people heard our footsteps, faces peered out from behind windows, curious to know what was happening. Only the odd sniper broke the strange silence that reigned. Soon we could see the Italian forces approaching and our pace slowed in anticipation, but we still kept moving forward. As the gap closed between us I kept silently rehearsing, in Italian, how I would introduce us to the Italian forces. Suddenly, as we turned a corner, about a dozen Italian soldiers appeared with fixed bayonets. They seemed even more surprised to see this strange band shuffling along the street. Waving their bayonets in front of us they ordered us to stop and to put our hands above our heads. I was petrified, but I tried to keep my composure and quickly translated the soldier's orders into German. An officer then approached me demanding to know who we were. I began my rehearsed speech, but as soon as he heard the word *tedeschi* (German), he shook my hand enthusiastically and shouted with pleasure that 'Germans and Italians are friends'.

Whereupon he told us to lower our hands. As he had not let me finish my prepared explanation he obviously did not realize that we were Jewish refugees. I decided at that point just to tell him that we were a small group living together in one large house, which we had left only that morning when the shooting had begun and that we were just making our way back home. He ceremoniously assured me that he and his soldiers would honour the friendship which now existed between the Italian and German people. I did not think it prudent to point out that although we held German and Austrian passports we were not considered German citizens under the Nazi regime. He offered us a guard to accompany us back to our house, which had survived the invasion intact, though the neighbouring police station had suffered a direct hit from one of the shells fired from the warships.

The officer insisted that his men should search our rooms, just in case there had been any unwanted guests in our absence. While the rest of our group waited anxiously outside, guarded by one lot of soldiers, I was asked to show the other soldiers round the house. As they looked in cupboards, under beds and through all the various boxes I was terrified at what they might find. I suddenly thought that one of the Albanian policemen from next door might have decided to hide in our house or at least might have hidden some of their weapons there. I was certain that if the Italian soldiers were to find anything it would be impossible to explain. Thankfully nothing was found and we were allowed back into the house. We were left with two soldiers to guard us whilst the rest of the troop moved on. We were never sure whether these guards were there to protect us or to imprison us. I decided to try to engage them in conversation in order to ease the tension. One soldier told me that he was from a farming family near Naples, while the other was from Milan. Both were devout Catholics and very much resented having to fight on Good Friday. The soldiers kept repeating over and over again how pleased they were to have met some Germans and kept reassuring me that no harm would come to us. I wanted to laugh at the irony of the situation, Hitler's allies helping his enemies, but knew I was under close supervision.

Finally, exhausted after the events of the day, I returned to our room at the back of the house. No sooner than I had closed the door I heard a whistle from outside the window. I peeped out and saw a young man standing in his underwear pointing to the uniform bundled up beside him that he obviously wanted to discard. He begged me to give him civilian clothing so that he could escape without being taken prisoner by the Italians. Although I knew it would be dangerous to help him and we had little spare clothing, I motioned to him to hide while I tried to find him something. I grabbed a pair of my father's pyjamas and tossed them out of the window. He quickly put them on and disappeared into the back streets. I never found out whether he managed to escape, but at least I felt I had managed to repay a little of the kindness that many Albanians had shown us.

*

It took just one day for the Italians to complete their rounding up operation of Durres. The following morning the large convoy of their troops took Tirana, Albania's capital. Large posters were pasted all over the town, and vans with loudspeakers toured the streets informing the residents that Albania was now under Italian rule and that until all resistance had ceased a strict curfew would be enforced. Our two guards were withdrawn and we were left much to our own devices. We kept a low profile so as not to attract the attention of the newly established Italian authorities. I even continued teaching my two young pupils, but I stopped my afternoon walks with my band of followers so as not to worry my parents.

A few days after the occupation of Albania an official car stopped in front of our house and the driver delivered a letter addressed to me. None of us had any idea what it might contain and we all feared the worst. I opened it slowly and could feel everyone's eyes boring into me. I gave a huge sigh of relief when I read that it was from the Italian consul, whom I had been teaching German. He had now become the first Italian governor of Albania and was writing to me to request that I continue my German lessons, as he was now keener than ever to acquire a reasonable command of the language. The committee representatives immediately asked me to put in a good word for them all when I returned to my job with the new governor. The journey to his residence took me through numerous inspection points, so I was issued with a document that stated that I was a personal friend of the governor. Thus I had free access to travel throughout Albania. The document was covered with a series of impressive looking stamps and signatures and was extremely effective in getting guards to let me pass. When I met the governor he was as charming as ever and showed me how he had continued studying German in my absence. As I was leaving I mentioned to him how worried our little refugee community was about the possibility of the new Italian rulers being as anti-Semitic as the Germans. He assured me that as long as he had any power, no harm would come to any of us. He kept his promise, and we continued our lives largely undisturbed by the change in government.

Mussolini's occupation of Albania temporarily suspended all civilian travel outside the country, which made Mama and I panic. We had to be in England by the end of April when our entry permits would expire. The obvious route was to fly via Italy and France, but even transit passengers needed French visas and these were not issued for passports that bore a large red 'J'. The one and only travel agent in Durres, who had been a member of my Albanian entourage, suggested we take the freighter from Naples that was due to leave there on 20 April, arriving in England nine days later. With no other option open to us we gladly accepted his advice, and he duly booked passages for Mama and myself. As arranged we boarded the steamer at Durres for Bari, from where we travelled by train to Naples, to catch the freighter for England.

Saying goodbye to Papa was one of the hardest moments of my life. I so desperately wanted him to come with us, and I felt so guilty about leaving him behind. We clung to each other tightly and I wondered if I would ever see him again. He was already resigned to never seeing us again and when he held me for the last time before they raised the gangplank he made me promise that I would look after Mama for him. We stood on the deck waving madly at the crowd who had come to see us off. As the ship slowly left the port, the figures of those left behind became smaller and smaller. Mama and I stood embracing each other, both sobbing as we watched Papa's figure slowly disappear into the distance. We were worried how he would cope on his own without us and had talked to the committee to ensure that they would look after him. Feeling sad, but also a sense of relief and a glimmer of excitement as the next stage of our escape was to unfold, I tried to cheer Mama by reminding her of our imminent reunion with Otto and Kurt. Our trip to Bari and Naples passed without incident, and we checked into the hotel that my travel agent friend had reserved for us. It felt like a palace after our long months sleeping on makeshift beds and sitting at orange-box tables and chairs. We had our first proper meal in months and my stomach ached as it tried to accommodate the plateful of food. I started to feel euphoric and giddy with our new-found freedom, but Mama continued to fret about having had to leave Papa behind.

First thing in the morning I ventured to the shipping-line for which we had vouchers to catch the freighter to England. When I reached my destination an official casually told me that the freighter was three weeks late and that there was no other ship leaving Naples that would reach England before the end of the month. I was devastated: and the roller-coaster existence was suddenly more than I could bear. I had no one to turn to and knew that there was no point in asking Mama. The International Jewish Aid Committee had provided us with our fare money and we also had a large sum of money which one of my Greek Jewish friends, whom I had met in Durres, had asked me to put into his London bank account. He only agreed to hand it over if I promised him that I would use part or all of it should the need arise. To avoid the currency restrictions we had hidden the money by wrapping it in paper and winding knitting wool round it. We had placed the balls of wool in our suitcases and I retrieved one before I left the hotel. Now that I had the money I didn't know quite what to do with it, so I simply sat on a nearby bench to consider the possible alternatives. As we knew no one in Naples the outlook seemed somewhat bleak.

As my eyes wandered about looking for a clue or a sign, I suddenly saw across the road a branch of CIT, the Italian travel bureau. I marched straight in and explained our predicament to the kind clerk. He did not take this young girl seriously at first, but once I had presented him with our visas for England as well as some money he assured me he would be able to book us air tickets to fly via France. He did not believe me that the French authorities refused to give refugees transit visas, but a quick call to the French consulate proved me right and seemed to convince him that I knew what I was talking about. He then asked me to sit down while he explored other possibilities. After waiting what seemed an eternity to me he explained that the only way we could possibly reach London before the end of April 1939 would be to fly KLM, from Rome via Milan, Frankfurt, Cologne, Rotterdam and Amsterdam. I was horrified at the idea of having to pass through Germany, but there was no other option and nobody I could consult so I decided to take the risk. The Italian clerk clearly understood the difficult situation and after I had paid the bill and gathered up the tickets he took my hand in his and said 'Good luck! I shall pray for your safe arrival in England.'

On my way back to the hotel I cabled Otto that we would be flying to England via Germany, so that if we failed to arrive he would know where we had been detained. I was aware on one level that there was nothing anyone could do if we were stopped in Cologne, yet on another level I had such faith in Otto's abilities that I believed that he would somehow manage to get us released. I so desperately wanted to cry and have someone put their arms round me and take care of me, but I knew that I had to pull myself together to keep Mama going. I tried to concentrate on the reunion with my brothers, and when I found Mama pacing the hotel room I cheerfully announced that rather than going on a lengthy sea journey I had managed to arrange to fly to London.

As an afterthought I quietly added that we would be flying via Germany. Mama seemed more worried about the dangers of air travel than about our passage through Germany, which I found reassuring.

We spent the rest of 20 April 1939 in Naples. It happened to be Hitler's birthday and there were posters and birthday greetings plastered all over the city. I took Mama for a bit of sightseeing, for I thought that if things went wrong in Germany then at least we would have enjoyed our brief stay in Italy. That night we took the night train to Rome where early in the morning we boarded the KLM flight for London.

It was the first time I had ever travelled by plane and I was so excited when the engines started to rev up for take-off. Unfortunately, Mama did not share my excitement and sat, eyes closed, murmuring something to herself. She seemed totally prepared to die for she never believed that a plane could fly and land safely. When we touched down at Milan airport she realized that air travel was not quite as dangerous as she had feared and she began to relax, while I became increasingly anxious about our next touchdown in Germany. I tried not to worry Mama and pretended to share her admiration for the impressive marble display at Milan airport, but deep down I was very much afraid.

When we reboarded the plane I thought I would try to explain our predicament to the steward. I had hoped that he would be able to reassure me that transit passengers could stay on board while the plane refuelled in Germany. He politely stated that this was impossible: the German authorities insisted that all passengers disembark and have their passports checked. I couldn't help it, my face fell and the tears came to my eyes – and now I had given us away. I cursed myself for having taken such a dangerous course of action but I knew in reality that it had been the only possible choice. The steward then gently asked whether there was anything he could do to help, whereupon I showed him our passports with the red 'J' and the English visas and gave him Otto's address, asking him to let Otto know in case we would not be allowed to continue on to London. The KLM steward obviously knew about the unpredictability of the German authorities and their treatment of Jews. He had seen a number of victims of the concentration camps board his flights at the various German airports and had been horrified at the state they were in. They were frail and shook uncontrollably, their eyes were hollow and their skin jaundiced. As he recounted this to me he shook his head sadly, and when he had finished he whispered to me that he would do everything that he could to ensure that we reach our destination safely.

As we began our descent into Frankfurt I told Mama as calmly as I could that we would have to go through the German passport control. She did not seem to grasp the full implication of this for she showed little concern. Only when we had landed and she could see the flags with the swastika and officials in Nazi uniforms everywhere did she begin to suspect the danger we were in. I took her by the hand and whispered to her to keep her head high and not to show any fear. The official to whom I showed our passports when our turn came immediately said 'Rückwanderer' (returned emigrants). I immediately explained that we were on our way to London and had no intention of returning to Germany. He then inspected our English visas and let us pass. I heaved a sigh of relief when we reboarded the plane and exchanged a big smile with our steward. He appeared genuinely pleased that everything had gone all right for us so far. However, he warned me to be prepared for worse treatment at Cologne where he knew the authorities were notoriously tough.

As soon as we had touched down in Cologne and the doors had been opened we heard our names called over the tannoy. We were told to report to a special office. On hearing this I went limp and could hardly walk. I was terrified. It had all gone wrong and it was because of me. I should have tried to stay on in Naples and found a safer way of getting to England. I should have contacted Otto and consulted him as to what action to take. I had let Papa down. However, I did not have long for this self-flagellation as soon we were being marched through Cologne airport by two female Nazi officials. They led us to a tiny room in which there was only one table and one chair. Their steely blue eyes looked first at poor Mama, who had become so afraid that she could hardly control the trembling of her body. Then they turned their gaze upon me. I attempted to return their stare and I tried not to show my fear. Again we were declared 'Rückwanderer'. Once more I explained that we were on our way to England and pointed to the English visas in our passports. One of them snatched our passports and left the room while her companion remained to watch us. When the first official returned without our documents she ordered us in a harsh voice to strip completely saying, 'Wir wollen sehen was Ihr Juden alles herausschmugelt' (we want to see all that you Jews try to smuggle out of the country). Thank goodness the balls of wool were packed in the suitcase which we had checked in with our luggage.

Within minutes I was standing there stark naked, while poor Mama's fingers were shaking so badly that she could not undo her suspender-belt. When I tried to help her the younger of the two female officials jerked me away saying 'Die alte Saujüdin soll sich allein ausziehen!' (the old dirty Jewess should undress herself). Terrified, though I was, their inhumane treatment of us enraged me. I tried my best to control my emotions and not display my embarrassment as they continued to stare at me standing before them naked. They then proceeded to examine every piece of clothing. They emptied each pocket; they checked each hem and collar. On rifling through my wallet they found the letter the Italian governor of Albania had given me to allow me free movement around Durres. It was an official-looking certificate with numerous seals and stamps. They looked at it with great interest and I could see they were impressed. They asked me to translate the document, which I duly did. The elder of the two Nazi officials, who also appeared to be the more senior, took me by the shoulders and shook me while shouting that if I had lied to her we would be severely punished. Quickly realising that this certificate could save us, I coolly advised her to try to find one of their own officials who could translate the document for her and verify what I had told her. I added that there were several copies of this certificate around: one with the governor of Albania, who I said knew that we were on this flight to England; another with my father, who was still in Durres; and a third with my brother, who was to meet us at London airport on our arrival. Throughout this lengthy discussion Mama and I were still standing there with no clothes on and Mama's whole body was shaking like a leaf in the wind.

The senior official ordered us to get dressed again and marched off with the document. When I put my watch back on I noted that the whole encounter had lasted over two hours, and I knew that our plane was intended to have only a 45-minute stopover at Cologne airport. I was beginning to believe we were fated – just as we escaped from one situation we were presented with another. I felt as if I was constantly being tested and wondered at what stage it would be that I would finally fail. I was sure the plane would have left without us and my mind went into overdrive trying to figure out what to do. After what seemed an eternity to me but was in fact no more than ten minutes, the Nazi woman returned and in a harsh voice told us to get back on to the plane. Relief flooded through me, but as I saw the effect our ordeal had had on Mama I nearly broke down. Her face was as white as a sheet and she was still shaking, she looked as if she had shrunk and aged. I wanted to kill this woman for doing this to my mother, and I truly believe I would have enjoyed watching her suffer. Instead I simply asked her to return our passports, which contained our visas for England. At this, she just laughed, pushed me out of the room and told me in no uncertain terms that we should consider ourselves lucky to be allowed to continue our journey and that I was in no position to make any demands.

Through the window I spotted our KLM plane on the tarmac and saw the steward standing at the top of the stairs. When the steward saw us approaching he dashed down the steps to meet us and, with a big smile on his face, welcomed us back like long-lost kin. I immediately told him that although we had finally been permitted to reboard our passports had been confiscated. He advised us to take our seats and said he would try to negotiate with the German authorities to release our passports. As Mama and I walked along the gangway to our seats the passengers applauded and tried to show us how pleased they were to see us back. (I assumed most of them to be Dutch or English.) We subsequently learned that the plane had been delayed for us and our fellow passengers had been informed as to the reason. Alhough I was greatly relieved to be out of the clutches of the dreadful Nazi women I was still worried what would happen to us if we arrived in England without our passports. I feared we would end up like the German couple whom we had met on the ship travelling from Yugoslavia to Albania, endlessly sailing the seas as they were not allowed to disembark anywhere. Lost in thought, I hardly noticed the steward running towards our plane waving something in the air. Then when I saw him bounding up the steps, two at a time I dashed to meet him at the door where he proudly handed our passports to me. I flung my arms round his neck and hugged and kissed him while most of the passengers began to sing 'For He's a Jolly Good Fellow'.

Within a few minutes we were airborne and the experience of the previous few hours began to seem like a nightmare. Watching as Mama sat white-knuckled and drawn, murmuring to herself, I knew she would relive this nightmare for some time. I sat back in my seat and pondered the events of the day. I wanted so much to contact the governor and thank him for his prescient words – little did he know that he would be able to keep us from harm. It seemed that the list of people to thank for our survival was getting longer and longer.

Once the steward had settled everybody down I caught him, as I was eager to know how he had managed to retrieve our passports. He explained that the captain had refused to take off unless all the passengers had their travel documents. After arguing with the German officials for some time, the latter had finally agreed to return our passports. I then told him what we had experienced during our stopover in Cologne. He was appalled on hearing my account of our treatment.

When we arrived in Amsterdam we had to change planes and therefore part from the steward. I kept shaking his hand and thanking him profusely, but I was so preoccupied with our arrival in London that I forgot to ask his name or where I could contact him. When Mama held her hand out to him he kissed it, muttering how sorry he was for what she had been made to suffer in the course of her journey. I have often wondered since then what happened to him and whether he survived the Second World War.

We finally landed at London Airport at about five o'clock in the afternoon, having left Rome at seven in the morning. After queuing to see the British immigration official and again to reclaim our luggage, we were finally allowed to go through to the arrival hall. I scanned the crowds for Otto. (I was secretly looking forward to the praise and recognition I thought he would shower me with when I told him of all our exploits.) There was no sign of him or Kurt. I couldn't believe it: after all we had been through to get to England and they couldn't even turn up to meet us! I wanted to cry, but the tears wouldn't come and in my now customary fashion I settled Mama in a chair before going off to find Otto. Since I did not know a single word of English I could not ask anyone what to do or where to find my brother. Then I spotted a lady sitting behind a desk wearing a badge with the Star of David and a placard saying 'Jewish Aid Committee' in large letters. I timidly went up to her and asked her whether she understood German. She nodded, and on hearing our tale immediately put her arms round me and said that we would be safe in England – which was just what I needed to hear. She asked me whether I knew Otto's London address and suggested that we take the airport coach to the city terminal and from there a taxi, showing the driver Otto's address. By this time I was getting worried that something might have happened to Otto, but she reassured me that it was much more likely that he had been given the wrong information about the time of our flight arrival and might still be on his way to the airport. I thought maybe we should wait a little longer, but on seeing Mama she told me to get to Otto's as quickly possible. She insisted on buying our tickets for the airport coach and even gave me money for the taxi. I thanked her, collected Mama and left the airport, overwhelmed by all the kindness we had been shown.

On the ride to the city terminal I had my first glimpse of London. It seemed vast after Durres. The streets were lined with small houses which had handkerchief-sized gardens in the front, whilst in Vienna there were mostly large apartment blocks. I was like a child in a toyshop with all these new things to look at. I gasped at the red double-decker buses that I thought were like small houses on wheels. I was also struck by the absence of soldiers. (We had become accustomed to seeing soldiers everywhere.) Once we had transferred to a taxi I showed the driver an envelope with Otto's address and uttered my first words in English, 'No speak English'. I sat in the front, peering out of the window searching for the right street name. All of a sudden I saw a sign saying Marchmont Street, where Otto lived, and spotted Joschi, a young man I knew from Vienna and who I knew shared the flat with Otto. I shouted 'Stop' and the taxi skidded to a halt. I then called Joschi, who, though surprised to see us without Otto, immediately took care of everything. He assured us that Otto was perfectly all right and as far as he knew had gone to meet us at the airport. Joschi took us to his parents' flat nearby and we were given a warm welcome. From there he phoned the airport and left a message for Otto with the news that we had already safely arrived. As we waited impatiently we were joined by other Viennese refugees who had managed to escape to England and who recounted their horrific experiences in German concentration camps. I had been eager to tell them about our great escape, but I now realized that we had in fact been extremely lucky. When Otto eventually turned up I just mentioned in passing the episode at Cologne airport. Otto then hugged me and declared admiringly, 'What a girl you have become.' At last I had the recognition I had been craving for so long.

Despite her ordeal Mama perked up as soon as she saw Otto and became positively joyful when she heard that he was confident about getting a visa for Papa within the next few weeks. I allowed myself to relax for the first time in days, and I was encouraged to see that some of our Viennese friends had managed to establish the kind of family life to which I had been accustomed while still in pre-Hitler Austria. Our refugee existence in Yugoslavia and Albania had been so unsettling that I had lost hope of ever being able to lead a 'normal' life again. Otto kept reassuring me that although it would not be easy for us in England it would certainly be a lot safer than life in Albania. He had managed to find a job as a packer, which shocked us as he had obtained an engineering degree in Vienna. He explained that most refugees found employment as unskilled labour, and that their qualifications and degrees were not worth the paper on which they were written. His job paid reasonably well and he had managed to save enough money to pay for Mama and I to stay in a nearby boarding-house for the first few days. We were so excited to be sleeping in proper beds with clean white sheets, eating decent meals and living without a constant threat over our heads.

The following day Kurt joined us from Manchester. He looked like a different person and had lost his former bewildered expression. Our family reunion was a joyful occasion with much hugging and kissing, marred only by Papa's absence. That evening we walked along Oxford Street, down Regent Street to Piccadilly Circus, which my brothers told me was the centre of the world. I was mesmerized by the flashing lights that lit up the sky, the huge shops with colourful displays of all the latest fashions, the wide avenues and the throngs of people scurrying by. Otto, sensing my excitement, told me that before anything else I had to concentrate on learning English. I agreed, already planning in my head how I would start studying to be a doctor and getting my life back on course. That evening I stupidly allowed myself the luxury of dreaming only to be brought up short by a group of Nazi demonstrators. I could not believe it: they were carrying posters with swastikas and shouting the same slogans that I had heard in Vienna. I felt as if I had been slapped – to fight so hard to escape only to meet the enemy face to face here on the streets of England. My euphoria evaporated and my dreams disappeared. I was empty. Nobody seemed to pay much attention to the demonstrators, but they had cast a dark shadow, and I could not help but wonder what life would really be like in England.

# 6 • *Accepting Responsibilities*

After our brief stay in the boarding-house we moved to a fully furnished two-room flat in Tavistock Square which had been offered to Otto by a couple of friends who had gone to America. The two rooms were very narrow and had originally been one large room. There was no separate kitchen, only a tiny stove in one corner, and the bathroom and toilet were shared with three other tenants on the same floor. The furniture had come from Vienna and provided almost everything we needed. Compared to our orange boxes in Albania, our new flat seemed luxurious to us. Mama regained her energy and started to enjoy her shopping expeditions and new-found freedom. However, as soon as she received a letter from Papa she plummeted back into a state of depression. His letters were desperate and it was impossible to know how to answer them.

I spent my first few days in London wandering the streets, exploring and marvelling at the shop-window displays. I had not realized how much I had missed the colour and vibrancy of life, and now I revelled in it. I knew, however, that it could not last for long and I would soon have to face my future.

Mama's domestic job had simply been a ruse to get her an entry permit, and I assumed the same applied to my hairdresser apprenticeship; however, Otto thought otherwise. At the end of my first week he insisted on my meeting Mr Cohen to make the necessary arrangements for me to start work at his premises. Mama was determined to come too, so the three of us made our way to the East End, where Otto pointed to a dilapidated hairdresser's shop and ceremoniously introduced it as my new place of employment. I was horrified – what had happened to my studies? I was better than this – surely I was not going to spend my life snipping old ladies' hair in a shabby hairdresser's? I wanted to flee. Had it not been for Otto yanking me across the road I would never have set foot in the place. Otto ushered us inside and there I was faced with Mr Cohen. I couldn't meet his eyes and stood staring at my feet as Otto chatted away in English. Otto kept nudging me and telling me in German that I should smile and be polite to my new employer. I refused, and thankfully could see that Mama was sympathetic to my feelings. Yet she too asked me not to be so stubborn and give it a try. She was understandably worried about the financial implications if I would not take the job.

After Otto had been talking with Mr Cohen for some time, he turned to me and asked me in a harsh tone whether I had any questions. I answered that I wanted to know what my duties would be. When I heard that I would be expected to sweep the floors, clean the basins, wash the brushes and combs and generally help out, I wanted to cry. In exchange for this I would receive board and lodging as well as sixpence a week, which I knew was not even enough to pay for the bus-fare to visit Mama. I was appalled but not surprised by this stinginess. Then my sadness turned to anger. I decided that I would rather starve than accept his terms. I asked Otto to thank Mr Cohen for having helped me come to England but to explain that I had somewhat different ambitions and did not want to work in his shop. Otto tried to make me change my mind, while at the same time muttering a few polite sentences to Mr Cohen to make him believe that I was just a shy young girl afraid of leaving her mother. When he finally realized that I was adamant he had the unenviable task of explaining that I did not want to learn hairdressing after all. Mr Cohen did not seem terribly upset at this news for, as Otto subsequently told me, he had five daughters of his own who were already helping in the business. He had simply thought that his family could easily absorb another young girl, particularly as he would not have to pay much for the additional help, and it would be an easy *mitzvah* (charitable act). I knew I had embarrassed Otto and felt guilty at having ruined his plans, but I was certain that I had made the right decision.

As we were leaving the shop I turned to Otto to apologize to him, hoping that he would understand and forgive me. However, before I could open my mouth he took me by the shoulders and said in venomous tones that I had never heard before: 'Listen young lady, do you have any idea how hard it was to get your visa to England? Do you have any idea how many people I had to ask in order to get someone to sponsor your application? For some reason you seem to think you are better than the millions of girls who would get on their hands and knees to be given the opportunity you have just thrown away. If you think you can just flounce in and out of jobs, you are very much mistaken. I can't believe how selfish you are. What about Mama? What about Papa? What are they going to live on? As far as I am concerned you are on your own now.' He went on and on in this vein for sometime as I just listened, bristling with indignation. Didn't he know how much I had done in Albania? How dare he call me selfish! Why should I accept my menial job when Mama was not expected to become the domestic for which she had been given her visa?

I reminded him how I had coped without him during the many incidents we had encountered on our escape route from Vienna to London, via Yugoslavia and Albania, and told him that I would continue to be able to do so. Having delivered my speech I fell silent, wondering just how I was going to manage this time. I could not even hold a conversation in English, let alone read or write, but I kept muttering to myself that I would find a way without his help. I would show him!

The next morning I set off for Bloomsbury House, the headquarters of the Jewish refugee organization in London. I had hoped to be seen at once so that I could start my job search immediately. I had set myself the goal of having a job by the end of the week. However, that morning there was some commotion at the entrance and I could not get through. I soon found out that the latest *Kindertransport* (children's transport) had just arrived from Germany. There were about 200 little boys and girls, all dressed nicely, with nametags tied round their necks. Most of them were screaming or sobbing quietly to themselves as their foster-parents tried to take them to their new homes. I could hardly look at them in their misery, but their pitiful cries kept ringing in my ears. I could only guess how hard it must have been to part with their parents and realized how unlikely it was that they would ever see them again. It must have been even worse for their parents having to send their children away to a fate they had no control over and to be left behind with no hope of ever seeing them again. I could feel the pain as tangibly as if they were my own children. That night I had nightmares as their pale faces and vacant eyes flashed before me and their screams ripped through the silence, crying out their names. I would have this same nightmare for years to come.

As I turned away I felt guilty at my own good fortune in managing to escape with most of my family. However hard it had been, I had never been totally on my own. I felt that I needed to pay someone back and the only way I could do this was to start earning and making a contribution. I ran up the steps in Bloomsbury House, two at a time, to the youth office, where I joined the queue of teenagers. As I stood there waiting impatiently, I heard one after the other ask about continuing their education. I had decided by this time that my dream of being a doctor would have to wait – I needed to earn some money. I could hardly believe that little more than a year ago I had been so fixed on my career, but now I felt angry that my education had failed to equip me with the simple skills required to earn a living.

When I was finally called into the office the kind lady behind the desk asked me whether I was yet another student looking for a scholarship. I surprised her by answering emphatically 'no', explaining that I wanted to find a job to earn my keep. She was delighted to hear that and said that she was sure she could help to find me something suitable.

It was spring 1939, a few months before the start of World War II, and the British economy was already short of labour, particularly unskilled female workers. Numerous Jewish firms had posted notices of job vacancies at Bloomsbury, and after my personal details had been taken, I was given a list of a dozen names and addresses of firms. It seemed that I would have no difficulty finding work. I was thrilled with my morning's work and left the office as if walking on air. I dashed back to convey my good news to Mama, who I thought would be pleased with my list of names and addresses. However, she started to weep and hugging me cried out that this was not what she had hoped for me; this was not what Papa had wanted for me. I tried to console her, but felt deeply frustrated. I could do nothing right. I decided to wait for Otto to return from work before I mentioned my work plans again. As soon as he walked through the door I proudly presented my list to him, fully expecting him to throw his arms around me and congratulate me. He simply looked at me coldly and asked me how I intended to pay for the bus fare on my job-search. I promised him that I would pay him back out of my first week's wages. He then laughed and asked me how much I expected to earn per week. I was stunned into silence. I had forgotten to ask the most obvious and most important question. Otto just smirked and I was furious at my own stupidity.

I departed early the next morning equipped with a map, the instructions Otto had prepared for me and some money for bus fares. Not knowing any English I showed the bus conductor Otto's note, which gave the name of the stop I wanted, and asked him to show me when to get off. The bus conductors had become accustomed to their many passengers who could not speak a word of English and kindly went out of their way to help them find where they were going to. I found my way easily to the first factory on my list. At the reception I produced the introduction letter given to me at Bloomsbury House. The receptionist then looked at me and asked me a question, which of course I could not understand. It had obviously never occurred to her that I would not be able to speak English and she must have decided I was deaf, as she just repeated the question more loudly. I tried to make her understand that I would never understand what she was asking me, however loudly she shouted, but my attempts just seemed to infuriate her. Finally she called into a back room from where a man emerged. When he saw my card he immediately understood the situation and motioned me to follow him. I could hear the humming and whirring of machines and soon I found myself in a large room with about 40 girls all hunched over machines making goggles. I nearly burst out laughing, I had never operated a machine in my life and here I was expecting to get paid for it. The manager quickly got one of the girls to show me what to do, and I looked on mesmerized by the hypnotic motion of the levers. I could not imagine spending my days doing nothing else but pressing down this lever countless times. I shook my head as we left and tried to explain that I would not be starting work at his goggle factory. My triumphant mood changed as I sought out the next factory on my list. I began to think that maybe being an apprentice hairdresser wouldn't have been so bad after all.

That morning I saw five other factories, all exactly the same as the first. I became increasingly despondent. I had to find work, but it all seemed so tedious and soul-destroying. As I walked into the next office I made up my mind that I would at least give it a try. Once again the receptionist resorted to shouting at me in an attempt to get me to understand. Fortunately, the owner of the factory, Mr Redford, happened to be walking past and enquired what all the shouting was about. Turning to me he addressed me in Yiddish, which being similar to German I could grasp. He then invited me into his office, where I wearily sank into a comfortable armchair. While answering his many questions about what I had experienced during my emigration I looked around the room and liked what I saw. He sat behind a big executive desk on which there were two telephones, one ivory and one red. The office displayed signs of comfort and affluence and success, which appealed to me after all the greyness in my life. I imagined myself working in this environment and hoped he would offer me a job. Therefore, when he asked me if I wanted to work in his factory I eagerly agreed. In my new-found enthusiasm I completely forgot to ask what I would be expected to do and how much I would be paid. Mr Redford then took me along to the personnel office and kindly stayed long enough with me to act as interpreter. When I left to go home I knew that I had to turn up at 8 a.m. the following Monday and report to the forelady on the first floor of the factory.

My spirits restored, I returned cheerfully and gave Mama the good news about my new job. When later I repeated my good news to Otto he could not believe how stupid I had been not to ask what I would be paid and what the job would entail. I felt small and humbled. I tried to keep my self-composure and kept saying how nice Mr Redford had been to me and how clean and well-run his factory looked. I had reasoned that whatever I would be expected to do there could not possibly be as bad as the other jobs that I had turned down. Otto just laughed sarcastically and said, 'Wait and see, my girl.'

The next day when I returned to the youth official at Bloomsbury House to report my job, the kind lady advised me that I would be paid 15 shillings per week. I had no idea how little this was. It was only when she subsequently told me that she would arrange for me to receive a weekly grant of an additional 15 shillings per week until my own wages were increased, that I realized what a paltry sum it was. I only hoped that Otto would consider 30 shillings a week enough for my upkeep.

The day I began my working career I realized how right Otto had been. The factory was no different from the others I had seen. The large building had four floors, each of which housed about a hundred women at electric sewing machines. Suddenly I heard a bell heralding the start of the working day. I was swept upstairs by the rush of women trying to get to their respective machines on time. As instructed, I sought out the forelady on the first floor. She was a kind young woman who tried to get me to understand through sign language rather than screaming and shouting at me. Relieved, I tried to explain to her that I had never learned to use a sewing machine, but that I was eager to give it a try. She motioned me to follow her to a bench where there were ten machines in a row, half of them empty. I sat down on one of the little chairs, ready for my first sewing lesson. As she deftly threaded the needle I noticed her oddly shaped hands and realized that she had only two stumps left on her right hand. I recoiled and wondered how long it would be before I lost my first digit.

Weeks later I learned what had really happened. The belt had broken on her sewing machine and instead of waiting for a mechanic to be called she had decided to save the time and try to repair it herself. Time was precious, as the better machinists were paid piece-rate and therefore did not want to lose the time when their machines were idle. She had climbed under the bench to try to slip the belt back on her machine, but as she was doing so she got her hand caught in the moving wheel. Everyone had been shocked, but had praised Mr Redford for having promoted her to forelady, even though she had broken the factory rules. On hearing this, I felt it was the least he could have done. I had seen the luxury of his own office and had come to resent what I saw as exploitation. Yet none of my fellow workers seemed to share my feelings.

At the end of my first working week I received a wage packet containing 15 shillings. It made me feel proud that I would be able to contribute to our household expenses. As I handed ten shillings to Mama she gave me a big hug and when I repaid Otto the bus fare he finally rewarded me with a kiss on the forehead. It made all the difference and I congratulated myself on living up to my promise. That first week was one of the most gruelling, as I sat eight hours a day at the same machine, with my head spinning at the speed of the needle. After a few weeks I began to enjoy my work in the factory as I was introduced to a number of other Jewish refugees who had been working there for some time. I was surprised how quickly I learned machining. At the end of my second week I calculated that I would have earned more had I been on piece-rate. The following week I reckoned I should have doubled my wages had I not been on time-rate. I therefore began to petition the management to be transferred on to piece-work. After one month in the factory I was labelled an 'experienced' machinist, and was paid piece-rate I began to earn over three pounds per week. Subsequently my wages fluctuated, not so much because of the variation in my pace but rather as a result of the different kinds of work we were given. For instance, to sew black lace on black silk underwear took a lot longer than to do the same thing on other coloured materials, yet the pay was identical. I used to get so worked up at the injustice of it all. Soon working in the factory became not only a source of income and self-respect but, more importantly, a social occasion.

I enjoyed listening to the different experiences my friends had in their attempts to escape from Hitler's fascist regime. My friend Ruth told me how she had sailed from Germany to Cuba, but when they had arrived the Cuban authorities refused them landing permission. They had been sold false landing permits and were now stuck on a boat which was no longer seaworthy, with nowhere to go. After a few weeks at sea, during which nobody on board knew what was to happen to them some committed suicide. The American Jewish Joint Distribution Committee was alerted and managed to get America, England and France to accept a third of the passengers each, on humanitarian grounds. Ruth had wanted to go to America, but as they were given no choice, was sent to England instead.

Ruth was 18 years old when we met: tall, dark-haired and rather overweight, but full of fun and worldly wisdom. She often told about the times she had shared with her boyfriend on that fateful voyage. She would pull out his photograph and gaze at it lovingly as she talked about how he had been the first man in her life to whom she had given herself completely and how on warm nights they lay together on deck, dreaming of a future when they would be married, have children and live happily ever after. I asked her what had happened and she explained that when they were allocating the refugees to the different countries he was sent to France. I never really understood her as she had such a philosophical view about life, always telling me to grab happiness wherever and whenever I could. According to her, each individual only ever has the chance of a few moments of true happiness in their lifetime, and if those are missed a golden opportunity is lost.

One day in July she arrived at work jubilantly waving a letter in her hand. She had finally had news from her boyfriend. She was beaming all day and started to plan for their romantic reunion. However, as war broke out they lost touch with each other and two years later when I met Ruth again she had become resigned to the life of a spinster. She told me that she was lucky to have experienced her few moments of happiness: what more could any individual want of life, she asked philosophically.

Once I had started work my English improved considerably, but it was still somewhat stilted so I welcomed the invitation extended by a group of Quakers to organize evening classes for us. Our teacher turned out to be a non-Jewish German journalist on *The Times* who had recently been rescued from Germany. His life had been in grave danger since he had published an article critical of Hitler and his policies. Being bilingual he was well qualified to teach us English. My mind thrilled at the chance to be learning again and I looked forward to his lessons. Sensing my excitement, he started to pay me more attention. After some weeks he took me aside and said that he thought I had great potential. When I told him of my earlier ambitions to become a doctor he excitedly told me that one of the professors of medicine at London University, who was a good friend of his, had expressed his intention to finance the studies of a promising young refugee. Next time we met he said, 'My professor friend is keen to meet you. I have written his telephone number down so that you can arrange when and where to meet him. If you convince him of your aspirations to become a doctor, which I am confident you will be able to do, then he will sponsor you and you can give up working as a machinist.' This sounded too good to be true. I could not believe it and happily rushed home to where Otto and Mama awaited my return. I burst in and blurted out my news. They both looked at me and I was bewildered as to why they didn't share my joy. Otto then said quietly, 'What about your mother? I don't think your sponsor will have considered supporting your mother as part of the deal. How do you think she will manage without your financial help? You always put yourself first; you seem to have completely forgotten your responsibilities to your family.' Otto's words were like a blow to the stomach and I was winded. I could not believe that they wanted me to spend my life as a machinist and I felt trapped and angry. I had thought they would be so proud of me; instead I was berated for being selfish. The next lesson I explained the situation to my teacher, who was disappointed but respected my reasons.

As the weeks passed I became quite fluent in English and tried to get to know some of the English machinists with whom I worked side by side. The majority of them were young women, most of them recently married and still without children. Gladys and Mary worked on the machines on the other side of the bench immediately opposite me. They were friendly and cheerful young women in their early twenties and they always went out of their way to be helpful. Several times when I was given lots of black underwear to sew three or four days running, while they had received pink material, they volunteered to change the work with me so as to take the strain off my eyes. Doing this was of course in breach of the prevailing factory rules, but they did not care about this and nor of course did I. It gave me a great feeling of solidarity and warmth of belonging to find that my English co-workers were prepared to accept me as an equal.

During these first few months of my stay in England going to work provided my only enjoyable social stimulus. I enjoyed the rather carefree life of factory work in contrast to the sorrowful atmosphere that prevailed in the flat I shared with Mama. Since I was quick in acquiring the skills of machining I had become one of the fastest and best-paid workers on the shop-floor and could, therefore, afford to slacken off periodically and enjoy the social aspects of work. I got to know many young women and became real friends with a number of them. I did not reveal much about myself, but I learned a great deal about others.

Returning from work tired but usually quite cheerful I had to brace myself to face the various problems that Mama and often Otto presented me with. Our flat had become a sort of debriefing place for refugees who had managed to get out of German concentration camps. Whenever I put the key in our front door I prepared myself for the sight of at least one shaven-headed person with hollow, sunken eyes. To me they represented the symbol of Nazi victims and I did not want to be confronted with them on a daily basis. But I did not dare admit to anyone my ambivalence about meeting Otto's old friends and colleagues. It was strange how I almost needed to hear how they had managed to survive under the most dehumanizing conditions, yet at the same time I despised them for allowing it to happen to them.

When Karl turned up one day I was particularly interested in his tale. He had been not only a leading patent engineer in Vienna but also a gifted poet and musician before Hitler annexed Austria. He explained that in one of the many street round-ups of Viennese Jews during the autumn of 1938 he was taken away and deported to Dachau, one of a number of German concentration camps in which he was imprisoned over the past eight months. On the evenings when Karl had dinner with us, I quizzed him about how he had managed to survive all the atrocities he was telling us that he had been made to suffer. He explained that he had a number of different ways of trying to retain his sanity. He had decided to make a mental diary to keep an objective record of his experiences and observations, and every night when he was too cold to fall asleep he would recite to himself his accumulated daily accounts. Even after many months he still remembered the daily entries he had made in his mental diary. Most of his daily accounts focused on his extreme hunger and how it had driven him to scavenge through the rubbish that was thrown out of the camp guards' canteen. Even that he had to do secretly, for on the few occasions he was caught he was severely punished. He also used to train his memory to help him relive some of the happier times of his life. Karl proudly told me: 'My spirits managed to break through the camp's barbed wire fences without being electrocuted. Spirits are free, they cannot be imprisoned.' It was because of Karl that I began to believe in the power of mind over body.

As the weeks and months passed we became increasingly worried about Papa. We still had no news of when he would be able to join us in England and I knew that left on his own in Albania he would become increasingly more morose and downhearted. Though I realized that it was unfair of me to blame him for his state of mind, I could not help but resent his miserable letters to which we always had to reply so positively. I couldn't help but wonder why Papa couldn't be more like Karl. Finally, we received news of Papa's permit, and within a matter of weeks he reached London. Kurt joined us for another family reunion and for a few days at least life seemed free from worry. The five of us felt happy about being once more a united family: something which we realized not many refugees were fortunate enough to achieve. The only dark cloud on our horizon at that time was that Otto was due to sail to Australia a week later. Yet I remembered Ruth's philosophy and made the best of it while it lasted.

I had such mixed feelings about Otto leaving: although I had become somewhat alienated from him about my job I still adored him and desperately needed his guidance and support. However, I was so angry with him for leaving us again. How dare he call me selfish when here he was setting off to a new life leaving me to look after Mama and Papa! Having struggled so hard for the family to be safely reunited in England I could hardly believe that we would be split up again so soon. Otto kept trying to reassure us that as the advance party he would arrange for us to follow him to Australia as soon as possible. We desperately wanted to believe his promises, but we had gnawing doubts whether he would be able to fulfil them in view of the impending threat of war.

Otto's departure left a huge void in my life. I was used to being able to discuss all our problems with him and seek his advice. Now that he had gone I was on my own again, as Mama had stopped telling me what to do a long time ago. Now she waited on guidance from me. Papa was not much more of a help, for as soon as the few days of our honeymoon reunion were over he once more succumbed to his depression. Ever since he had to leave Yugoslavia he felt guilty about being unable to provide for his wife and children. He resented the fact that it was impossible for him to get a job, whereas I, his little girl, had already become a skilled machinist and the sole income-earner in our household. Poor Mama had the difficult task of trying to cheer him up. Every night before he went to bed he used to sigh and say, 'I wish I did not have to wake up again tomorrow morning.' Mama kept urging me to show Papa the respect he expected from his children. I tried hard to be his little girl, but it was difficult with our role reversal, for not only was I the breadwinner but I also had to act as his interpreter and English teacher. Papa was like a fish out of water and once again I had to assume total charge of the family. I wondered if my life would ever become my own.

# 7 • *Wartime*

It was September 1939 and the Allies were finally taking a stand against Hitler. However, we had such mixed feelings over the outbreak of the war. We were obviously eager to see Hitler defeated after all the suffering he had caused, but at the same time we were concerned about our many friends and family still left under German rule who would now have no chance of escape. Most of Mama's relatives were still in Yugoslavia and Papa's were in Czechoslovakia. We had been trying to help them get out and had visited many offices to secure their entry permits, but the bureaucratic processing of applications was dreadfully slow. Now the war had started we feared they would almost certainly perish in the camps. The onset of war also meant that our plans to join Otto in Australia would have to be postponed.

We resigned ourselves to staying in England and prepared for war. We blacked out our windows like all the other households in England, but unlike British citizens we had to attend alien tribunals, where we were vetted for our loyalties to Germany and our allegiance to the Allied cause. We were obviously in an anomalous position since we had arrived with German passports and were therefore still citizens of a country with which England was now at war. However, each of our passports bore a big red 'J' on the front page indicating that we were Jewish and therefore regarded as undesirable subjects in Germany. This put the British legal system in something of a quandary. After much debate we were termed 'friendly enemy aliens' on our registration cards.

For the first few months of the war, life went on as normal. I continued to work as a machinist, while my parents attended English lessons and looked after the domestic duties. Kurt was then still in Manchester. Feeling increasingly isolated from us, he began to explore the possibility of moving us all to Manchester, so that we would all be together again. He came down to London to try to convince us, since he had already found a nice house that we could rent for less than we paid for our two-room flat. He said that it would be easy for me to find a job as a machinist in Manchester since there were factories springing up everywhere as a result of government contracts for soldiers' uniforms; he even hinted that Papa might be able to get work. This was the deciding factor, and within a couple of weeks we were on our way to Salford. I was sad to leave London where I had a well-paid job and a circle of friends, but I knew that if I had said anything my objections would simply have been quashed.

Kurt went out of his way to help us settle into a little street in Salford, the inhabitants of which were predominantly Jewish. The house was terraced, with a small but pretty front garden, and we soon felt at home. I was getting used to being uprooted by now, so life settled into a familiar routine very quickly. I found another job as a machinist, making denim trousers for army personnel. Papa busied himself at home making furniture out of orange boxes that he collected free from the nearby Jewish greengrocer's. Mama pottered round the house, trying to make it a home, and ventured out gingerly to get her bearings.

Soon after we had arrived, Kurt invited me to a meeting of Young Austria in Great Britain, a youth group formed by young Austrian refugees of which he was a prominent member. He introduced me to many of his friends, and for the first time in years, I began to enjoy myself and have some sort of social life. I realized what a nun-like existence I had led in London and threw myself into my new social life with a vengeance. In London my factory work had been my social life, while in Salford I looked upon it as simply a means to an end and found my entertainment elsewhere. Kurt was much happier and healthier than I had ever known him. He had become an extrovert during our time apart; and for the first time in our lives we got on really well. His good looks attracted numerous girls, who thought that one way to his heart was to befriend his sister. Thus I became popular very quickly not only with the boys – since I had become a proficient flirt – but also with the young female members of the group.

I was just getting used to this enjoyable existence when the fortunes of the Allies changed and France fell. This threw the British authorities into a blind panic. Afraid of German spies in their midst, they rounded up all male enemy aliens, including those registered as 'friendly enemies', and placed them in internment camps. Papa and Kurt, together with thousands of other Jewish refugees, passed through a number of internment camps before they ended up on the Isle of Man in fenced-in boarding houses. Once again I was left to look after Mama and the household. However, it was easier this time than it had been in Vienna, as I was older, more experienced and had made a number of close friends who supported me.

Our youth group was depleted as all the boys had been interned except for Ken and Ernst, who for reasons unknown to us had not been taken away by the police. However, the girls voted to continue the activities of Young Austria in Great Britain and Mama agreed we could hold the meetings in our house. Our social life became severely restricted by the curfew that was imposed on all aliens, as everyone had to be indoors, at their registered address by 10 p.m. every night. This meant that Mama and I were left on our own and often chatted till late in the night. We became close in a way that we had not been for years and we exchanged confidences in a way we had never done before. It made me realize how much I had missed her strength and support over the last few years. I also became close to two girls, Eva and Miriam both of whom had confessed that they were in love with Kurt and during his internment they became my close and invaluable allies.

One day when I was chatting with Eva, she confided to me that she wanted to study and get into higher education. She was ambitious and hoped for a chance to prove herself. As I listened to her, I realized how frustrated I had become with working just to earn a living. I needed more stimulation and more of a challenge. I knew that I had to continue earning money and that the only option open to me was to attend night school, which would preclude me from studying medicine, but I was still determined to enrol in something.

The factory where I worked was conveniently situated near Salford Technical College, which offered a number of different evening classes. One day, early in the summer of 1940, I rushed to the college in my lunch hour and insisted on seeing the head of the chemistry department. Surprised by the request, the administrative assistant ushered me into the professor's office. He was a kindly looking man in his early fifties, and asked what he could do for me. I told him about my interests in chemistry in general and pharmacy in particular and showed him my Viennese school reports. He was impressed by my determination and chatted to me at length, by which time I was getting increasingly worried about getting back to work on time. Finally, I felt compelled to explain that I had to dash back to work as my lunch break was almost over. He assumed that I must have been working for one of the local chemical companies – for why else would I be interested in studying chemistry – and calmly assured me that he would square it with my employers should I return late from the college. He could not believe it when I told him what I actually did. At last I managed to disentangle myself, and while dashing out of the college I heard the professor call after me that I must be sure to enrol on the specified night. I ran back to the factory, arriving just in time to hear the whistle blowing.

I felt triumphant. I had been concerned that I would not qualify for entry to the college and suddenly I could see doors opening ahead of me that I had thought closed forever. I vowed to study hard to ensure that I passed all examinations. I was positive that when they saw my grades they would allow me to study medicine. Mama seemed delighted, and for once I could share my happiness without having someone dampen my spirits. She had come a long way from our days together in Vienna and I was pleased to see how she had changed her earlier views about girls' education. She assured me that she would not mind if I left her alone not only during the days but also three evenings a week as long as she knew it was all in a good cause.

I discussed my study plans with Eva, who decided to join me. That September I entered my first classroom in over three years. From the moment the lecturer began I hung on his every word: it was like the first drop of rain after years of drought and I felt giddy with the sensation. I walked home that night as if I were drunk, and in a sense I was: drunk with happiness; drunk with the experience of learning new things; drunk with the dream of a different life.

Those months studying went by blissfully quickly for me, but for Mama every night seemed an eternity. Every night the sirens sounded and I would return home to find her cowering under a table, shaking uncontrollably. I volunteered to give up my studies at least until bombing had eased off a little, but was pleased when Mama would not hear of it. I was so thankful that my studies were able to continue uninterrupted. That was until one evening, having run home from college in the middle of an air raid to beat the curfew restrictions, I found Mama lying unconscious at the bottom of our stairs in the entrance hall of our house. From the bruises on her face and arms I could see that she must have fallen down the steps. I tried to lift her on to the couch in our downstairs living-room, but I was unable to move her on my own and was surprised how heavy she felt. I tried to revive her with a cold flannel but as I applied it to her forehead she started to gurgle, which terrified me. I desperately wished that there was someone around whom I could consult, but I was entirely on my own with Mama in the house and we were in the middle of a fierce air raid. I could hear bombs exploding continuously and they sounded horribly close. I didn't dare open the door without turning out the light in the hall but I didn't want to leave her in darkness while I went for help. I put a cushion under her head, covered her body with a blanket and tried to make her as comfortable as possible. Finally, I decided to switch off the light and open the door to call for help from the air raid wardens, who I knew would be nearby helping with the injured and the homeless. A warden soon came by and asked me where the bomb had dropped, assuming that an incendiary bomb had landed on our house. When I told him of Mama's accident and that I needed an ambulance to take her to hospital he began to shout at me for having bothered him for no good reason: did I not know that a warden's primary duty is to take care of air raid victims? Having had his say he stormed off, leaving me standing there shivering in the cold, not knowing what to do next. I considered alerting our neighbours, but then decided against it because the old mother had a weak heart: if I rang their bell in the middle of an air raid I might cause her to have a heart attack and that was the last thing I wanted to do. So I went back into the house and hearing Mama breathe a little more easily I waited until the 'All Clear' had sounded, when I once more ventured into the street in search of a more sympathetic air raid warden. After a few more abortive attempts I found one who promised to call an ambulance. When I returned I realized that I had tried so hard to be strong, but now all I wanted do was lie down next to Mama, cling to her and cry my heart out.

I must have been lying like that for at least half an hour when I heard a knock on the door and a voice calling through the letterbox that the ambulance had arrived. I let the men into the hall and they gently lifted Mama on to a stretcher. I then noticed that her face looked oddly asymmetrical: the right side was lower than the left. I followed her into the ambulance wondering whether this might have been the result of the injuries she had incurred falling down the stairs. It seemed an eternity before we reached the hospital, as the ambulance had to pick its way along roads covered with rubble. Mama was admitted as an accident case but not a casualty, which meant we had to wait until all the air raid casualties had been seen by the staff before they could attend to her. I never knew if she could hear my words, but I sat stroking her head gently, murmuring how I would sort everything out and she would be back to normal very quickly. I felt so guilty for having been at college just when she needed me by her side. She looked as white as a sheet except for where she was bruised, and her lips were dark blue instead of their usual red colour. Her face still looked out of kilter. I watched her every move and noticed that she was beginning to open her eyes and wake up. She was trying to say something, but seemed unable to put the sounds together to formulate any words.

Finally a doctor came to examine her. He asked me to wait outside the cubicle. I paced anxiously up and down until he came to me and explained that she had suffered a slight stroke, which accounted for the facial paralysis that I had noticed. He was unable to say for sure if the stroke had caused her fall, or whether it was the result of her fall down the stairs. Either way, he assured me that she would recover completely within about two or three weeks, provided she had complete rest and was undisturbed by any worries. I thought the doctor was joking when he asked me if I would be able to ensure these conditions for her recovery. How could I possibly keep her calm when she got upset every time she heard the air raid warning? How could I undertake looking after her 24 hours a day when I had to go to work to provide for the two of us? I decided that the only way I could manage was to worry about one thing at a time, otherwise I would become so overwhelmed that I would end up doing nothing.

The doctor suggested that it would be best if my mother had a few hours sleep in hospital before arranging to have us taken home in an ambulance, for which I thanked him profusely. The nurse gave Mama a sedative, and while she slept I settled into a chair beside her bed wondering how I would cope with her illness. She had always been a textbook mother, putting her family first and neglecting her own interests. Looking at her frail appearance I thought what a remarkable person she really was and how scared I had been at the thought of losing her. All our lives she had tried to be our guide as well as friend and companion, and I berated myself for having been so cruel and ungrateful to her after all she had suffered in her life.

A few hours later we arrived home. As the ambulance men lifted Mama on to her bed she uttered the first audible words since her accident, saying: 'I did not fast yesterday.' Hearing this I thought at first that her mind might still be disturbed and she did not quite know what she was saying. But when she repeated the same sentence several times I began to realize what she was trying to convey to me. Her accident had happened on the evening of Yom Kippur, the Jewish Day of Atonement, on which Jews are expected to fast. Though Mama had always adopted Papa's agnosticism in terms of her children's upbringing, as long as I could remember she had always fasted on Yom Kippur. She used to explain this to us by saying that she was doing so in memory of her own parents, who had been Orthodox Jews. She never admitted that she was fasting as a sort of insurance policy in case God existed after all. That year for the first time since she was a child herself she had refused to fast. She later told me that the atrocities and the cruelty millions of people had suffered under Nazi rule had convinced her that there could be no God, as if there was a God surely he would punish the guilty instead of allowing the innocent to be tortured. I realized that she regarded her accident as God's punishment for her doubts about his existence. Since that day, she always fasted.

Mama was highly agitated and insisted on seeing a Jewish prayer book before she was prepared to settle down for a rest. I rummaged through various drawers before I finally found her an old one. She solemnly took it into her hands, closed her eyes and said a prayer to make peace with God in whose supreme power she once more believed.

As the day wore on, numerous neighbours and friends called on us with offers of help. Mama wondered why I would not let anyone in to visit her, but I had decided that it would be best if she did not know about her stroke, and I was worried that visitors might remark on her somewhat strange appearance. I felt certain that if she knew she had had a stroke it would have an adverse effect on her recovery, so I stalled when she asked to see a mirror, explaining that her facial paralysis and slurred speech were due to her fall and subsequent bruising.

That evening I called Eva and Miriam for a crisis meeting to discuss how I was going to cope with juggling work, studies and looking after Mama. After discussing all the options we concluded that I should arrange to work mornings only, since we calculated that I could probably earn 75 per cent of my full-time wages if I took no breaks and worked straight through. We then agreed that my two friends, who were staying at a nearby youth hostel where they also had to pay for their board and lodging, should move in with us to make up the shortfall in my income. This meant they could help in looking after Mama and share the household chores. After much deliberation Eva and I decided to discontinue our studies. It seemed so unfair: I kept grabbing at my dreams, clasping them for a few glorious moments only to have them slip through my fingers. I began to wonder if there was an evil spirit playing games with me, always raising my hopes and expectations only to squash them again shortly thereafter. I wanted to cry, but I knew that my tears would not help Mama recover.

On the following day Eva and Miriam went to record their intended change of address. However, the policeman went into a back office and returned some minutes later stating that they had been refused permission to move to a house where underground political meetings were taking place. I was stunned when I heard this news and couldn't believe that our Austrian youth group was considered subversive. I could only assume that the strong socialist element was disapproved of and even considered potentially dangerous. In those days everything we did seemed to be seen as a threat, with the security services on high alert for any German uprising in England. Once again I became terrified every time the doorbell rang, expecting some policeman to be standing there waiting to take me away.

The next few weeks passed by in a blur. I was exhausted; my eyes were tired from concentrating so hard for such long periods of time and my head ached. There was little time to rest as I spent the nights trying to calm Mama from the relentless air raids. Finally, I managed to get a prescription for sedatives, which meant we both could get some much-needed rest. Within two weeks of her accident Mama's facial paralysis had almost completely disappeared, and I was able to let her look at herself in a mirror. I never told Papa, Kurt or Otto about Mama's stroke, but simply advised them that she had had a bad fall. I reasoned that there was no point in worrying them unnecessarily, since there was nothing they could possibly do to help.

Much as I was afraid of the police, I decided to continue our youth group meetings at home because they provided some respite for both Mama and me. As I had expected, the day soon came when I opened the door to two policemen who interrogated me in turn about what we did at our meetings. Their questions confirmed my fears that I was under suspicion for organizing illegal political meetings and would be arrested. As soon as they had left I rushed over to see my friends from the group to ask their advice. They thought that I needed to find a public cover so that the police would not suspect or harass me. We came up with a number of ideas, each more ridiculous than the last, until Ken suggested that we get married to throw them off the scent and make them believe that I was more interested in love and marriage than any subversive politics. The group all thought this a brilliant idea. However, I was thrown into a quandary. I was then only 18 years old, and while I seemed mature in the ways of the world I was a novice when it came to love and relationships. Ken seemed intelligent, gentle and was reasonably goodlooking, but emotionally he left me cold. As I lay awake at night pondering what I should do, I felt the resentment well up inside me. Was I to have nothing in my life that I had chosen for myself? My future seemed so much out of my control: first my career and studies, now even my choice of husband. Eva and Miriam kept urging me to accept Ken's offer and he himself began to woo me by bringing me small gifts of books and flowers.

I remained undecided for some days, until a second visit from the police forced me into a decision. The following day I announced to Mama that Ken and I had fallen in love and were planning to get married. I tried to sound excited, but I was crying inside. I was desperately hoping for someone to tell me that I shouldn't marry him. But no one did. My family were all surprisingly pleased at my decision. There was no turning back.

Ken and I began to see a lot of each other, and together we consulted the Rabbi of the local synagogue about marriage arrangements. Shortly afterwards Papa and Kurt were released from their internment camp and returned home, which made things a great deal easier for me. I had convinced myself that I was doing the right thing, and by this time had even begun to feign some feelings for Ken, so when he insisted that I move in with him after the wedding I swiftly agreed. My parents could see no reason why Ken and I should not live with them, even after our marriage, but we stressed the need to start our married life on our own. The Ladies' Guild of the synagogue thought our marriage was very romantic and, appreciating the financial difficulties facing Jewish refugees, offered to arrange the wedding reception. As we prepared for the wedding we played the part of a young couple in love: we held hands, embraced and even kissed. For me it was all role-play, and I assumed it was the same for Ken.

Our wedding day was set for 21 June 1941, which happened to be the day that Hitler's armies attacked the Soviet Union. I had scraped enough money together to buy a new suit and a little hat.

I thought I looked the part, until I showed up at the synagogue and the Ladies' Guild could not hide their disappointment that I was not wearing a traditional white dress and kept telling me that had they known they would have provided one for me. They quickly made a makeshift veil, and I entered the synagogue with Papa. I thought back to the stories Mama had told me of how they had met and felt sure that their wedding had been a different affair. I glanced sideways at Ken and wondered what I was doing, but it was much too late to change anything.

At the reception Ken's speech was very short and showed his nerves. I felt he had let me down already, and not wanting to leave it at that I immediately stood up to say a few words, which in those days was unheard of. I did not want the reception to end and my married life to begin. However, before I knew it Ken and I were making our way back to our one-room bedsit. As soon as we were alone Ken put his arms round me and tried to make love to me. I suddenly had the dreadful realization that this was not just a charade for him and that his offer of marriage was not just the cover-up I had taken it to be. I didn't know what to think. I was still a virgin, and though I had heard a great deal from my fellow machinists (who often spent their days discussing the most intimate of details), I had had no first-hand sexual experience. Ken was clumsy and groped at me wildly, while I lay waiting for it to be over. As we rolled away from each other I lay crying quietly trying to understand how I had got into such a mess. I felt trapped in a way I had never felt before.

Over breakfast the next morning I reminded Ken of the reason why he had proposed to me. It was horribly embarrassing, and we could hardly look at each other. I think he was relieved when I told him that we could not live together as man and wife. We agreed simply to live together as friends for the duration of the war. Yet having to share a bed every night took its toll on both of us. My young body harboured desires which were out of tune with my emotions. I started to have stomach problems, stopped eating and lost a great deal of weight. My parents became extremely worried and Mama spent many hours trying to coax me into telling her what was troubling me. But how could I tell her that I had married Ken out of fear of being interned and because I was scared that she would be left to fend for herself?

Fortunately, after a few months Ken volunteered to join the army and soon left to serve in the Engineering Corps. His departure was a great relief to me and I soon regained my health. The police had left me alone since my marriage, which in a way gave my marrying Ken some validity. Now that I was a soldier's wife I had good credentials, and I quickly moved back in with my parents.

As the remainder of our youth group were released from the various internment camps, an Austria House was established in Manchester where our youth group meetings were then held. Once again I became an active member of the Austrian youth group, now that I was the wife of a soldier serving in the British army and therefore beyond suspicion. At one of these meetings I saw Ernst again; he was tall, goodlooking and also came from Vienna. I found out that he had been fortunate enough to find a sponsor to support his university studies, hence the university scarf he always flaunted. I was immediately attracted to him for he represented everything I wanted but did not have. We began to meet quite frequently and I found myself looking forward to our time together, so much so that I began to think about little else. One evening, as we were walking side by side, we stopped suddenly and turned to face each other. As he pulled me close to kiss me I just melted into his arms, overwhelmed by such powerful feelings. He kissed me deeply and I kissed him back with a passion that surprised both of us. I knew at once that I was in love, and from Ernst's murmurings in my ear I knew it was reciprocated. As we parted we made plans to meet again the following evening, and I floated home, feeling truly alive for the first time. My parents soon noticed my strong attachment to Ernst, and although they liked him they disapproved of their daughter betraying her husband. However, this did not deter me; if anything, my love for Ernst increased daily. Work became an unnecessary evil which kept us apart, and I longed for the final bell to ring to release me into his arms. We spent most evenings together until on his graduation he joined the army. Fortunately he was stationed near Manchester, so we still managed to see a great deal of each other.

We began to make plans to get married and tried to find out how quickly my divorce would come through. We had become quite open about our relationship and were completely taken aback by the Victorian attitude displayed by many of our youth-group friends. Even Kurt, who I felt should have been more understanding, attacked me. At the time he was the leader of our youth group, and instead of talking to me in private about how he felt, hauled me up in front of the committee and told me in no uncertain terms that unless I stopped going out with Ernst, both he and I would be expelled. He even suggested that I stop meeting Ernst and move back to London, where I would be allowed to join the movement there. I was furious. How dare he talk to me like that! I wanted to humiliate him and hurt him in the same way he had me, so I reminded him that I was the only breadwinner in the family and that what he proposed was ridiculous. I then handed in my resignation and ran home shaking with anger as tears poured down my cheeks. Kurt never realized that this episode would cause an irreconcilable breach in our relationship. I would never forgive him.

The following day, as soon as I saw Ernst, I collapsed into his arms, sobbing. As soon as I recounted my experience he also sent Kurt his letter of resignation. About this time, Ken was due back on leave. I was rather nervous, as I had not told him anything about my relationship with Ernst because I had wanted to tell him in person. I did not anticipate that there would be issues, as Ken knew that our marriage was in name only. Ernst had consulted a lawyer about how I could get a divorce and he had insisted that he, Ken and I should get together as soon as possible to sort out our relationship amicably. After all, it was still wartime and Ken was likely to get a posting overseas soon, and we would need to get things moving. Ernst promised me he would get leave on the Sunday after Ken's return home. I now awaited Ken's return eagerly, anxious to get the whole business over and done with as quickly as possible.

I welcomed Ken back warmly, which he unfortunately mistook as an expression of at least some feelings for him, and he got very upset when I rejected his advances that night. I kept thinking that it would be only a few hours before Ernst would arrive and we could openly admit to our love for each other. I anxiously awaited the dawn, and as the sun rose I started to watch the door, hoping to hear a knock. Sunday morning came and went and as the hours slowly ticked by I knew he wasn't coming. Finally, I could stand the tension no longer. I broke down and confessed my love for Ernst to Ken and my parents. Ken was outraged, hurt and disbelieving all at the same time. His first response was to flee, and he started to pack his kitbag straight away. Mama tried to stop him and make me accept my responsibilities. The night wore on as I cried, Ken sat morosely and Mama served hot cups of tea. Ken left the next morning, but as he was leaving he demanded to know Ernst's army unit and where he was based. I didn't think anything of it at the time as I was so exhausted by the previous day's events.

1 Lina Loebl, Scarlett's maternal grandmother

2 David Loebl, Scarlett's maternal grandfather

3 Theresa and Leopold Grünwald, Scarlett's paternal grandparents

4 Outside the Karl Marx Hof, 1935

5 With her parents and brothers, 1936

6 Scarlett (front row, far left) and her classmates at the Glasergasse Realgymnasium, 1936

7 Southern India, 1955

8 Bidding a farewell to Mangala's headman, 1955

9 Scarlett and Bill signing their marriage contract, 1957

10 Scarlett after receiving her PhD, 1958

11 The New Guinea Pavlova

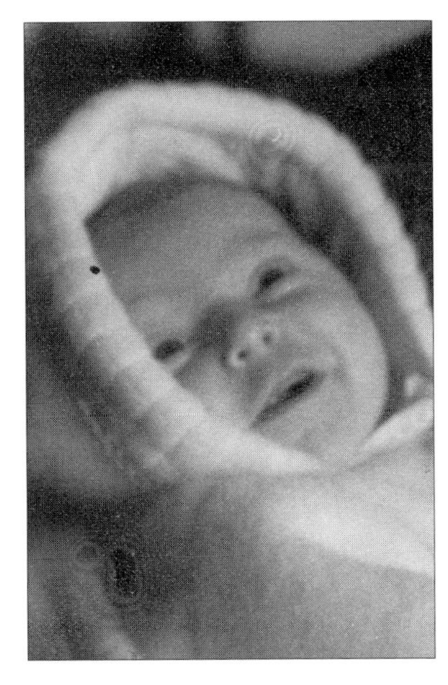

12 Michelle smiling at Scarlett, 1963

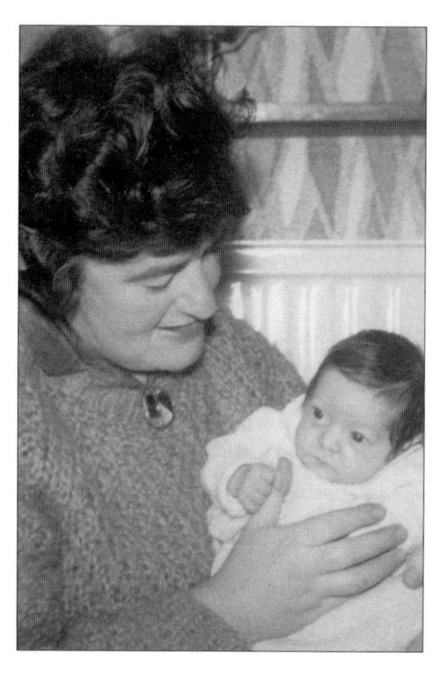

13 Scarlett with Debbie, 1964

14 Scarlett and Bill at Michelle's wedding, 1989

15 Return visit to Mangala, 1996

16 Ruby wedding, 1997

17 Scarlett and Bill shortly before his death in 1999

18 With her brothers, 2002

19 Surprise eightieth birthday party, 2002

I never found out what happened to Ernst and why he never showed up. I wanted to believe that he must have been injured or gone missing in action, as I could not accept the thought that he might not have loved me enough. However, a couple of weeks later I received a letter from him, explaining that Ken had lodged a complaint against him for having tried to take his wife away, and since this was a breach of the officer's accepted code of conduct he hoped I would understand that we had to break off our relationship. I was devastated. I did not believe that Ernst could so coldly and so easily dismiss a love which he had sworn would last forever. I hated him. I was so confused: how could I stop loving someone with whom I had wanted to spend my life? I never wanted to see him again. From the euphoria of first love I was now spent and devoid of all emotion. I reverted to being the child my parents loved, vulnerable and in need of their protection.

I never quite recovered from the shock that I received from Ernst's letter, and it was a long time before I would trust another man. I felt I had been let down not only by my lover but also by my husband and my brother. From that moment I decided that I would never become so vulnerable again. I had opened up the crack in my shell and it had cost me dearly. I was not going to make the same mistake again.

# 8 • *Great Expectations*

I found it difficult adjusting to the idea of living a life of solitude and struggled to find a purpose. It seemed pointless trying to map out a life for myself, as every time I tried to take control of my life it went sadly wrong. Miriam became my only solace, as she felt equally betrayed by men since Kurt had married Eva some months after his release. We became very close and spent many hours discussing our disappointment in love and life. We managed to get jobs as machinists working side by side, which helped us cope with our sense of rejection. However, it didn't last for long. I became increasingly dissatisfied with being a machinist and longed for the bell to sound so that I could escape. Miriam felt the same, and thus we spent the next few months moving from one factory to another to try to relieve the boredom. In one place we machined sailor dolls; in another we worked on a conveyor-belt, making coats for air raid wardens.

The constant changes made us realize that we needed to do something drastic if we were to ever escape from the factories. We examined our school reports and discovered that both of us had done well in mathematics. We tried to come up with ideas for jobs for which we would qualify. This took hours and we laughed at how little we were actually qualified for. Finally, I suggested that we might make good wages clerks. When we presented ourselves at the Labour Exchange we were sent to an electrical engineering firm. There we were interviewed, given a test in arithmetic, and to our greatest surprise we were both offered employment immediately at a salary considerably higher than anything we had managed to earn as machinists working on piece-rate. We looked at each other agog, unable to believe our luck. We burst out laughing: it had been so easy! We felt as if we had just won first prize in a lottery.

Life took on a different routine as I moved from the shop floor to office work. The working day started at nine instead of eight o'clock, the surroundings were more pleasant without the continuous noise of machines and we used our brains rather than our hands. I felt as if a heavy load had been lifted off my shoulders since I no longer had to try to beat the clock to increase my earnings. It made me realize what a strain piece-rate machining had been for me. To be a salary earner and to get paid even for public holidays was a luxury I found difficult to accept. Mama was delighted with the change in me. I became more relaxed and more as she expected a girl of my age should be.

While the intensity of the war increased, things became easier for us. Papa got a job as a packer, which, though he kept complaining was below his dignity, at least occupied his days and brought in an income. During the first years of the war when the German fascists were winning on all fronts we remained in dread of what would happen if we fell into Nazi hands again. We could never quite believe that we were safe until the Second Front was established and the Allies began to force the Germans to retreat. We then began to voice our worries about our family and friends who had been left behind. Previously we had not talked much about them, though of course we were all worried about what might have happened to them. The thought that they might not have survived was too horrific to contemplate.

Finally, the war was over and crowds filled the streets, rejoicing in the victory. I tried to join in, but was completely overwhelmed. Strangers were hugging and kissing each other in the streets, people were dancing and singing. A half-drunk sailor was thrust against me by the crowd: he tried to kiss me and when I did not respond he jeered and called me a cold fish, or was I perhaps a German sympathizer? I was frightened and tried to escape down a side street. The mob violence that I had seen in Vienna had left me with a deep-rooted fear of crowds and I stuck to the back streets as I made my way home.

I could not understand why I did not share the people's jubilation – to me it just seemed like a huge anticlimax. During wartime everyone referred to everything in terms of 'only for the duration of the war', assuming that peace would provide the panacea for all our problems. Now the war was over, what next? What difference would it make to my own life? I was 21 years old and living with my parents. My only skills were machining and being a wages clerk. I had no prospects and unlike those around us who could at least return to the lives the war had interrupted, I had no way back, I could never return to my schooldays or my childhood. Some of my German and Austrian friends discussed the possibility of going home, but I could not face living where I suspected everyone of having been a Nazi and party to all the terrible atrocities I had witnessed.

A Jewish clearinghouse was established soon after the war had ended to try to help locate those left under occupied territories. We queued up and handed over the long list of our relatives and many of our friends. Day after day we waited anxiously for news until we learned that one after another could not be traced but was assumed to have perished in the concentration camp at which they were last heard of. Like many others, Mama and Papa went into a state of shock and were like zombies. It was impossible to conceive what had taken place in Germany, the magnitude of the cruelty. When we heard that my grandmother had been marched into a gas chamber, Papa went white and sat with clenched fists, unable to speak for hours. I had a strange cloak of general grief, as I hardly knew the numerous relatives who had died at the hands of the Nazis. I did not mourn their loss any more than I mourned the millions of other Nazi victims who had been murdered. I hated to see my parents' misery and instead of grief I felt anger.

I decided to discard everything that identified me as Austrian and as soon as it was possible I applied for citizenship, which I obtained without any difficulty. I also decided to change my name from the Germanic 'Trude' to something that sounded more English. I searched and searched for the right name for me until Miriam suggested 'Scarlett'. We had both seen the film and read the book *Gone with the Wind* and had loved it. Miriam convinced me that I had a streak of Scarlett O'Hara in me: a fighter to the end.

My new name also gave me a new identity. I reread *Gone with the Wind* innumerable times and tried to absorb some of Scarlett's determination and her will to succeed. I so desperately wanted to prove my Nazi teacher wrong. I would not end up in the gutter, as he had predicted, but would fight to make something of my life. I just didn't know what it was. I had had bad experiences with men. When Ken was demobbed from the army he came back to me suggesting that we give our marriage another chance, but I flatly refused. I did not care that we were not divorced, for at the time I could not imagine that I would ever want to get married again. Marriage and children were out of the question. Fascism, and the brainwashing it represented, had completely disillusioned me from becoming a political activist. I continued to struggle to find a meaning and would not accept that my sole purpose in life was to care for my parents. I could see myself becoming a frustrated spinster, old before my years, with no joy in my life. I tried desperately to put my mental house in order, but I had no one with whom to discuss my fears. I hardly spoke to Kurt and Eva was too wrapped up in her life with him to want to spend time with me. Miriam had moved to London, hoping to return to Austria, and we now had such different aspirations that we sadly drifted apart. Mama was the only person left to whom I could talk. She was perceptive enough to realize that I was going through a difficult phase, but she spent most of her energies on Papa, trying to keep him cheerful. The anticlimax following the end of the war was even worse for them than it was for me. There was nothing to go back to Vienna for and there was little in England to keep them there. Hitler had robbed us of something that we could never recover: a normal life.

I could not burden my parents with my problems, I had no friends on whom to unleash my frustrations and I soon became listless and lethargic. I dragged myself to and from work on auto-pilot. I had been promoted to skilled costing clerk, but I was still bored. I operated like a human calculator and felt totally dehumanized. I needed the interaction and stimulation of others. This gave me the idea that I should train for a job that involved dealing with people rather than machines, and I resolved to train to become a personnel manager in a large firm. I quickly discovered that I would need to attend evening classes and went to enrol at the Manchester College of Technology. The head of the Industrial Administration Department talked me into taking the full four-year night school course leading to a diploma rather than just the personnel management course, which meant that I had to take six subjects per year, attending two one-hour lessons three nights per week. It was the first year that this diploma course was offered and there were only 15 students enrolled, among whom there was only one other woman.

After a couple of weeks my spirits started to soar as my mind responded to the new challenges. I attended my classes eagerly and threw myself into my studies. I had some catching up to do as I was the only one who had never studied English, but I soon came top of the class. However, balancing my work life with my studies became increasingly difficult, so I placed an advertisement in the local paper that read: 'Young woman with organisational skills and managerial abilities, with working knowledge of French and German, seeks challenging work.' I was amazed when I received six replies. I went to several interviews and decided to work as secretary of an export company that sold British textile machinery in various European countries. The boss explained to me that he needed someone whom he could trust to place incoming orders correctly in this country and make the necessary shipping arrangements for exporting the machinery while he spent most of his time travelling. I thought this kind of work would suit me well, and I happily changed from the engineering firm to a nice new office in the centre of Manchester. My new job demanded quality rather than quantity of work, which gave me additional time to pursue my studies. On most days I had to do no more than write a few letters, in German or French, and make some phone calls. Yet my boss was very pleased with the way I quickly managed to run his business and he rewarded me with a handsome bonus every Christmas.

As the course came to an end I became restless again, wondering what I would do with the diploma and how I would fill my time. I no longer knew if I actually wanted to be a personnel manager. Once again, the decision was made for me. I studied economics in my final year and thought that the lecturer was truly brilliant. He was an ex-miner from Newcastle, who had been sponsored by his trade union to go to Ruskin College, Oxford, and subsequently won a scholarship to Oxford University. After our term examinations in economics, in which I came top of the class, he asked me to stay behind. I had no idea what to expect and was flabbergasted when he suggested that I should go on to university to study economics.

Going to university had always been a secret ambition of mine that I had never dared voice. I had always watched the university students enviously when I turned up for my evening classes and had come to regard their long university scarves as the symbol of achievement. I had seriously considered buying myself a scarf, just to try to gain the self-confidence I was certain went with it. I was flattered by my lecturer's words and greatly encouraged, but I could see no way that I would ever be able to attend university on a full-time basis. I never thought that I would qualify for a scholarship, and even if I did qualify, it would never be enough to support my parents. My lecturer tried to dispel my doubts and strongly recommended me to apply to Ruskin College, where he himself had begun his academic career. Once I had a place at Ruskin a scholarship would follow automatically, and he assured me that in special hardship cases like mine the authorities might be prepared to increase the grant.

We talked for over an hour while he painted a bright new future for me. He explained that at Ruskin College I could only get a diploma, but from there I could apply to go on to university. He was so convincing that I agreed to submit an essay to Ruskin College with my application for admission. The following weekend I worked feverishly trying to produce the essay.

I did not have the courage to tell Mama what I was doing, as I knew she would only worry how she and Papa would cope if I moved away. I was not only the main breadwinner but also acted as a much-needed buffer. The difficulties and hopelessness that they both faced, and their inability to admit this to each other, made both of them, but Papa in particular, very irritable. Even the most trivial of disagreements would escalate into a huge argument, and Papa would then shout about how no one listened to him now that he was no longer the breadwinner and would rush out of the house, slamming the door behind him. Mama had learned that it was best to keep quiet when Papa got into these rages and just sat there motionless, drained of all strength. I would then be dispatched after about an hour to fetch him home. Mama always welcomed him back rather than reproaching him, and all was forgotten until the next incident. How could I leave them to go to Oxford? I reasoned with myself that I had already made enough sacrifices for them and I also felt resentful towards my brothers who had simply left me to cope with the situation. Surely, it was someone else's turn to bear the heavy burden? And so I wrote and rewrote my essay countless times until I was satisfied.

I knew it would be at least three weeks before I could expect a response from Ruskin College, but even so I raced to check the post every day and was nervous and on edge. Mama noticed me hanging round waiting for the postman and teased me that I must be waiting for a love letter. Finally it arrived. I didn't know whether to laugh or cry. I turned it over in my hands, not wanting to know the contents. I couldn't believe that I might have been accepted, but nor could I believe that I might have been rejected. All my hopes and fears lay in this one slim white envelope and I was desperate to delay the moment of truth. I took the letter, unopened with me to the office. After settling myself at my desk I slowly sliced it open and read the brief contents. I was overjoyed and immediately jumped up and began dancing round the office clutching the letter. It said that the principal of Ruskin College had read my essay with great interest and hoped that I would be able to come for an interview the following week. Needing to share my news with someone, I rang my economics lecturer.

When he heard my rapturous ranting, he simply said, 'well done', and that it was just as he had expected. I felt completely deflated and started to wonder whether my rejoicing was somewhat premature, as I still had the interview to get through.

I had such mixed feelings that I no longer knew what to think. I so wanted a friend to confide in and I realized how totally alone I was. I felt that I would burst if I didn't find someone to talk to, so against my better judgement I decided to confront Mama. On my way home from work I bought her a bunch of mimosa, her favourite flowers, to help soften the blow of my news. She was delighted with the flowers, but was immediately suspicious. She mistook the twinkle in my eyes as a sign of a new boyfriend, which made me burst out laughing in the light of my experiences. She looked confused, but as I braced myself and handed her the letter her expression changed to one of scorn. She grabbed me by the shoulders and railed at me, 'Who do you think you are to believe you are clever enough to go to Oxford? Surely you realize you will never get through the interview?' I was shocked and hurt by her contempt and selfishness. I so needed her support and encouragement and I thought that she would have at least been proud of my achievement even if she had not wanted me to go. That evening I stayed in my bedroom, staring blankly at the walls and refusing the food Mama had cooked. The next few days I hardly said a word to my parents and stayed in my bedroom as much as possible. On the morning of my interview, as I was preparing to leave for Oxford, Mama grabbed my hand and pulled me to her in a tight embrace, whispering: 'If this is what you really want, then I do hope you get it.' I set off, reassured by her hugs and kisses, but I was too preoccupied to respond.

As I sat on the train, I became increasingly nervous and unsure of myself. I tried to pull myself together, remembering how I met Mr Maidanatz, faced the Albanian invasion, survived the ordeal at Cologne airport and supported my parents over the years. One interview should not deter me from my dream. By the time I reached Oxford I felt composed and reasonably sure of myself.

I arrived at the college puffing and panting as the train had been late and I had had to run all the way from the station. I found the college secretary who welcomed me and told me how pleased he was to meet me after all the nice things his old friend, my economics lecturer, had written about me. After a few minutes he ushered me upstairs to meet the principal and vice-principal who were to interview me. They too were very friendly and tried their best to make me feel at ease. They began by telling me how much they had enjoyed reading my essay and we discussed that topic for a while. They then asked my views on some of the economic problems concerning the world in general and England in particular. I began to feel out of my depth and when they enquired whether I had read a particular article in the previous week's *Economist* I had to admit that I had never even heard of the journal, let alone read the article they were referring to. They smiled knowingly at each other and then dismissed me after a final few pleasantries.

I was mortified. I left the college in tears, even forgetting to bid farewell to the kind secretary. How could I have been so stupid? Mama was right! The very thought of returning home in this dejected state filled me with dread. I sat on a college bench and tried to collect my thoughts when suddenly I heard a voice calling my name. I looked up and saw the college secretary running towards me. He berated me for having left without stopping for a cup of tea with him. But as soon as he saw the state I was in he sat quietly beside me as I explained what a mess I had made of the interview and how miserable I was. I had set my heart on going to Ruskin College and now it was all ruined. He patted me gently on the back and, smiling, told me he had just heard the principal dictate a letter offering me a place for the coming academic year. I was stunned. I thought he was making fun of me, but he reassured me that he was telling the truth. As the news began to sink in I threw my arms round his neck and hugged and kissed him. He seemed somewhat surprised yet pleased at my response. He offered to show me round the college and as we walked back to the college together I felt as if I was walking on air.

I left the college the second time in a very different frame of mind from the first. I wanted to shout from the rooftops about my triumph. As I passed students in the streets I was tempted to go up to them and tell them that I would be studying at Oxford soon. Instead I treated myself to an English cream tea to celebrate and kept pinching myself to check if I was dreaming.

My return rail journey was pleasant. I started chatting to a couple who had been to see their son who was studying at Oxford and proudly announced that I would be starting the following year. It was odd that I found it easier to share my happiness with complete strangers than with my own parents. I was not looking forward to breaking my news to them. Mama was very sweet when I gave her my news and she congratulated me and told me how proud she was of my achievement. She must have spent the day adjusting to how she would manage without me. Papa was not quite so positive but he too could not hide his pride.

Once I knew for certain that I was going to Oxford in the autumn, I proudly told all my lecturers and colleagues about it. My economics lecturer chuckled to himself when I gave him my good news after telling him about my humiliating interview. He was obviously pleased to find that he had put me on to the right road. I never discovered what part he played in getting me admitted to Ruskin College, but I suspect he wrote about me not only to the secretary but also to the principals, and his recommendation may have weighted their decision heavily in my favour. After I finished my evening classes I never met him again. I later heard that he had moved away and gone to another college. I often think about him and what a huge debt I owe him, for without him my life would have taken a very different path.

I completed my evening class course with flying colours, was given the diploma in industrial administration and was awarded the 'Sir Murdoch McDonald Prize' by the Association of Mechanical Engineers for the best student of the year. Prize-giving came and I was thrilled to see how proud my parents were at a function at the Grand Hotel when they watched the mayor of Manchester formally handing me the books I had chosen as my prize and heard him praise my extraordinary commitment to study. The occasion has always stuck in my mind as one of the first times I had encountered true sexism. The functionaries of the association, all of whom were men, had turned out in large numbers, and were surprised and embarrassed when they saw that the prize-winner was a young woman. It had never occurred to any of them that a woman could come top in what they regarded as a man's domain. They were somewhat loath to invite me to their all-male dinner at which the award winner was supposed to be the guest of honour. One of them casually mentioned the possibility of my joining them for a meal, but warned me that I would be the only woman and that I might have to listen to jokes not usually meant for the ears of a woman. Smiling inwardly, I gladly accepted his invitation, much to his surprise and acute embarrassment. I will never know if they were on their best behaviour that evening, but I certainly enjoyed my evening out.

During the summer months of 1949 I busied myself with preparations for my move to Oxford. I had received my scholarship, but it was not enough to leave a surplus for my parents. I therefore discussed finances with Mama. We explored several possibilities, finally agreeing that it would be best if I found them a lodger whose rent would help meet their expenses. I managed to find them a nice, quiet young man, who fitted into the household and whose payments more than compensated for what they lost because of my departure. Though I knew perfectly well that the course I was embarking on at Oxford was for two years I thought it best to assure my parents that I would be away for no more than one year. I had tried my best to lessen the pain of leaving and felt that I had done everything in my power to ease the financial burden. However, our farewell was tearful and emotional. It was if we were back in Albania and they did not believe that we would ever be reunited. I had to reassure them continuously that Oxford was only a train-ride away and that I would be back to visit as I often as I could.

Ruskin College had been established in order to provide an education for mature students who had missed the opportunity to study earlier in life. So it was a motley crew that gathered on that first day at the hall of residence. The majority of students were men, but I was surprised to see the number of different nationalities: Africans, Americans, Asians, Indians and Europeans. I later found out that most of them had been sponsored by Labour Party groups or trade union branches in their respective home countries.

Lectures started soon after and I immediately struggled with the routine of the day. I was used to studying at night and working during the day, but now I was free to spend my days reading in the library or preparing for essays. I felt guilty as it seemed immoral, to be paid to do something I enjoyed. I decided to try to finish the two-year diploma course in one year. The college principal tried his best to dissuade me and pointed out that even if I could get dispensation from Oxford University to do this and succeeded in qualifying for the diploma, I would miss out on so much of the full life that Oxford had to offer. I remained adamant, however, and he gave way.

Thus I spent my time at Oxford buried in books and essays, while my fellow students attended guest lectures, joined in debates and generally enjoyed the life that Oxford offered. Days, weeks and months rushed by as I thirstily drank from the fountain of knowledge. I never stopped to consider where it was going to lead, but for once in my life enjoyed my epicurean existence. Like my namesake Scarlett in *Gone with the Wind* I kept saying to myself, 'I won't think of it now, I'll think of it tomorrow.'

At the beginning of 1950 the previous year's college intake began to scramble for the limited university places. By that time I had come to appreciate that it was not really immoral to spend one's days learning new things and discussing theoretical propositions while being paid to do so. I therefore decided to apply for the various adult scholarships on offer. Together with two other female students I even sat for the qualifying examination at St Hilda's, one of the few Oxford colleges for women. I was under no illusion that I would pass and so was surprised some days later to be summoned to the principal's office. As I entered her office she congratulated me on my performance. My mind raced, and for a few moments I allowed myself the luxury of believing that I had achieved my ultimate ambition to become an Oxford undergraduate. But as I looked back at the principal's face I knew I had been dreaming in vain, for she proceeded to tell me that though I was academically gifted, my social background would preclude my entry to any college. I was enraged as I listened to her entrenched upper-class ideology and left the room in a fit of pique. As I did so I heard her mutter to herself: 'These girls have no manners.' When the other Ruskin students heard of my experience, and also discovered that neither of the other two girls who had sat for the St Hilda's scholarship examination had been accepted, they wanted to stage a demonstration outside St Hilda's branding it a symbol of class discrimination. However, I no longer wanted to be a part of Oxford's class-conscious establishment and I certainly did not want to become the centre of a political incident at Oxford. It took all my powers of persuasion to prevent them from holding that demonstration.

I succeeded in getting the Oxford diploma in economics and political science in one year, which had previously been unheard of, and on the strength of this was offered a scholarship to Manchester University to study economics. My parents were thrilled when they heard that I would be able to live with them again, and by the autumn of 1950 I was ready to become a fully fledged undergraduate. Just as I thought life was becoming a little too easy I was brought up short. I realized that my scholarship did not provide enough for me to contribute to our household expenditure. Stricken, I consulted some of the lecturers who had taught me at night school, and when they heard that I was about to give it up and go back to work they kindly volunteered to help me find a part-time job to supplement my meagre scholarship.

Thus at the same time as I became a first-year undergraduate student in economics I also became an instructor at Bradford Technical College, where every Wednesday evening I taught three courses: industrial relations, social psychology and social philosophy. I felt ill-equipped to teach these courses, but could not refuse the offer because I desperately needed the money. I therefore got hold of the relevant textbooks and managed to stay one lesson ahead of my students. The fact that we were learning together seemed to spur my students on and made them regular attenders. Thus my course continued for the whole academic year, unlike many others which were discontinued because of poor attendance. I congratulated myself on overcoming yet another hurdle. I was past waiting for someone to give me a sign of recognition, Otto was miles away and my parents would never have understood.

As soon as term started I treated myself to the university scarf I had so coveted. However, I was disappointed that I did not immediately gain the self-confidence that I thought went automatically with the scarf. I tried my best to fit in with the other students, but it was not easy since I was about ten years older than most of them. Not only did my fellow students eye me with some trepidation, but the junior lecturers also seemed to consider me a threat. I always used to sit in the front row of the lecture theatres, right under the eye of the lecturer, and if I did not understand what was being said I would unconsciously shake my head. The lecturers mistook this as a sign of disagreement and that I was questioning their knowledge. This irritated some of the younger ones so much that to the amusement of the rest of the class, they often stopped their lecture to find out what it was that I disagreed with.

Since the boys greatly outnumbered the girls on the course, we were much in demand. I became a favourite, as I was older than most of the other girls and presented a fantasy figure to the many 18-year-old males in my class. I often used to find little bags of sweets or even a few flowers from anonymous admirers when I returned to my library desk after a tea-break. One tall, spindly boy with dark hair and a face covered with spots seemed to have fallen head-over-heels in love with me. He presented me with poems he had written, in which he declared his undying love. He saw me as an enigmatic woman to whom he wished to devote the rest of his life. For a while I was amused and flattered by the attention. Then one day, I accidentally discovered a note in his handwriting in which he described, in obscene language, how I had responded to his lovemaking. I was disgusted and confronted him, telling him that I never wanted to speak to him again. He was obviously upset and embarrassed and pleaded like a little boy with me. However hard I tried to keep away from this young man it took months before he finally cooled off and began to pursue with equal commitment a girl more his own age.

I attended a number of wild student parties. However, much as I tried to join in the fun I always felt the outsider. Not only was I considerably older but I also had so many different kinds of experience, whereas most of them were still novices in the school of life. I envied them their carefree ways and found myself thinking how unfair it had been that by their age I had suffered the trauma of fascism, emigration and what felt like a lifetime behind a sewing machine. What I had struggled so hard to attain, they would have considered as their birthright. I tried to swallow the bitter pill and simply enjoy my days at university. However, I so wanted to fit in and join their lengthy debates that many days I would return to my bedroom and cry into my pillow. I wanted their self-belief and blithe confidence that they could change the world, yet my life had been so different from theirs that I found them naïve and foolish.

I spent most of my time with a group of adult students who, having served in the forces, were catching up on their education. It was then that I met Beccie. Beccie was Jewish and already in her late forties; she was married to a prosperous businessman and had two teenage daughters. I took to her immediately and over the next three years we became close friends. Now that I had found a group of kindred spirits at the university it was not long before I paired off with one of them called Ron. He had a great sense of humour and I thought he was extremely intelligent. He made me realize how earnest my youth had been and how little I had laughed in all those years. Ron tried his best to help me make up for lost time. We spent almost all our free time together and I became very fond of him. I even began to wonder whether I was at last beginning to fall in love again. This made me nervous and I constantly quizzed him on his feelings and his commitment. We behaved like a couple of kids in love for the first time. I guess both of us had missed out on the usual early innocent encounters with the opposite sex: he because of his war service and I as a result of emigration.

As our first year at university neared its end I began to explore vacation jobs. The long summer vacation was an unaccustomed treat for me. I searched for opportunities that would enable me to maximize my earnings and at the same time be instructive and enjoyable. One day, as I was passing a travel agency, I noticed an advertisement for couriers to host package tours on the Continent. It occurred to me that I might make a reasonably good travel hostess. Ron agreed, and together we composed a letter offering my services. I was asked to go to an interview in London. Ron offered to accompany me, and we hitchhiked together, having great fun on the way. I had moments when I began to be afraid that things were running too smoothly, and I was scared some disaster was bound to happen to spoil it all. I quickly dismissed the thought from my mind and reminded myself of Ruth's motto: 'Grab happiness while you can.' How could I be unhappy while travelling on a lovely June day through the lush English countryside, sitting next to a young man who kept whispering in my ear how much he loved me? It was all too good to be true!

My interview went well and I was immediately offered the job of resident hostess in a small Austrian village near the border with Italy and Switzerland. I was jubilant and notched up another success on my mental scoreboard. I rushed back to Ron, who I had left waiting for me at a nearby café. From the expression on my face he could see that everything had gone well and hugged me, jokingly saying, 'You look as if you've been appointed director of the travel agency rather having just been given a summer job.' He then offered to take to me out for a meal to celebrate. We had a lovely time together until we prepared to pay. While Ron went to the toilet he handed me his wallet to pay the bill. As I pulled out the money, a small paper cutting dropped to the floor. I picked it up and to my horror found myself reading the engagement announcement between Ron and a girl called Sylvia. I was dumbstruck and had to reread it several times before I would let myself believe it. As I stood waiting for the change Ron joined me, wondering why I had turned white. I simply thrust his wallet and the announcement into his hands and ran out of the restaurant. He tried to follow me, but I hid in a doorway and watched as he raced past me. I crouched down, feeling unable to move. I could not understand why he had lied to me. How he could treat me like that? Why I was so unlucky in love? I began to wonder whether it was my fault. What did I do to make men always let me down? I was furious with myself for opening up and allowing myself to feel for Ron.

I was on my own again and found myself having to hitchhike back to Manchester by myself. I arrived home safely, no thanks to

Ron, and told Mama about my summer job. She was surprised by my lack of enthusiasm, but I couldn't explain to her about what had happened with Ron. I avoided all the places I used to frequent with Ron in an effort not to have to face him. However, he cornered me after one of my classes and started quickly on what seemed like a well-rehearsed speech. He explained that his engagement had been arranged by his parents, that until he met me he never thought he could really love any girl and was therefore prepared to marry the girl his parents had chosen for him. Since he had met me he had come to realize how much he could get out of a relationship and had decided to terminate his engagement. I wished I could believe him, but the damage was done. I would never again let him penetrate my protective outer shell. I was not prepared to listen to or accept any of his excuses and explanations. After the crowd around us had dispersed and we were left on our own I simply said, 'I never want to see you again!' and walked off, hoping that he would not have noticed my tears. I was deeply hurt and angry. I became a solitary student, happier in my own company rather than risking being hurt again.

I concentrated on my studies and my first year was soon over. I did well in my preliminary exams, but as soon as they were finished I turned my thoughts to Austria. I felt strangely excited about returning to Austria for the first time since I had escaped in 1939. It seemed an eternity ago and so much had happened in the intervening period. I felt finally that I could prove that I had not ended up in the gutter. However, as I journeyed to Austria, my feelings turned to dread and I despised myself for having wanted to return to a country which had caused so much pain and suffering. I felt torn: I would never forgive the Austrian people, yet there I was heading for a summer in the Tyrolean Alps, I felt like a traitor.

On my arrival in the village I was charmed by its glorious alpine setting. The Hotel Post, where I was to be stationed, was a nice place, with friendly staff and excellent food. A Scandinavian travel agency also used the hotel and I soon struck up a friendship with Knut, my Scandinavian counterpart. He was tall and blonde and had years of experience as a travel host, which made him extremely useful in showing me the ropes. He taught me how to increase my salary by earning a commission on the purchases my tourist group made. All I had to do was to arrange to stop at the various gift shops during our day-trips. I accumulated what at the time seemed to me quite a considerable amount of money, which became a welcome supplement to my scholarship.

As our friendship grew I told Knut about my refugee background – a fact that I did not admit to anyone else throughout the whole summer. Knut in return confided in me that he had been one of the Norwegian underground leaders involved in fighting the German occupying forces, many of whom were Austrian. I felt much happier having found a kindred spirit who shared my unease with the Austrians with whom we were expected to mix. I tried to enjoy myself, but every time I met an Austrian I could not help but ask silently, 'Where were you when Hitler tried to kill us? What did you do to help us? Were you one of the murderers?'

During the summer I tried to keep my distance from the local men and those in my tour groups. However, this only seemed to add to my appeal. I received several proposals of marriage during those few months. I have always wanted to know if they would have been as interested in me had they known I was Jewish.

As a courier I was entitled to cheap train fares and hotel discounts, so I arranged for my parents to have their first holiday in years, in Bad Gastein, one of their favourite spa resorts in Austria. I even had Mama to stay with me in the Tyrolean village after Papa had to go back to his job in Manchester. Mama was happier in the two weeks she was with me than I had seen her for years. Her eyes sparkled in a way that they had not done since before we had left Vienna. I saw her as I had when I was a child and I realized how the refugee experience had aged her far beyond her years.

The summer passed all too quickly. It had been a welcome break from the emotionally charged university life I had left and I had learned a great deal about establishing relationships. I put into practice Mama's little idiom 'A smile and a kind word costs you nothing, while it may help you a great deal', which seemed to work, as I was on good terms with the villagers, the hotel management and staff as well as my demanding tourists.

After the last tourists had left Knut and I had a couple of days to make the final arrangements for closing the season. As we prepared to leave the villagers held a party for us which completely overwhelmed us. We felt so guilty at having questioned their allegiances. However, since no one had mentioned the war throughout the summer our imaginations had been left to their own devices. I returned home suntanned and pleased with myself for having earned enough money not to need to teach evening classes. This allowed me to concentrate on my own studies. I submerged myself in my books and enjoyed my days in the library toiling over my essays.

That Christmas I decided to make use of all my contacts in Austria and organized a student skiing trip. The travel agency I had worked for in the summer was not offering winter holidays, so I felt it would be a good opportunity to have a break and earn a little extra. I put posters up around the university campus and was soon oversubscribed and ended up taking 25 students. When we arrived I was greeted like a long-lost friend and made so welcome. Knut was also there with a group of tourists and together we had a fairy-tale Christmas. The village was covered in snow and the only way to get around was on horse-drawn sledges with little bells jingling on the side. On Christmas Eve we crowded into the local church for midnight mass and on New Year's Eve we organized a big party. The two weeks sped by and since I had enjoyed it so much and made quite a bit of money out of my first travel venture I promised to organize one again for the following year.

However, on my return I received a letter from the travel agency. The management of the Hotel Post had informed them that I had organized my own tour and had written to advise me that my services were no longer required. I was fuming when I read this – it seemed so unfair. I had not taken any business away from them. There was no point in arguing with them and shortly afterwards I was offered a courier job with another agency for the following summer.

My next summer assignment was far more taxing than the previous one had been. This time I had to take tourists on special trains through Austria and Germany and make short stops along the way. I was therefore continually on the move and at the end of the season I was exhausted. In recognition of my hard work my employers treated me to a week's holiday in Vienna. I was not sure that I should accept their offer, but shortly afterwards, early one September morning in 1952, I found myself back in Vienna.

I was keen to see what had happened to the city and the people since I had left 14 years earlier. It seemed a very different city from the vibrant Vienna I had known. It was still under Allied occupation and had become run down and drab. Gone were the smart shops and fashionable people. Many of the official buildings and private apartment blocks and houses were dilapidated and badly in need of repair. I took some solace in the fact that Vienna had not survived the war unscathed. I found myself actively seeking out signs of suffering and revenge for the atrocities I had witnessed. I wanted to see whether justice had been done.

It was strange, I had grown up in Vienna, yet there was no one for me to visit, no one to turn to. There was no one left: either they had escaped and were scattered around the globe or else had perished in the concentration camps. I spent some time in the university library collecting data for the essay I was submitting and which focused on Austria's postwar currency reforms.

It was a very different woman who walked up the library steps from the girl that had viewed them with such reverence. I wondered what would have happened if my life had not been so cruelly disrupted. Would I have become a doctor? Would I have married Willie? I sat on the steps and began to weep for my lost childhood. Whatever I did with my life I would never win back those years. I returned home from Vienna with much of my hatred and desire for vengeance dissipated. I knew I could not change what had happened, but I also knew that my fate now lay in my own hands.

When I arrived home, Mama and Papa were so excited to see me: they could not wait to give me the glad news that Otto was coming to visit. I had not seen my brother in thirteen years and in that time he had been married and divorced. I had never really forgiven him for leaving me to look after our parents while he started his new life away from the war, away from anti-Semitism. But I still looked to him as my role-model and after all these years would still ask myself, 'What would Otto do?' when I was in a quandary. As his date of arrival approached I became increasingly excited and kept wondering how he would have changed. Finally the day dawned. Papa and Kurt went to London to meet Otto at the airport and together they flew back to Manchester. Otto had anglicized his surname from 'Grünwald' to 'Grant' and Kurt had changed his to 'Greenwood'. Thus Papa was travelling together with his two sons, each of them with a different surname, which struck me as rather funny. Mama and I met them at Manchester airport where we had an emotional reunion.

Otto and I arranged to spend a few days touring England and we were able to renew our close bond. He had become an amateur actor in Sydney and was brilliant at imitating Lawrence Olivier in various Shakespearean roles. We went to Stratford-upon-Avon to see *Romeo and Juliet*. Although the theatre was completely sold out we managed to obtain the VIP seats which were always kept to the end. We were the perfect partners in crime, and although our time together was short-lived Otto once again became an integral part of my life.

After Otto's departure I threw myself into my final year at university. During the spring term the university appointments board had arranged interviews for those students who were expected to get top degrees. I was therefore thrilled when I found myself among the select few who were invited by a number of large British firms to come for interviews. They seemed to believe that economic graduates would make the most promising candidates for managerial and executive positions. Being a mature student with shop-floor experience, with a diploma in industrial administration and another one from Oxford University, I seemed a particularly attractive candidate to them. I received a number of conditional offers dependent on the results of my final examination, one of which I thought was just perfect. It was from the John Lewis Partnership, offering me a trainee post as one of their buyers. The salary was more than I had ever earned and the prospects were good. Images of me in a smart suit, driving a little sports car to meetings with suppliers where I carefully picked product lines, whirled before my eyes. Feeling confident about my future I attacked my books with extra vigour. I was ready to say goodbye to my university days and start my life in the real world.

# 9 • *The Obstacle Race*

On the first Sunday in May of 1953, just one week before my final examinations were due to start, I sat in my room trying to revise from the piles of lecture notes sprawled out on the floor in front of me. As I was feeling a little chilly I switched on the electric fire Papa had made for me. (He had acquired the elements for the heater from the electrical engineering company he was working at and had fixed it on to an asbestos board without bothering to fit the statutory guard.) I had used the heater previously without any problem and was grateful to Papa for having gone to the trouble of making it for me. However, that day, as I turned to pick up my notes from the floor, the edge of my nylon dress caught fire. Worried that my revision notes might be destroyed I rushed to the bathroom to try to extinguish the flames. However, as I opened the door of my room the sudden draught fanned the fire and within seconds I was engulfed in flames. I screamed with pain and fear. (I later learned that I could be heard several houses down the road.)

As soon as Papa saw me standing at the top of the stairs like a flaming beacon he rushed to save me. As he was trying to tear off my clothes he lost his balance and fell down the stairs. Fortunately, Mama managed to break his fall and within seconds he was again tearing at my dress, his hands alight. Shortly afterwards he gently wrapped a sheet around my body as I stood there naked and numb with pain. I had no idea how long the whole incident had lasted. It seemed like an eternity to me, but it could have been no more than a couple of minutes. No one had thought to call for an ambulance, so even in my state of shock I had to take charge and ask Papa to use our neighbour's phone to call the emergency services. Once again it felt like an eternity before the ambulance arrived and all I could think of was my final exam and my dream job disappearing before my eyes. Papa, whose hands were also burned, accompanied me to Manchester's Jewish hospital, which was the closest to where we lived. I was admitted with third-degree burns, bandaged from shoulder to knee and wheeled on to a ward with a saline drip stuck into my left arm. Poor Papa did not quite know what to say or do as he stood next to my hospital bed. On the one hand he obviously felt guilty because the electric fire he had somewhat carelessly put together caused the accident, on the other he was proud that he had at least managed to save my life.

Soon the pain-killing injection I was given began to have an effect and the pain receded. As I lay there the reality of what had happened began to sink in. Tears began to stream down my cheeks and I knew that however badly burned I was and however much pain I would have to suffer I could not afford to miss my final examinations the following week. Therefore, I decided I had to find a way for me to sit the exam as planned. I looked down my bandaged body and realized that there was no chance of me returning to university within a week. My mind began to race and I wondered how I could convince the university to change their exam policy and let me take them outside the university grounds. I thought that if anyone could help me persuade the authorities to let me continue with my exams it was Beccie. As Papa was preparing to return home I sent him off to phone her and ask her to come to see me as quickly as possible. Within less than an hour Beccie was by my bedside. At first she was shocked when she saw what had happened to me, but she soon rallied. She immediately appreciated my concerns about my examination, for she knew she would feel the same in my predicament. Reassuringly she told me to leave matters to her. She hoped to be able to give me some positive news by the following evening.

As soon as Beccie and Papa left the hospital I allowed myself the luxury of succumbing to the sedative and fell asleep. I woke after dark and saw the night nurse sitting by my bedside watching over me. This made me wonder how badly hurt I might be. I reasoned that it must be pretty bad if the hospital allocated a night nurse specifically to me. But I refused myself the self-pity of worrying about my injuries and kept telling myself that I must concentrate on preparing for my degree examinations. So the next day, in the midst of the most agonizing pain, I tried to force myself to recollect what I had learned day by day during the last few months. As I lay there I remembered what Karl had told me, all those years ago, about how he had managed to survive the most atrocious experiences in the German concentration camps by keeping a mental diary and how he had told me that the human spirit can overcome anything. I have subsequently been told by some of my medical friends that burning and drowning are the two most agonizing experiences for human beings, but I was determined not to allow my bodily affliction to interfere with the workings of my mind.

For the first time I was completely helpless and totally dependent on others to look after me. I was burned all down the right side of my body, the fingers on my right hand were heavily bandaged, and with a saline drip still in my left arm it was impossible for me to drink or feed myself. While all this was obviously distressing, I was actually more concerned about news from Beccie.

As promised, Beccie turned up late in the afternoon, beaming. I took this to mean good news and was thrilled when she told me that it was all arranged. I was to sit my exams in hospital the same time as my fellow students and under the supervision of an academic invigilator as required by the university authorities. Faculty members had immediately volunteered to come and sit with me and even the secretaries had offered to come and take down the dictation of my answers since I would not be able to use my right hand. I was ecstatic and gave my fellow patients a shock as I started to shout for joy. I wished I could hug Beccie, but had to make do with thanking her again and again. It was so generous and kind of her to have given up some of the time she badly needed to prepare for her own examinations just to make arrangements for mine. She too was pleased with her own achievements. However, she then told me that we still had one more obstacle to overcome. We had to get the hospital to let me have a private room for the duration of my examinations. I could not possibly be expected to concentrate amidst the hustle and bustle that was part of the large ward. Yet she was pretty optimistic that she could sort that out too. When she had entered the hospital on her way up to see me she had established that the hospital administrator was an old friend of her husband's family. She thus decided to go and tackle him right away.

She returned half an hour later, once again beaming with success. All was arranged now for me to take my final examinations. Beccie had done it all in one day. I thought it a tremendous achievement and found it amazing how she had managed to get the university and hospital bureaucracies to make their decisions so quickly when it was the first time they had ever been confronted with such a problem. Beccie admitted that she had emphasized my difficult refugee experience and how I had had to struggle to earn money to help my parents while studying at the same time. I did not really care what their motivation had been, I was just so happy that it had all been organized so quickly and efficiently. Beccie then left to fetch my notes and books from my home so that I could try to do some final revision.

As I lay in bed, however, my previous elation disappeared and I began to worry whether my mind would ultimately let me down and I would fail. I felt so alone, I couldn't discuss my fears with Beccie, now that she had organized everything – she would think I was ungrateful. I couldn't talk to my parents as they would never understand, and I certainly couldn't talk to my fellow patients, particularly as in the bed next to me was a young woman who had just had a miscarriage and was herself deeply distressed. I therefore forced myself to continue my revision and test my memory. When Beccie brought me my notes and books the following day she also got the hospital to fix a special gadget over my bed which enabled me to read without holding a book or note. Thank goodness the next day the drip was removed and I could at least use my left hand again.

I soon became a hospital celebrity as the news that I would be taking my final degree examinations in hospital spread round the wards like wildfire. Newspaper reporters came to interview me, but I did not want the publicity just in case I failed the exams. I therefore asked the nurses not to let any journalist in. The doctors and nurses who treated me kept looking at me with awe and admiration as if I was about to undertake a death-defying feat. The young doctor looking after me kindly prescribed medication that reduced the pain without making me feel drowsy, which was just what I needed. I tried to keep calm and work through my notes. Periodically my worries resurfaced whether I would be able to pass the exams in my present condition. What if I failed? I would become the laughing-stock of all around me. I pushed these worrying thoughts aside. Like Scarlett O'Hara in *Gone with the Wind* I kept telling myself: I won't think about it today, I'll think about it later on. During the few days before the great event only my parents and Beccie came to see me, as the doctor had advised that it would be best not to tire me unnecessarily. Poor Mama looked at me with deeply sorrowful eyes. This convinced me that her suffering in watching me was worse than all the pain I had to put up with myself.

On the Sunday, exactly one week after my accident had occurred, the hospital administrator, a small man in a dark pin-striped suit, came to see me. With an official air on his face he formally told me that the hospital board had generously decided to let me have the free use of one of their best private rooms. This would enable me to remain undisturbed during the examinations the university authorities had kindly agreed for me to take in the hospital. He was so obviously full of his own self-importance as he told me what I already knew that I was tempted to give him a short and rather rude response. Fortunately, I thought better of it and instead politely thanked him and the hospital staff for all their kindness. After he had left me, two orderlies came to move me to the private room on the ground floor. I was wheeled out of the ward amidst cheers and good wishes from the nurses and the other patients. The eight papers that made up my finals were spread over three weeks. This meant that I would be in the private room for the duration, which cheered me up as after the busyness of the big ward I longed for some space and privacy.

Doctors and nurses groomed me as if I were a horse about to enter a big race. They spared no effort to try to make me feel more comfortable. The next day, about five minutes before my examination was due to start, one of the university secretaries arrived and settled down on the left-hand side of my bed where a typewriter, table and chair had been provided for her. One of my lecturers was also there as invigilator and he had brought the sealed envelope containing the questions. He explained the procedural rules to me: I would be handed the paper at exactly the same moment as the rest of the students would see theirs at the university; I then had three hours to dictate my answers to the typist; no extra time could be allowed for me except under very exceptional circumstances, which he hoped would not occur. Everything was handled very formally until the door of my hospital room suddenly burst open and cameras began to flash while reporters shouted questions at me. It took a few minutes before the hospital and university staff managed to expel the newspaper people and things were under control again. This unexpected excitement added to my nervousness and I began to fel that perhaps I couldn't go through with it after all. But I knew I had no choice. The invigilator tore open the envelope and while handing me the question paper reassured me that I need not worry about him listening to my dictation: he had brought a book to read and would therefore not even hear what I was saying. I thanked him as I had been feeling embarrassed about having to display my ignorance in front of one of my lecturers, but seeing him sitting there engrossed in his book I ceased worrying about his presence.

As I looked down at the question paper I felt relieved because I saw that I would have no difficulty in answering the required number. I knew what to say. The only problem I encountered was that I had become accustomed to scribbling down a structure for my answers before writing them down at greater length. Without the use of my right hand I was in no position to scribble anything. To overcome this handicap I tried to organize my thoughts so that I would provide a logically argued coherent answer. Yet when I read my answer to the first question I was not happy with what I had done. I thus asked the secretary to take down my notes first, which she did, and with these notes as guidelines I managed much better to answer the questions that followed. I finished just in time, and my paper was handed to the invigilator who put it in an envelope, which he sealed immediately. Realizing the strain I must have been under, he and the secretary kindly stayed on with me for a little while. To help me unwind he conveyed to me the best wishes from the faculty and students of Manchester University and told me that they were all hoping and praying that I would succeed in my endeavours. Listening to him was such an anticlimax for me after having just been under great stress that I could not contain myself and burst into tears. The poor young man did not know how to handle this situation and after calling a nurse he and the secretary beat a hasty retreat.

The following day my room began to look like a fruit and flower shop. One fruit basket after another and one flower-arrangement after another kept arriving. All were beautifully wrapped with labels, most of which just said 'From an anonymous well-wisher who admires your courage'. Some came from groups of lecturers and fellow students while others were from the people who had been with me while I was a travel hostess during my summer vacations. The nurses rushed in with the morning papers to show me my story on the front page, together with a picture of me lying bandaged in my hospital bed. It was obviously this publicity that had brought the many gifts from so many people. I was overwhelmed by this generosity but felt that I did not deserve it. People seemed to consider me as outstandingly courageous, whereas I knew that deep down I felt frightened and was scared of not being able to complete the remaining seven papers. I cursed myself again and again for having been so foolish to undertake a task that I was so ill-equipped to complete. Yet I had no option but to put on a brave face and continue. These thoughts and the persistent pain prevented me from sleeping and I became increasingly exhausted. I desperately needed to talk to someone, but I had become such a symbol of strength and courage no one would want to hear of my fears.

At the end of my second week in hospital, after I had completed another paper, my burns began to go septic. The doctors put me on penicillin. As a result I came out in big red itchy welts wherever I had not been burned. The irritation was even worse than the pain of the burns and without the use of my right hand I couldn't even scratch myself properly. I was in such distress that the doctor who was in charge of my case took me off penicillin and ordered a nurse to cover me in cooling lotion. I felt like a boxer whose injury had been patched up only for him to get back into the ring to fight the next round.

One morning Professor Gluckman, under whom I had studied social anthropology, turned up as the invigilator. He realized that the examination he had come to supervise was in the subject he himself had been teaching me. Thinking I would be embarrassed, he assured me he would be engrossed in his book – but by now I no longer cared. The pain was so overwhelming and my allergy to the penicillin so irritating that half-way through the exam I declared that I could not carry on any longer and would have to give up fighting for my degree. When Professor Gluckman heard my outburst he came to my bedside, looked deep into my eyes and said in a commanding voice: 'You must not give up now. I shall get the doctors and nursing staff to give you at least temporary relief, and I will allow you extra time for this. You must carry on, if not for yourself then for my sake, for I have put my faith in you and I would hate to be disappointed.' I was so surprised by his words that I agreed to his action. The doctor came and gave me a sedative injection, while nurses put more cooling lotion on my itching body. And after ten minutes' break I was back in the ring, continuing the fight, and managed to finish the paper in the time allotted me.

Professor Gluckman stayed and chatted with me for over an hour after the end of the exam. He asked me what I was planning to do after I had obtained my degree. I took strength from his optimism and answered that I was still hoping to take up the job to become a buyer. On hearing this he asked me whether I might be interested in a graduate scholarship to enable me to go on to do a doctorate. I thought he was just trying to make me feel better; either that or he was out of his mind thinking that I was capable of attaining a doctorate. I had already resigned myself that the best I could expect was a pass and I knew that graduate scholarships were only awarded to those with at least upper second-class degrees. I told Professor Gluckman all this and stressed that I wanted no allowances made for me; I wanted no charity. He laughed in reply, assuring me that I wouldn't get any, as external examiners have no idea of the circumstances under which an exam is taken, nor do they know the student's identity. Thus I could be sure that the marks I received were a true assessment of my performance rather then due to any special consideration for my circumstances. I was greatly relieved when I heard this for I wanted to be treated like any other student rather than the invalid I then was.

The itching disappeared after a couple of days, but without the application of any further antibiotics the infection spread quickly. I began to stink and I could see the revulsion in Mama's eyes when she bent over to kiss me on her daily visits. The smell made me feel nauseous and I asked her to bring me large bottles of eau de cologne to mask the stench, which made it slightly more bearable for my many visitors.

Finally, I finished the exams and was transferred back to the main ward where I had been admitted. The nurses welcomed me back like a returning hero and the few patients who knew me clapped enthusiastically as I was wheeled in. Expecting that I would have to remain in hospital for some time, I was allocated a bed in a corner by the window. It was the best position on the ward, but I was too exhausted after my three-week ordeal to appreciate how much the nurses had put themselves out to get me that place. My return to the ward symbolized to me that my exams were now over and I knew I had to wait another four weeks before the results were due to be announced.

Once the mental anguish of the exams was over I became more aware of my injuries and how little my condition had improved. The infection was preventing the burns from healing and the doctor admitted that he knew no other effective remedy, but that at least my youth was in my favour. I could not believe that I would simply have to lie there until my body's strength returned to fight the infection, and began to fear that I might never fully recover. I was thankful that I had not realized the seriousness of my condition when I was first admitted or I would never have been able to concentrate on my exams. To ease the pain and boredom I turned to alcohol and my bedside locker became the local bar. When visitors asked me what I would like them to bring me, I always requested spirits. I built up quite a stock over the weeks. The night staff often spent the quiet hours of the early morning by my bed sipping my 'special medicine' from the dispensing cups. I became very popular with the nursing staff and they could not do enough to make me comfortable. They were marvellous in helping to occupy my time, particularly as the day of the results drew nearer.

I had arranged for Papa to go to the university and phone the hospital ward as soon as he had found out my results. The nurses for their point had agreed to relay the news to me as soon as they received it. As the day of the results dawned everyone was filled with apprehension, and each time the phone rang a hush fell over the ward. The phone was located in the ward sister's office, round the corner from my bed, so we designed a system whereby on receiving the message from Papa the ward sister would convey it by sign language to the patient opposite, whose bed was strategically positioned to relay the news to me. I had never felt such tension, not even on the plane journey to Cologne – my body was shaking and my mouth was dry. After numerous false alarms the phone rang again. I strained to hear the ward sister and watched anxiously for a sign but could hear nothing. Suddenly a nurse skidded round my curtain and in her hands she held up a piece of paper on which was written 2:1. I was shocked. There must have been some mistake. How could I have been awarded such a good degree when I had taken the exams under such adverse conditions? The patients on the ward burst into a round of 'For She's a Jolly Good Fellow' and the nurses rushed to congratulate me. I dissolved into tears as the news sank in. Shortly afterwards Papa ran into the ward bearing a huge bunch of red carnations. He was grinning from ear to ear and he looked happier than I had seen him for a long, long time. It was the recognition which I had been waiting for for years and it felt wonderful. We toasted my success and drank to my speedy recovery with our little medicine glasses.

After my various visitors had left and the initial excitement had worn off I began to reflect on my future. I felt optimistic. I had a number of options to choose from and the world was finally my oyster, or so I thought. A few days later Professor Gluckman arrived to congratulate me on my exam results and offer me a graduate scholarship. He had even arranged to have it backdated to the end of the previous academic year. I thought he was just being charitable and refused his kind offer. He was, understandably, furious. He went on to explain that he had been trying to attract an economist for sometime to conduct social anthropological studies. He assured me that he did not support charity cases but had pursued me as he had been impressed by my intellectual calibre and physical stamina, of which he had first-hand knowledge. My eyes lit up and without hesitation I accepted his offer. I was going to become a doctor after all.

I informed John Lewis that I would reluctantly have to relinquish the position they had offered me, as I did not know how long it would be, if ever, before I would be well enough to start work with them. I was in fact completely absorbed by the idea of an academic career. I had come a long way since my Ruskin College days when I had thought it immoral to be paid for something I enjoyed doing. However, before I could even begin to think about taking up my studies again I had to concentrate on getting well. I became determined to secure my release from hospital as quickly as possible and started what I termed 'Operation Hospital Release'.

Beccie had continued to visit me regularly and on one occasion I asked her to find out from her medical friends if there really was no quick cure for my burns. The same day she returned and told me that there was a special burns unit in another Manchester hospital where they specialized in skin grafting – a new technique that had been developed during the war to help the air crews who were badly burned when their planes were shot down. In order to be admitted to that unit I would have to convince my hospital doctor to transfer me, or I would have to discharge myself and ask my GP, an old family friend, to admit me to the unit. When I suggested to my hospital doctor the possibility of having some skin grafts he immediately rejected it. I thought he selfishly wanted to claim the glory for my recovery and therefore would keep me there until I was fit enough to walk out of the door. I then discussed with Mama the option of discharging myself and getting myself admitted to the specialist burns unit the same day. Since I still could neither walk nor look after myself I needed her approval to take me home before the hospital was prepared to release me. I was so angry with her when she refused, after all I had done for her. I appreciated that she was worried about me, but I couldn't believe that she wasn't prepared to help me.

The days and weeks continued to pass and I could see that there was no improvement in my condition. When they came to change my bandages I eagerly looked for signs of the healing process, but the infection remained as bad as ever. I felt dejected and totally helpless. I began to fear that Professor Gluckman would change his mind and I would be left to rot in hospital. As I poured out my heart to Beccie she stopped me and said she had an idea. She promised to get Phil, her husband, to discuss my case with the ear, nose and throat specialist who had been the senior doctor on duty the day I was admitted to hospital and who was therefore in charge of my case although he had little knowledge of how to treat burns. (Her husband was a member of the same Masonic lodge as the ENT specialist.)

A few days later I was informed that the director of the burns unit was due to see me later that afternoon. An impressive-looking tall, grey-haired gentleman duly arrived, followed by the entourage of doctors and nurses who had been caring for me. He introduced himself and said to me, while shaking my left hand vigorously: 'Young lady, you have made quite a name for yourself. I don't normally do house calls but I was so intrigued by you that I felt I had to come personally.' A nurse then took off my bandages and he wrinkled his nose in disgust. He immediately ordered one of my doctors to take a swab and told him that he would be taking it for testing and that he would call with instructions of what antibiotic they should administer as soon as they had grown a culture. I could tell that he was not greatly impressed with my treatment so far, and heard him mutter to the doctor: 'After all, you must know quite well that penicillin is not the only antibiotic on the market.' Two days later I was put on to aureomycin, which worked like magic, and within a few days the infection had cleared up completely.

My wounds were now ready for skin grafting. I was jubilant as I could finally see light at the end of the tunnel. That night the ward nurses arranged a party for me. They wheeled my bed into the middle of the ward and made speeches and sang songs they had made up in my honour, then presented me with a huge bouquet of flowers made up from all the different bunches that were dotted round the room as a token from my fellow patients. I didn't know quite what to say. My time with them had been painful and traumatic and I felt that had I received the right treatment I would never have been there for such an extended stay. I didn't want to tell them that I could not wait to leave, but instead managed a few words thanking them for having made my stay more bearable.

In the morning an ambulance arrived to transfer me to the burns unit. I was in an exuberant mood and laughed and joked with the ambulance men. I had no doubt that the skin grafts would be a success and at last I could see an end to my invalid state. As I was wheeled into the unit I was surprised that everyone seemed to know about me, as staff crowded round congratulating me on my courage and success. They had all seen the report of my exam results in the press. I was given VIP treatment and allocated a side-room all to myself.

Two days later I was taken to the operating theatre for skin-grafting. When I recovered from the anaesthetic I found myself back in my bed with my body tightly bandaged. The ward sister explained that the bandages would be removed in a few days when the surgeon would assess how much of the skin graft had taken. I had foolishly expected that the place on to which the skin had been grafted from my left thigh would look like normal skin, so I was aghast when I saw how raw and red it all looked. The surgeon carefully examined my skin and only nodded to me with a smile. He then ordered the nurse to put a cage over my body and cover it with a sheet so that air could circulate round the graft. Left on my own and naked – for nothing was allowed to touch the newly grafted areas – I kept gazing at my own body. I assumed that the operation must have been a failure, bearing in mind how my body looked.

At that moment I lost all will to live. I decided that I had been through enough and was tired of fighting, tired of waiting for my life to begin. I became withdrawn and refused any food that was offered to me, hoping that starvation would be a quick route to death. I turned my visitors away, desperate to be alone. The ward sister became so worried that she told the surgeon about my hunger campaign. The eminent surgeon came and sat down by my bedside for a little talk. I had not expected that he would understand what was going on in my mind, but to my surprise he did. He explained to me that the skin graft he had undertaken was a 97 per cent success, which was one of the highest success rates he had ever achieved. However, to ensure that the grafted skin gets its full strength my body must be fed well. My refusal to eat right now was in fact undermining all that he had taken great care to achieve. I was still not convinced. What if he wanted to get me back to eating again just to prepare me for another operation? I put this question to him and told him I had had enough. For a few seconds he sat there silently looking at me with a sad expression in his eyes. Then he said, 'I know how you feel, you have been through a lot during these months. You have never seen grafted skin before and you obviously didn't know what it would look like just after the operation. But you must trust me. I promise that if you eat well you will recover quickly and you will walk out of this ward within two weeks. If this turns out not be so then I shall agree to let you do whatever you decide.' He added, with a warm smile, 'Do I have a deal?' I nodded grudgingly. He called the nurse to bring me some food right away, which I ate while he watched over me with a smile.

Seeing my skin improve daily encouraged me to keep my part of the bargain. Within a few days I was fit enough to get up again for the first time in months and to put on a nightdress and dressing-gown. I ventured out for a walk round the ward and was shocked to see the injuries of the other patients. I saw a little girl, who could have been no more than 6 years old, whose face had been so badly burned that she had no nose, ears or eyebrows. Another girl had half her face burned. She told me that she had been in the unit for over four months while the surgeon was rebuilding her face. Seeing these cases made me realize how lucky I had been in comparison and that I owed my survival to so many people. As the surgeon had promised, I was released from the burns unit on the fourteenth day. I had recovered sufficiently to dress normally once more and only a tiny area of my body was still raw skin that needed attention. It was a great moment for my parents and me when at last I faced them fully dressed and ready to go home. I felt as if the surgeon had achieved a miracle but unfortunately, I never got to tell him that.

On the way home I looked around me in amazement. Suddenly the world seemed a beautiful place and it felt wonderful to be alive. I drank in the air and the sunshine as if they were intoxicating substances. Every moment seemed precious. As soon as we had arrived home the house became full of friends and neighbours all wishing me well.

After a few days at home recuperating in the garden I began to get restless. I longed to have a break somewhere on the Continent. As if God had heard my silent prayers I received a letter asking whether I was interested in acting as hostess for a package tour to the French Riviera. I was overjoyed. My parents thought I had gone mad when I began to dance around them waving the letter and shouting at the top of my voice: 'I am off to Monte Carlo!' I had not given a thought to the state of my body as I accepted the job offer, but as I packed to leave I started to have second thoughts. Though my skin had completely healed the scars of the burns and the skin graft were still red and unsightly. No one would suspect what I had been through unless they saw me naked. I began to panic and decided that I would simply never wear a swimming costume or let any one get close to me. I reasoned that no one would ever want to love me if they saw my scarred body. Having decided this, I allowed myself to enjoy my holiday and together with some of the younger tourists in my care I went dancing every night and flirted unashamedly with many of the young Italian and French men who were attracted by my vivacity. To avoid any advances I wore an engagement ring on my finger and told everyone that I had a fiancé waiting for me in England. This put most of the men off except Carlo: a tall, dark and handsome Italian who danced the tango beautifully. I was immediately attracted to him and loved to dance with him as he held me tightly round the waist whispering into my ear how much fun it would be if we went to bed together. He was persistent and would not listen to the story about my engagement. Exasperated, he thought he would win me over by pronouncing that English men do not have the stamina to make love properly. *Una volta* (once) a week was as much as any Englishman could manage, he said. By contrast he could promise me *cinque volte* (five times) a night if only I would listen to his pleas. I couldn't help but laugh at his absurd claim, which marked the end of our relationship.

I had managed to keep Carlo at arm's length, but I started to wonder whether I would ever meet any one to whom I would be prepared to expose myself, both emotionally and physically. My emotional scars had never fully healed and now in addition I had my physical scars. But in true Scarlett O'Hara style I pushed these worries out of my head saying to myself: 'I won't think of this now, I'll deal with it when the time comes.'

# 10 • *Life Begins at 30*

On the first day of the new term I walked slowly to the campus, wondering what was in store for me and rather nervous of whether I was actually clever enough to be a graduate student. I had thought that I would be eased in gently, but when I met with my professors I was given an extensive reading list and topics for the long essays they expected me to write. I scanned the questions and was relieved to see that I could cope with most of them; indeed I was sure I could get the marks I had been accustomed to receiving as an undergraduate. However, I soon realized the difference between undergraduate and postgraduate studies. The objective for an undergraduate is to score the highest marks possible in their degree exams. In contrast postgraduate students are judged not on their answers to examination questions but rather on the basis of their original essays or dissertations and the quality of their research. At first I struggled, but I soon found the exploratory style refreshing and my brain responded to the new challenge.

As an undergraduate I had always felt the odd one out: my age and previous experience made me different from my fellow students, many of whom were jealous of my exam success. However, it was much easier to merge with the postgraduates as they were older and many had had varied work experience before starting their doctoral research. I loved to listen to the tales of the band of social anthropologists who had already completed their field studies and gave fascinating accounts of the exotic places they had studied. The more I listened, the more I felt that this was where my future lay, and I decided that I wanted to conduct my own field research, live in a village in some far-flung land and study the community. When I told my economics supervisor Professor Lewis what I wanted to do he thought I was mad and that it was a waste of time. I ignored his comments and became even more absorbed in development anthropology. At that time it was almost virgin territory and my study was among the first. I scoured the literature for anything and everything I could find on economic development and spent hour after hour pondering what would be the focus of my research. My personal experience of persecution, discrimination and deprivation made me want to apply my knowledge to benefit the poorer strata in society. I also wanted to make it action-oriented, as I could not see the value of theoretical 'ivory-tower' academia. I wanted to make a difference.

Professor Gluckman appreciated the potential importance of my research and became an invaluable source of help and inspiration. He had not only a fine mind but also a warm and generous personality. I was the first student whom he had taught both as an undergraduate and a postgraduate. On the one hand he treated me like a daughter, while on the other he regarded me as a racehorse on whom he had placed a high bet. We spent many hours discussing my proposed doctoral thesis and exploring possible field-study locations for me. He favoured central Africa, where he himself and most of his other graduate students had carried out their studies and where his wide network would easily secure funds for the kind of research he expected me to conduct.

As I was deliberating where to spend the next two years I had a long discussion with Professor M.N. Srinivas, an eminent Indian social anthropologist who was visiting Manchester. He was keen for me to do my research among South Indian societies and suggested I should investigate the impact of a large canal irrigation scheme on the socio-economic system of villagers. Having been fascinated by India ever since I was a little girl, I immediately made up my mind. I was nervous about going against the wishes of my supervisor, but I finally plucked up the courage to tell Professor Gluckman that I was much more attracted to India than to Africa. While I could see that he was disappointed he was magnanimous enough to help me to secure a Rockefeller fellowship for my field studies and arranged a departmental assistantship for me. This provided me with funds to spend two years in South Indian villages as well as for the subsequent writing-up period. I was ecstatic.

In August 1954 I left home for my journey to Bombay. I was exhausted. During the weeks leading up to my departure I had lain awake at night, full of anxiety. What had I been thinking of, going off to India on my own? I had never conducted field research before; how would I know what to do? Would I be able to communicate? Would I be able to learn the language of the people I had gone to study? I tried to reassure myself that I had overcome so many hurdles already that this was just another one; but the questions would not stop.

As I said my farewells to my parents and friends and took my seat on the train to Southampton my spirits rose and I could not contain the bubble of excitement that was spreading rapidly through my body. I loved travelling and the prospect of seeing new places and meeting different people made the blood run faster through my veins. I could not sit still for the whole journey and when I boarded the ship I felt that finally my life was beginning.

The boat trip to Bombay took 26 days and I enjoyed it thoroughly. I shared a cabin with a young missionary who had already spent several years in India. A soon as we met she warned me of seasickness when we would pass through the Gulf of Biscay. And just as she had predicted, the whole body of passengers retired to their cabins overcome by the swell of the sea. To my surprise I was completely unaffected and enjoyed my solitary strolls on the deck and the empty dining-room where I gorged myself on the array of oriental dishes the ship's cooks had prepared.

I met many people from different nationalities and backgrounds and I sat fascinated listening to their accounts of their lives. Among them were two English girls who were on their way to Pakistan. They were dancers and attracted a great deal of attention from the crew. Sue was thin, tall and fair, while Liz was a medium-sized redhead. Both oozed sex appeal. Their appearance and flirtatious ways offended many of the passengers and they became social outcasts. I, however, did not care about their dubious moral standards and spent much time in their company, listening to their bawdy tales. At the end of the first week on board Sue struck up a friendship with the captain and Liz with the purser, which enabled them to move into first-class cabins. They insisted on rewarding me for my friendship by arranging for me to have free access to all first-class amenities on board, though I retained my tourist-class quarters. At each port where the ship docked the captain and the purser had hordes of local traders trying to bestow gifts upon them, which they immediately passed to the girls. Sue and Liz in turn generously shared their presents with me. By the time I left the ship I had enough Nivea cream and eau de cologne to last me a lifetime. Sue and Liz disembarked in Pakistan and we promised faithfully to write each other. We subsequently lost touch and I often wondered whether they became the cabaret stars they set out to be.

The next stop was Karachi, where we were allowed to go ashore for the day. It was my first real taste of Asia and I had imagined that it would be magical. Instead, as I walked down the gangplank, I was overcome by the stench of rotting food, the sight of the malnourished children and the filthy hovels that were their homes. It was only a short time after the partition with India, and Pakistan seemed totally unprepared and unable to cope with the massive influx of Muslim immigrants. Karachi was full to bursting and the lovely tree-lined avenues of central Karachi, where the homes of the wealthy stood behind high walls, were now surrounded by makeshift homes. I admired their ingenuity and the craftsmanship in building their improvised lean-tos and shacks which had been made out of various bits of scrap: tin if they were lucky, but sacks served predominantly as roofs and walls.

As soon as they saw me, children and beggars crowded round. I wanted to give them everything: my money, pens, pencils – everything. I felt so guilty in the midst of such extreme poverty and misery. Just as I started to hand things out I was grabbed by an Indian doctor who had befriended me on board ship. He rescued me just in time, pulling me away from the hordes of beggars explaining to me that whatever I could give them would not alleviate their suffering. I would only encourage them to beg and fuel the street fights that always broke out as they argued over their booty. As I turned my back on the crowds of people and made my way back to my comfortable cabin the injustice was all the more apparent.

As we made our way into the port of Bombay I was met by a very different scene: men dressed in loincloths were milling around touting their wares, while women carried baskets of food with all sorts of interesting titbits. They looked beautiful with their colourful saris billowing in the wind. As soon as the ship had docked, hordes of Indian porters pushed and kicked their way up the gangway fighting over the customers: 'Need porter?' they kept shouting. I was scared of drowning in the sea of people and thankfully spotted Professor M.N. Srinivas in the crowd waiting ashore. He had kindly agreed to come and meet me. He was a softly-spoken man with a brilliant mind and a great sense of humour, so I knew I would enjoy our journey together to Mysore. I admired him greatly and considered him my 'guru', as he had been instrumental in bringing me to India.

During the long train journey to Mysore I listened attentively as he explained all the different rites and rituals and tried to initiate me into Indian life. I could not believe how different it was to my life at home. I tried to make a mental record of everything I saw and heard, and as I looked around me I immediately noticed the caste system in practice. Third-class passengers were accommodated in what looked like cattle-trucks while the first-class passengers had comfortable carriages and seats. All the windows had metal bars to prevent monkeys and thieves from getting into the compartments. At one stop I saw a small monkey swing on to the bars while it was being fed bananas by the passengers; it made me smile and I felt I had arrived.

Most people had brought bedrolls for the long journey, but of course I had come ill-equipped. After two nights on the hard benches my body ached for a bed and I desperately needed some sleep. Finally, we drew into Mysore station. I had become hardened to the many beggars stretching their arms out to me and I pushed my way through the crowd, trying to stay close to Professor Srinivas.

I had thought that I would be able to find lodgings with an Indian family where I could learn the language and gain an introduction to the local community. How naïve I was! I quickly discovered that no self-respecting Hindu family would have a white person to stay in their house because we are all polluted by virtue of the fact that we are known to be beef-eaters. I immediately began to have visions of being left to my own devices, but Professor Srinivas reassured me that he would not leave me before I had found somewhere suitable to live. He seemed to feel responsible for me and I was grateful. He even asked me to call him Chamu, the name by which his family and close friends knew him.

Chamu made some enquiries and the vice-chancellor of Mysore University, who was a Goan Catholic, came to my rescue with the offer of a room at the local convent hostel. Unfortunately the nuns and their students were all from the neighbouring state of Kerala and thus spoke a different language from Kannada, the vernacular I had to learn. I was beginning to despair when Chamu arrived a few days later, grinning from ear to ear. He had made arrangements with the daughter of a language professor, who had a degree in Kannada, to teach me the language. The following week she came every day and I felt optimistic that at last I was beginning to learn the basics of the language. She not only taught me Kannada but also initiated me into the customs of the orthodox Brahmin household to which she belonged. I listened carefully to what she told me and tried my best to remember it all. I used to laugh at myself as I lay in bed practising my new words.

At the start of our second week she turned up formally dressed and in a somewhat stilted style announced that her father wished to meet me. I immediately tried to think what I might have done to have offended her family. I had been so careful in my behaviour. I had taken to wearing a sari and blouse, and was sure that I had remembered to take off my sandals and pour water over my hands and feet outside the front door of their house whenever I had been invited to visit the family. I desperately tried to discover what I had done wrong, but she only answered quietly, 'My father wants to tell you himself', which made me even more nervous. When we arrived I found her father, dressed in a sparkling white shirt and *dhoti* (loin-cloth) sitting cross-legged on a mat on the floor. After politely welcoming me he motioned me to sit down on a mat opposite him. I demurely sat down, anxious to find out what all this was about.

He began by thanking me for having been auspicious for his family and explained that for a number of years he and his daughter had applied for scholarships to Poona University. Previously they had always been rejected. However, that year just one week after his daughter had begun teaching me they had both received an offer of a scholarship. He was, therefore, convinced that I had brought them good fortune. I was delighted, until he told me that he and his daughter would be leaving in ten days. As if reading my mind, he said: 'We knew you would be worried about losing your teacher. So in gratitude for having brought us luck we would like to invite you to move into our house while my daughter and myself are away. You can have my daughter's room and share the house with my wife and two younger children, none of whom speaks any English. This should give you a good chance to pick up the language.' I was overwhelmed by his offer as I realized how rare it was for a white European woman to live with an orthodox Hindu family. Without taking time to consider exactly what it would mean to live with his family I enthusiastically agreed to become their lodger and thanked them profusely for their invitation.

To help me adjust to the family customs I moved in two days before father and daughter departed. My time with them was a social anthropologist's dream. The wife and the younger children tried their best to help me learn their language and make me feel at home. I went everywhere with them and met their wide network of their family and friends. I even joined in numerous family rituals and ceremonies. I felt so privileged to be allowed to lead the life of an orthodox Hindu woman. The only restriction the family imposed upon me was that I should not enter their kitchen; otherwise I was included in everything. I tried hard to adapt to the different rituals, many of which I could not see the sense in. However, I realized that to try to reason with an act that was steeped in tradition was beyond my remit. I started to see the role of a field-worker as that of subordinating oneself and becoming completely immersed in the local culture. Despite this realization, I found it hard to cope with so many things that I was supposed to do or not do. I felt very lonely, but the only person I could talk to was Chamu and he had left for North India to take up his university position: there was no one left in whom I could confide.

My hostess was perceptive enough to notice that I was struggling to fit into the lifestyle. She therefore arranged for me to meet Krishna, one of her relatives, who only recently had returned from America where he had completed a doctorate in chemistry. I was delighted to be able to converse with him in English rather than having to struggle in the vernacular. He offered to take me to the Mysore sports club, which was a legacy from the days of the British Raj, when a considerable number of Europeans had lived in Mysore.

As we entered the club I was reminded of some of Somerset Maugham's accounts of colonial life. The place was dimly lit and trophies decorated the walls. The large hall was almost empty of guests except for a group of men gathered in front of the bar. There were numerous servants in their white starched uniforms and high turbans, waiting to attend to their masters' every need. The guests were mainly Europeans, but there were also a few well-dressed Indian men. The formal suits and ties struck me as somewhat out of place in such a hot climate; it made me wonder how they coped in the heat. One of the Europeans must have just told a joke for the men were shaking with laughter. None of them noticed as we entered, as they had their backs to the door, but as soon as we approached the bar we were suddenly surrounded. My presence seemed to cause an uproar and before I realized what was happening I was trapped in a close circle of men. They began firing questions at me: 'Where are you from? What are you doing here? Where do you live and how long will you be staying?' They all vied for my attention and fell over themselves to buy me drinks. Initially I had thought it amusing that all these men wanted my attention, but after a few minutes I felt like a performing animal and was desperate to be taken offstage. I looked pleadingly at Krishna, hoping he would rescue me, but he had become a different person since we had joined his friends at the club, and he simply laughed at my predicament.

My merry band of men began to play games with me and every time I tried to refuse another drink they ordered yet another one for me, singing 'One more for the road!' I had not had a drink for some time now and this, combined with the heat, made me feel quite intoxicated. I knew I needed to get away, but did not know how to disentangle myself from this bunch of men. There seemed to be nobody whom I could trust. I searched the faces of the men who were closing in on me and spotted a European who stood out from the crowd, dressed in a casual open-necked shirt. He seemed a lot shyer than the others. I tried hard to compose myself and in the haughtiest voice I could muster I asked him whether he would be able to drive me home. His eyes lit up and he nodded quickly. The men immediately made a path through the crowd to where this tall and wiry man in his mid-fifties stood. He seemed to have the respect of this crowd of drunken males and I was impressed by the way they readily made way for him to escort me out of the club. This made me assume that he must be a man of some importance. He introduced himself as De Wet Van Ingen, and as he gently guided me towards his parked car I heard jeers from the men I left behind who were asking, 'What has he got that we haven't?' I nearly fainted as the fresh evening air hit me and De Wet took my arm to support me. He beckoned to his driver and soon we were driving swiftly out of the enclosure. He apologized for my treatment at the club and told me that I was safe with him.

He was well-mannered and charming, and I gratefully accepted his invitation to drive up to Chamundi Hill, one of Mysore's beauty spots, so that I could sober up before returning to my orthodox Hindu home. From the top, the view of the city was enchanting. Fireflies danced by the lights and the stars looked like millions of diamonds scattered over the night sky. As we sat there enjoying the cool evening breeze De Wet told me how his parents had come to Mysore before he was born and that he now lived with his elderly mother and younger brother. His father had been a skilled taxidermist and had trained his sons in the trade. He left them a well-established business with a prestigious list of customers, who included the Maharaja of Mysore. De Wet then asked what had brought me to Mysore. I explained that my forthcoming research was part of my doctoral studies, which satisfied his curiosity.

Before De Wet took me home he made me promise that I would join his family for lunch the following Sunday after the morning church service. He had taken it for granted that I was a churchgoing Christian. I didn't quite know what to say and blurted out that I was Jewish. I had half expected that he would not want anything more to do with me, but he graciously said that he would simply send his driver after church to fetch me. I was so glad that my gut-feelings had been right, as De Wet and his family became close friends during my stay in India.

Soon afterwards I moved to Mangala, a village some 30 miles from Mysore city, where I was to conduct the first stage of my research. The village was situated amidst undulating countryside and the canal irrigation ensured lush green vegetation. Most of the time it was very hot, but being situated on the Deccan plateau it never became unbearable. While I was aware how lucky I was to be in such a beautiful setting I felt completely isolated from the outside world, as I had no means of transport and no form of communication except for a few sporadic letters. De Wet often dropped in to check that I was all right and constantly urged me to buy a car. I didn't like to tell him that I would be hard-pressed even to buy a bicycle. However, soon I was the proud owner of a rickety old bike and was mobile again. I loved to explore the lanes around the village and meet the various people about their business. I felt it was a good way of getting people used to seeing me out and about, as a white woman was an unusual sight in the back streets of an Indian village.

One morning I was out for my morning ride and as I careered round the corner I came face to face with a farm bullock standing in the middle of the narrow road. I rang my bell to try to scare him into action, but he looked me straight in the eye and did not budge. I was so perplexed that I fell off my bike and got badly bruised, which made me scared of cycling again. After a few months of miserable isolation in the village De Wet offered to buy me a second-hand car provided that I could pay the running costs. It was too good an offer to miss and I gratefully accepted it. I reasoned that to have a car would not only be advantageous for me but it might also endear me more to my village friends. De Wet was shocked when he learned that I did not know how to drive and set about teaching me the rudiments, which got me through my driving test. Once I had a driving licence he presented me with an old Hindustan car that I called 'Sangi'. I was very proud of my first car and looked after it as if it were my first child. I even learned to carry out minor repairs. Whenever I drove during heavy rains the plugs would get wet and the car would stop. De Wet explained to me that if this happened all I had to do was take the plugs out, rub them against a matchbox and put them back again and the car would surge into action. He was right. My village friends were greatly impressed when I arrived with Sangi. Although they had accepted me without any difficulty right from the outset, having a car gave me extra credibility.

Not only had the lack of transport been an issue when I first arrived but also my accommodation. In fact when I first saw my new home I wanted to turn and run. I had been offered a house with a well in front and a pit-latrine at the back of it, but the house was old and dilapidated, having been built many years ago by the public works department for one of their irrigation engineers. Since the engineer had left about 15 years previously the villagers had used it as a stable for some of their farm animals. It was infested with rats and mice and the roof leaked; the latrine was also in a dreadful state. I tried to be positive: at least it was a house, which was more than was available in the other villages I had visited while searching for a field site. I set to with gusto and asked my cook and servants to whitewash the interior of the house. To my great distress I found that once the walls were dry again they were just as dirty as they had been before. It was the manager of the sugar factory in the nearby town of Mandya who came to my rescue. I asked him, when he visited one day, how I could possibly get the walls to appear white. He responded: 'You people will not want to do what we Indians would do, which is first to cover the walls with cow dung and then whitewash them.' I followed his advice and within a couple of days I had sparkling white walls. This made me realize that there was a strong basis for the widespread belief among Indians in the efficacy of cow-dung.

During my second week in the village I joined a gathering outside the local temple. It was a glorious moonlit night: the tall palm trees gently swayed in the breeze and the flames danced to the music that emanated from the temple. It was a beautiful sight. There is something so special about Indian nights that is impossible to explain; it just has to be seen to be believed. I was mesmerized by the scene before my eyes and was eager to find out what was going on. My grasp of the vernacular was still not sufficient for me to understand the lengthy explanation I was given. As I stood there watching, drums began to beat, louder and faster as the drummers frantically played on. Suddenly one of the villagers started to shake violently as if in the throes of an epileptic fit. The crowd circled him and watched as if spellbound. The man then threw himself about in time with the beating of the drums and as the pace of the beating increased so did the speed of his movements. Then suddenly the drumming stopped and the man stood still. At that moment he took on the role of spirit-medium. I was then told that he represented a specific Hindu deity. The villagers formed a single file, each waiting his turn to approach the spirit medium. I tried to get as near as possible to hear what was being said. I heard one man ask: 'Will my wife bear me a son?'; another enquired 'Will my son get well again?' Everyone asked similar questions, wanting to ascertain their future. The medium's response was invariably positive, but conditional on certain ritual observances. For example, one questioner was required to worship daily for a year at a temple that was two miles away to ensure that his wife would bear him a son. If his wife subsequently bore him a son this would obviously confirm the belief in the efficacy of spirit-medium predictions. However, if no son was born doubt would not be cast on the deity and its medium as failure would be attributed to that of fulfilment of the condition.

I was fascinated how close-knit the village community was and how everyone seemed to know all the details of each others' lives. As an anthropological researcher I felt cast into conflicting roles: on the one hand I was expected to be a participant observer and immerse myself as much as possible in the society I was studying; whereas on the other, professional standards required that I maintained my neutrality to ensure objectivity. To juggle these roles was not always easy, as many villagers wanted to manipulate my presence to their own specific advantage and the leaders of the two major opposing factions constantly vied for my support. One of these was a wise and impressive-looking white-haired old man for whom I developed a great personal respect, but I had to be careful not to give the impression that I was supporting his faction, otherwise I might well have been denied access to information from households loyal to his rival.

My home soon became the village meeting-house as the door to the main room was always open and I was the only one in the village who possessed a pressure-lamp. The lighting of the lamp, which my cook performed, became a daily ritual eagerly awaited by many. I was always amazed at their expressions as the bright light illuminated the room; they watched in awe and I realized how much we take for granted. We never stop to marvel when we switch on our electric lights or flush the toilet, and I silently vowed that I would never again take these luxuries for granted. A visit to the toilet was something I had taken for granted, yet in India it had became a major concern. Toilets were not commonplace and squatting in a sari was not only physically impossible for me but also unheard of in local society. I wished on a number of occasions that I was a man and found myself asking the women how they coped. They told me that I should reduce my food and fluid intake to ensure that I could last a whole day without using a toilet. This was not always easy because I frequently suffered bouts of diarrhoea and either had to spend my time close to my latrine or spend the day in agonies of discomfort. Yet all the problems of village life in India paled before the warm feeling of belonging I had which I had never truly experienced before.

Some of the village elders became my best and most reliable informants and talked with me at length, freely sharing their knowledge, particularly after they learned that I wanted to write a book about their lives. I felt privileged to be invited to their houses and allowed to listen to their long debates. The majority of these men were illiterate, yet in terms of their philosophical questions they would have easily qualified as intellectuals. I was fascinated to hear them discuss the meaning of life in the context of reincarnation and the transmigration of souls. Their profound religious belief was also accompanied by a healthy dose of scepticism. During the evenings in my village abode, when I sat listening to these elders, I learned more about Hinduism and its folk version than ever I could have done studying the subject at university.

While I enjoyed the company of the local elders I also established a kind of easy, jokey relationship with a group of young villagers. This had been facilitated by Suri, my Brahmin research assistant, who was a statistics graduate from Mysore University. Suri was about ten years my junior and not yet married. He was an earnest young man who took himself very seriously. Often when the two of us found ourselves on our own he would quiz me on how Westerners formed love marriages. He was at a loss to understand how young men and women could ever determine who would make them a good spouse. He was convinced that this was something the parental generation was best equipped to decide. Suri was a young man of conventional moral standards, who frowned upon extramarital relationships and I was amused how shocked he was at my easy banter with the young men of the village.

Bora, a newly wed young farmer, became my most frequent companion and I began to regard him as a close friend. One day I went looking for him and when finally I found him, feverish and crumpled up on a mat in his small thatched hut, I suspected that he was suffering from typhoid fever. (I had seen other villagers with similar symptoms.) I raced back to my house and drove to the nearest medical centre to alert the authorities of the dangers of a typhoid epidemic. The medical officer I saw there did not regard the matter as one of great urgency, but I insisted on taking back with me a medical team equipped with the necessary serum to protect the villagers against typhoid. (I myself had been inoculated before I left England.) When I turned up with these young health workers the *patel* (village headman) was summoned and the *Harijan* (scheduled caste) town-criers were sent round to advise that all villagers of all ages were to present themselves for an injection to avoid serious illness or death. My house became the headquarters of this exercise. We tried to assemble as many villagers as we could, but some went into hiding because they were afraid of the needle. I went out of my way to make sure that they paid a call on Bora. However, when I visited him two days later I was shocked to see him slumped on a mat by the door of his hut so that he could crawl out more readily whenever he had to relieve himself. He had deteriorated so rapidly and looked terribly sick. I couldn't understand it and wondered whether the inoculation had been effective. However, in a brief respite from his delirium he confessed that he had refused the injection. I was furious and wondered why he hadn't trusted me. I was so scared I would lose him.

Around 60 people contacted the fever and five of them subsequently died. It was a tense time in the village and people spent time praying and tending the sick. I sent nourishing food to Bora to help him regain his strength, while his grandmother called the witch-doctor to consult the oracle and thereby establish who was responsible for his sickness. It was impossible to know which, if any of our different methods helped Bora to recover from typhoid, but recover he did. It took weeks before he regained his strength and cheerfulness and during his recuperation I spent hours sitting with him, quizzing him why he had refused to have himself inoculated. He smiled at me sheepishly and said that he had been afraid of the needle.

The typhoid episode and the circumstances that surrounded it in fact brought us closer than we had ever been before. Bora was able to appreciate my rational approach, while I gained an insight into his culturally determined values and attitudes. It seemed ironic that Bora had to suffer from typhoid before we could bridge the gulf that separated our respective cultures.

Throughout my stay in the village I never managed to strike up a real friendship with any of the local women. In a segregated society it did not seem possible to cut across the gender barriers. However, since I considered the men to be my major source of information I tried my best to dissociate myself from any overt features of womanhood. I wore a loose bush-coat over khaki trousers and cut my hair short in the style of most of the Indian men. My appearance therefore differentiated me from the image of a woman held by most Indians, and in terms of social acceptance I seemed to take on the role of a neuter. I succeeded in forging links and even close friendships with many village men, but in stark contrast the village women remained aloof and reluctant to share their knowledge.

As soon as I was reasonably fluent in the local language I tried my best to get close to a few women. I particularly admired the *patel*'s wife, who always seemed to display such remarkable serenity. She was always nice and polite whenever we met, but it was obvious that she, like the rest of the women, wanted to keep her distance. On one of the rare occasions when I managed to sit together with a group of the village women I grasped the opportunity to ask them why they did not want to mix with me as freely as did their menfolk. One of the most articulate of them answered: 'You have the body of a woman, but the mind of a man and you behave like a man; you are so different from us village women that we feel that we have nothing in common with you. At an age when most of us are married and already have a number of children you have no children and are here without a husband. Our lives revolve round our families; you have no experience of this. Our paths therefore do not cross anywhere and this is why we remain remote.'

There was little I could say in response: these village women had obviously weighed me up carefully and found me wanting. I have often wondered whether my account of village life would have been significantly different had I concentrated my studies on the village women rather than rely, as I did almost exclusively, on the men. My training as an economist demanded that I collect a great deal of numerical data on different aspects of village life, this made me dependent on male informants as the women did not know the extent of their family's landholding let alone the details of cultivation costs. Subsequently I much regretted that I had allowed the economist in me to override my interest in discovering more about village women in South India.

As the end of my time in India approached I began to feel ambivalent about my return to England. I had come to feel at home with my Indian friends and was enchanted by their Hindu culture. I readily identified myself with the villagers; their joys became my joys and their sorrows my sorrows. At the same time my diverse set of friends, particularly the Van Ingen family, initiated me into many exciting new activities. They took me on elephant rides; they taught me how to shoot and how to handle a sailing boat. I even shot a panther that had been worrying the villagers, and the Van Ingens kindly presented it to me as a leaving present. It still adorns my study to this day.

I loved my time in India. It was intellectually challenging and allowed me the time to grow and develop on a personal level. I was finally allowed to enjoy myself without the responsibility of my parents weighing me down. But much as I did not want my time there to end I often longed for privacy and personal space, something I had totally sacrificed in the village. I also missed my family badly and couldn't wait to be reunited.

Though I corresponded regularly with my parents, Otto and some of my other friends from Manchester, my life in India was so removed from theirs that I felt there was little to connect us and I was nervous about seeing everyone again. Otto persuaded me to visit him in Australia before returning home in 1956. I discovered that most P&O liners were full between England and India but continued half-empty to Australia and offered low-cost return tickets from Bombay to Sydney. I could not believe that my time had gone so quickly and I was sorry to leave Mangala and my new family. I wondered whether I would ever return and what would become of my little house and car.

I spent the boat trip to Sydney relaxing and enjoying the Western comforts I had missed in my little village. I enjoyed the solitude and had time to put my thoughts in order before meeting Otto and his family. They gave me a royal welcome and introduced me to their little son Richard. I was touted round their group of friends like a celebrity, as they were all so eager to hear the tales of my village life. My elevated status surprised me and it seemed like a dream that Otto was actually showing me off and had therefore finally noticed me.

While I was in Sydney the Suez crisis worsened and P&O were unable to sail through the Suez Canal. Fortunately, they offered me a flight back to England instead of the long journey via Bombay, I was delighted. As I parted from Otto I felt a new age had dawned and the world was no longer such a vast place. Now that I had become a globetrotter I felt sure that it would not be long before we would be together again.

On the plane from Sydney to Singapore I met a number of British journalists who were returning from having observed a nuclear exercise in the Australian desert. We had an overnight stopover in Singapore, where the airline put us up at the Raffles Hotel. My newly acquired journalist friends asked me to join them for dinner. I felt like Cinderella going to the ball, but I tried to act as if dinner at Raffles with a group of well-known journalists was a frequent occurrence in my life.

In October 1956 I arrived back in England. I was deeply concerned how I would adjust to my old life. I realized how difficult it would be when I saw my old bedroom newly decorated in a floral paper with pink rosebuds and matching curtains. My parents had wanted to surprise me, but instead of exclaiming with pleasure as they had expected, I burst into tears. The conventional appearance of my parental home symbolized the straitjacket into which I was once more expected to fit. Before departing from India I had been planning how I would arrange my own rooms and I had brought back colourful handloom materials that I intended to use for curtains, wall-hangings and cushion-covers. When I saw what my parents had done I knew that I was no longer able to do as I pleased and I felt trapped. I loved my parents dearly and didn't want to upset them, but I also hated them for trying to tie me down to a dull and conventional life now that I had spread my wings and learned to fly. I rushed into my bedroom, locked the door and threw myself onto the bed. My parents were completely baffled by my behaviour and attributed it to jet lag and the strange life I must have been leading while outside their care.

Not only did I find home life stifling but also Manchester seemed grey and lifeless. I confessed to my colleagues how I missed the excitement of the field and they sympathized with my adjustment problems and offered advice on how they had dealt with traversing the different cultures. Professor Gluckman, who on my return asked me to address him as Max, obviously believed that hard work was the best cure, and within a week of my return asked me to set out the argument of my thesis in a lengthy paper. I was completely flabbergasted: I had so much material, but at no point had I considered how I would draw it all together in a single paper. However, I relished the challenge and enjoyed revisiting Mangala through my copious notes. After two weeks I smugly presented Max with a 50-page paper in which I had outlined my key theme. (I suspected he did not believe that I could put it together so quickly.)

When Max returned my paper every page had red lines scored through it. I was devastated. He laughed when he saw my despair and told me that there was nothing wrong with my thinking but that my writing was terrible. I argued that if my thinking was all right how could he have been so critical? Again he smiled and told me that intellect alone is not enough: ideas need to be articulated. He handed me back my essay together with a long list of English novels and insisted that I spent time learning how to express my ideas rather than just throwing them down on paper. Over the next two months I wrote and rewrote essay after essay and finally the red pen could be seen only here and there. Finally Max declared himself satisfied with my writing and gave me the all-clear to begin work on my thesis. I enjoyed becoming a fully fledged member of the academic community: my days as a machinist seemed now to belong to a different lifetime. The constant mental stimulation made me feel alive, yet I still felt unsettled and anxious to get back to the field. I decided that life in England was altogether too conventional and that I wanted to live my life differently.

# 11 • *Mr Right at Last*

At the beginning of 1957 Max introduced Dr Bill Epstein to one of our graduate seminars and explained that he had just returned from field studies in central Africa. I did not take much notice as there were always people coming and going and it was difficult to keep up. I would never have given him a second glance had we not happened to meet at the bus-stop after the class. We nodded at each and I lapsed back into my thoughts of escaping to some far-flung place across the globe. Suddenly I found myself wondering whether he too felt the same way. I plonked myself down next to him on the bus and by way of an introduction blurted out how fed up I was and, goading him, I asked whether he would like to travel the world with me. He turned to me and smiled, saying: 'Much as I would like to join you in your travels I am afraid it is out of the question.'

I was suddenly embarrassed by my outburst, realizing how forward I must have sounded. I wondered what he thought of me and as I looked up our eyes met for the first time. I was struck by their soulful expression but noticed a twinkle in the corners – he was laughing at me! I became flustered and scurried off the bus in a state of excitement. I hadn't felt like that in a very long time. I had lived my life in India largely as an honorary male and had forgotten the deep feelings that stirred within. I tried to convince myself that I should remain unattached, but at the same time I was yearning for love and close companionship. To this day I have no idea why I propositioned Bill, I hardly knew him, and was still extremely cautious with men. Yet there I was inviting a stranger to travel the world with me.

A few days after our encounter on the bus we met again across the seminar table. I couldn't concentrate on the argument of the person giving the paper and felt somewhat foolish when asked to contribute to the debate. For once I had nothing to say. I felt Bill would think I was an idiot and kicked myself.

During the usual after-seminar session in the nearby pub I was overjoyed when he came to sit next to me and felt the familiar tingle as his leg brushed mine. I had not experienced such feelings for years. We caught the bus together and this time he opened the conversation by asking me to a concert the following week. I was thrilled and accepted immediately, at which Bill gave me one of his lovely lopsided smiles and we arranged when and where to meet. I raced home flushed and happy. On seeing me Mama asked perceptively: 'Who is the lucky one?' I did not answer her. I was suddenly pleased that Beccie had insisted that I get a divorce from Ken and had arranged it all with Papa while I was in India. But it all seemed too good to be true and I wondered whether, like Ron, Bill was already engaged or even married. I realized I knew nothing about him and resolved to get to know him better before I allowed myself to fall in love with him.

The following day I made a point of catching Vic, another social anthropologist, with whom I knew Bill was staying and quizzed him about Bill's family. Vic suspected the motive behind my questions and gladly told me all he knew. I learnt that Bill was about my age and unattached and as far as he knew had never had a steady girlfriend. He had grown up in Northern Ireland and he came from an Orthodox Jewish family. He had trained as a lawyer and though he qualified as a barrister he never practised at the bar but instead turned to social anthropology. By the time we met he not only had his doctorate but had also established himself as an expert in urban anthropology. I was duly impressed and relieved by all that Vic told me. I made him promise that he would not mention his talk with me to Bill, as I wanted to make certain that Vic had not just spun me a yarn. The next time I met Bill I put him through my interrogation session and he passed with flying colours. He was somewhat bemused at my constant questioning, but did not object. I could now allow myself to love Bill. In any case I could not tell whether he reciprocated my feelings. He was shy and introverted and did not express his feelings openly, which I found somewhat exasperating.

I will always remember the early months of 1957 romantically as the 'spring of love'. Love had come rather late in our lives – we were both in our thirties. We were therefore eager to make up for lost time. I loved everything about Bill: his brilliant mind, his warm smile, his gentle concern for others and his sense of humour. We talked and laughed and loved, and I felt beautiful in a way I had never done before. I felt sure I had finally found Mr Right. I no longer yearned to escape but was happy just being with Bill. We went to concerts, parties and the theatre together and found more and more in common. It soon became obvious that we were a team and we were encouraged by our colleagues, who started to invite us as a couple to meals and parties. I even told my parents who were keen to meet him immediately and invited him for a meal. We were both nervous, but Bill could be very charming when he wanted to be and quickly won them both over. After he had left Mama told me how happy she was that I finally seemed to have found a nice young man and how pleased she was that he was Jewish. Papa, however, was more interested in any potential wedding plans and how they would affect the status quo, but I didn't care.

A few months later we were strolling through the streets of Manchester. It was a lovely mild spring evening and the sweet smell of cherry blossom filled the air, when Bill pulled me down on to a bench next to him and took my hand. At that moment I knew what they meant by the phrase 'my heart skipped a beat' because that was what mine did then. I looked at him as he struggled with his words and after taking a deep breath he proposed to me. I immediately said 'Of course', which was hardly the most romantic way of saying yes but it was all I could manage. He kissed me and we melted into one. If our words did not convey our feelings for each other, our kiss certainly did.

We left each other that night flushed and childishly carefree. We had agreed that Bill would come round the following day as he had insisted on formally asking my father for his daughter's hand in marriage. Papa was rather taken aback by our quick decision, but Mama was delighted. I supposed Papa had mixed feelings about my marriage as it would bring about a new stage in my life and to some extent he would be displaced. After we had toasted our engagement with my parents I was eager to do the same with Bill's. But whenever I questioned him about his parents' response he changed the subject. He rarely talked about them and I began to wonder if there was something he was trying to keep from me. Finally, during the engagement party our university friends held for us Bill decided to phone his parents to give them our news. As I stood next to him while he made the call I could tell they were not exactly delighted. Bill tried to prevent me from hearing the worst, but I knew then that it would take a long time before they would accept me. I was obviously not the kind of daughter-in-law they had expected for their only son and I began to wonder what I had let myself in for.

Bill subsequently arranged for me to join him at his parents' home in Ireland during Passover, which coincided with the Easter vacation. I flew to Belfast, where he met me with his father. I had misgivings about the initial meeting, but when I saw how like Bill his father was, I warmed to him immediately. I gave him a hug, which he seemed to enjoy, and I reckoned I had jumped the first hurdle. The second was not so easy. Bill's mother looked me up and down coldly and completely ignored me. Bill tried to introduce me to her, but she refused point-blank to respond. I could not believe that she could be so rude and hurtful. I was in no doubt that she did not approve of me, but I did not expect her to be so disparaging in front of everyone, asking what use was I if I had no dowry?

The week only got worse. Having never lived in a kosher household I made numerous *faux pas,* which were considered unforgivable by Bill's mother. When I asked for milk in my coffee after a meat meal she simply gave me a withering look. She turned to Bill and asked how he could contemplate marrying a woman who had no understanding of the laws of *kashrut*. Bill was crestfallen and said little, simply indicating that he would explain it all to me later. Bill's father, Morris, squirmed in his seat and looked less than pleased at the treatment I was receiving from his wife and her sisters. I wanted him to speak out and tell her to shut up, but I could tell that he was scared to.

Bill and I remained united against all the family objections to our marriage, but at times I seriously considered walking out and flying home on my own. His mother's family made me feel like a thief who had stolen their most prized possession. They took every opportunity to remind Bill that there were numerous excellent matches they could arrange for him with brides who would bring a large dowry that would, of course, also help his parents. I wanted to shake his mother and make her see that not only was I a worthy catch but I made her son happy – wasn't that enough? I had fought so hard to get to the position I was in and there I was having to justify myself to a prejudiced, small-minded bigot. I began to despise her superficial Jewish piety, her insensitivity and her complete lack of warmth. I could not believe how Bill had turned out, given his dreadful mother. When I told him that he smiled sadly and tried to reassure me that once we were married we would see very little of her.

I was still dubious, and while our love was stronger than ever, the strain of his family's interventions began to show. We started to criticize each other for the most trivial things and our tempers flared up quickly. I began to fear that our marriage was doomed and that I should never have allowed myself to fall in love again. Finally I decided to confront Bill and call it all off: I should have known that life would never be that straightforward. I tried to rationalize my feelings, but inside a part of me was dying. Gulping back the tears, I said: 'As anthropologists we both know that marriages not only unite individuals but also their respective kin-groups. The two of us may be overjoyed at the prospect of being together, but your family obviously disapproves of me and my kin. Do you really believe that our marriage stands a chance against such heavy odds?' Having said this I burst into tears and Bill took me in his arms, desperately trying to comfort me.

At that moment Bill's father knocked at the door and walked in. He saw my distress and asked me what was wrong. I almost laughed at his question. Didn't he know? Couldn't he see? I told him that I thought it was best for everyone if I left. I had decided to call the wedding off. He took me in his arms and held me close, stroking my hair until my sobs had subsided. He whispered softly that if it was what I wanted then he was sure that I would make his son the wife he had always wished for him. He then explained about the divide between his own family and his wife's. She came from a traditional Jewish family, her parents having immigrated to Belfast from Eastern Europe. Ethel was the eldest of four sisters, all of whom had married men who did not come from Belfast but had agreed to settle there. In time they all became prosperous moneylenders – all except for Bill's father who loved growing flowers and vegetables but never made any money despite all his prizes. For Ethel and her kin monetary wealth was the only value they knew. Morris's family, however, were modern thinkers and committed to the growing Zionist movement, hence they valued educational achievement much more than the accumulation of wealth.

The schism in Bill's family was best demonstrated by what name he was called and by whom. I knew Bill's first name at birth was Arnold. However, I had never heard him use that name. It was only in Belfast that I heard the name used by his mother and her family; his father always called him Bill. He explained to me that his brother Max (Bill's uncle) was chosen to hold the baby during the circumcision and when it had come to pronouncing his name Max was horrified and declared that he should be called Bill instead of Arnold. From that day though his mother's kin continued to call him Arnold, while his father's kin addressed him as Bill. I began to understand the difficulties Bill must have gone through growing up as an only child in that kind of family environment. It made me appreciate him more and intensified my love for him.

After I promised Bill's father that I would stay regardless of how rude his wife and her sisters were to me, he left. I cuddled up in Bill's arms and reminded myself of what Ruth had told me all those years ago: 'Grab happiness while you can!'

Having now been to Bill's home and seen how central Judaism was to his family life I promised him that I would learn how to keep a kosher home if this was what he wanted. In return I wanted him to pass his strong Jewish identity on to our children, should we have any. He seemed puzzled by my request so I explained my experience at school: how I had been persecuted for something I knew little about. I wanted to make sure that this would never happen to my children and, in my mind, developing a strong Jewish identity, was the best way to prevent it. Bill was evidently pleased to hear me say this.

Soon after we returned from Belfast, Mama, knowing that neither Bill nor I had much money, suggested that he became our lodger. We were delighted with the offer, for it allowed us more time together. We examined our financial position and decided to combine our savings and open a joint bank account. Our first joint purchase was a little black car, which we called 'Petrushka'. We used to spend our weekends exploring the countryside and were happy just being together.

Our wedding plans were beginning to take shape and we went to see the rabbi of the Manchester Reform Synagogue to discuss them with him. I had thought it would all be straightforward. However, he declared that I was not yet divorced according to Jewish law since I had only received the civil annulment. My heart sank and my previous feelings of hatred towards Ken returned. He had ruined my life! I looked at Bill helplessly and apologized. I didn't want to have to drag him through my past. The rabbi, seeing my distress, offered to try to get my divorce; but first I had to give him my former husband's address. Fortunately, I had Ken's address on the official divorce document I had obtained. (He lived in Canada.) A few anxious weeks followed during which Bill and I feared that Ken might still bear me a grudge and therefore might not agree to the Jewish *get* (divorce).

When the rabbi informed us that he had received notification from Ken and the *get* was approved we were greatly relieved and began to plan for our wedding in earnest. We told the rabbi of our limited finances and the difficulties with Bill's mother and her sisters, and he advised us to arrange a reception in the synagogue for our colleagues and friends and a kosher luncheon afterwards for family members. We managed to get friends to cater for the synagogue reception, but had to find a kosher caterer that we could afford, which was no mean feat. We sent invitations to all our friends and family and were saddened to see how short my list was. I had so few surviving relatives: Hitler had a lot to answer for. At least Bill's family would come, or so I thought. While we had lovely replies from Bill's father's side of the family we did not receive a single reply from his mother's people. I was shocked. I could not believe that they would go so far as to boycott our wedding.

The wedding took place on the morning of 16 August 1957. Bill's parents had flown over the day before. I was hoping that Bill's mother might have softened since last seeing her, but I couldn't have been more wrong. She refused to speak to either of my parents or me, and when she was supposed to kiss me under the *chupah* (wedding canopy) she refused even to look at me, for which I never forgave her. After the ultimate snub I decided to ignore her and concentrate on what was supposed to be the happiest day of my life. Once the ceremony was over we gathered in the synagogue for our reception, where our friends and colleagues made a great fuss of us and saw to it that we enjoyed ourselves. They made numerous speeches, many of which were hilarious. Then Bill gave a most touching speech, and I knew I had made the right choice. We gathered on the steps outside for photographs, and I could not help but laugh as I looked around me. The men, in their trilby hats, looked like extras from a gangster movie. Since few of our friends were Jewish no one wore the customary *yarmulkes* (skullcaps) so they had hunted out whatever they could find, knowing that Jewish custom demands that men cover their heads while in synagogue.

The subsequent kosher family luncheon was a sober affair in comparison and brought me down to earth with a bump. The aloofness of my mother-in-law made me grateful that the rest of her family had refused to come. I vowed to myself that I would not let her interfere with my happiness and I would think about how to win her approval later. I ignored her disapproving looks for the rest of the day and tried not to show how hurt I was. Fortunately, we had no plans to settle in Belfast so I would not need to see her very often.

Our honeymoon was spent touring Devon and Cornwall in

our little car. The sun shone and the skies were blue. I had never dreamed that I could be so happy. Bill not only told me how much he loved, me but he also showed it in many different ways. He would come home with a book in which he had put an appropriate Shakespeare quotation as a dedication, or he would present me with a big bunch of red roses or some little trinket he had carefully chosen for me. It was this thoughtfulness that I found so unusual in a man of his outstanding intellect. Life had a new purpose and I had someone I loved deeply to share it with.

# 12 • *A Marriage of Minds*

On our return to Manchester Bill and I moved into a small rented flat not far from the university. We loved traipsing round together finding second-hand bargains for our new home. My parents had wanted us to stay with them, but we had made it clear to them, as gently as we could, that we wanted to start our married life together – alone. I kept my promise and set up a kosher kitchen having read up on how to do it. It took me a little while to get used to separating milk from meat and I never truly bought into the principle. However, I knew it was important for Bill so I put up with the inconvenience.

As I adjusted to life as a wife I was also trying to complete my PhD thesis, which put me under a huge amount of strain. Having Bill around was like a tonic: he could empathize with what I was going through and was always ready to offer advice and discuss the problems I was facing. I felt so lucky to have found a husband with whom I could share not only my private but also my professional life. The last few weeks before submitting my PhD thesis were dreadful. I was convinced that it wasn't good enough and was finding it hard to sleep. I could not concentrate and constantly found myself scouring pans that I had forgotten to check and had burnt to a cinder. I felt totally inadequate not only as a scholar but also as a wife. Bill tried his best to help me regain my self-confidence, telling me that I was breaking new ground by combining the study of economics and social anthropology and that he was sure of my success. Much as I needed to hear this, I remained despondent, and had it not been for his constant encouragement I think I might well have given up. I had begun to question the very basis of my research and the numerous discussions I had with Bill only left me in awe of his brilliant mind and feeling ignorant by comparison. He was so widely read and seemed to have an encyclopaedic mind. In contrast my circumstances had made me a focused reader and I read the bare minimum even throughout my university studies. My refugee experience had given me confidence in dealing with the practical problems of everyday life but it had robbed me of the time to read widely and expand my mind. I was in a quandary: I was afraid that if I submitted my thesis I would fail and Bill would stop loving me, and also that if I didn't submit my thesis Bill would lose his respect for me and stop loving me. Bill could no longer help me, but simply had to watch as I tossed and turned at night. It was only our mutual love and respect for each other that helped us get through the strain of that period.

After deliberating at length, I finally completed my thesis and submitted it. Max arranged for Dr Eli Devons, Professor of Economics at Manchester University, to be my internal examiner and Professor Raymond Firth to be my external examiner. As the day of my viva approached I became increasingly nervous. Bill continued to reassure me in his gentle and patient way and I truly believe that I would never have got through without him. On the day of my exam Bill accompanied me to the exam room, all the while squeezing my hand and repeating over and over again: 'You will be fine, you'll see!' I felt as if my legs would give way under me as I entered the room. Max and the two examiners were already sitting there and I felt I was facing the oracle. I tried to read their faces for some sign, but I couldn't lift my gaze from the floor. Professor Firth stood up as soon as I sat down and shook my hand. I looked up and saw him smiling at me. I thought I heard him say: 'Congratulations Dr Epstein, you have produced a fine thesis', but I could not quite believe my ears. He said it again, only this time more slowly as he saw that it had not sunk in. He then went on to say that we should spend the remainder of the exam time discussing how it should be revised for publication. I was speechless and looked at the three of them with a dazed expression. Max smiled broadly and took my shaking hand in his own. The words 'publish' kept swimming round my head – all that worrying for nothing! Max then excused himself and said he wanted to let Bill know that there were now two doctors in the Epstein family. Bill had been pacing up and down the corridor outside the examination room like an expectant father and I heard him shout: 'I knew she would do it!' Grinning, I tried to compose myself for the rest of the viva and as soon as it was over I dashed outside into Bill's waiting arms.

My doctorate meant that Bill and I were now colleagues. We discussed our respective skills and talents and decided that we complemented each other perfectly. Bill was extremely widely read and had a brilliant mind, which made him into an expert theoretician, whereas my own strengths lay more in the applied field of socioeconomic development. We thus formed an ideal working partnership. As Bill's research fellowship at Manchester University was coming to an end he was looking for another position; fortunately, he was offered another research fellowship but this time at the Australian National University in Canberra. We were both excited at the prospect of moving to Australia: Bill because he had happy memories of the time he had spent there as a sailor during the war, and I because it meant a reunion with my brother Otto. My parents were very upset as they saw their daughter slipping away from them, but they managed to contain their feelings and allowed themselves to share in my new-found happiness.

I had been looking forward to the degree ceremony, the culmination of all that effort, and I beamed as I led the procession of graduate students who were to receive their doctoral certificates. I caught sight of Bill and my parents proudly watching me as I swept through the hall in my robes and I felt as if I were floating. Many of our friends had also come along to watch the ceremony and had arranged a party afterwards to celebrate my success. While Bill drove my parents home I enjoyed all the attention I was receiving. Suddenly, as I was being toasted yet again, I felt the ground coming rushing up and people closing in on me. The next thing I knew was that I was lying on a stretcher in Max's office. Everybody was exclaiming how the strain of the last few months must have been too much, but I knew better – I was pregnant. Two weeks before the degree ceremony I had tested positive and we were delighted, as we were both keen to have children. It was obviously too soon to announce our good news to anyone, so when Bill returned to pick me up and was told what had happened we just smiled knowingly at each other as he gently walked me to our car. On the way home we joked about how I had become the stereotypical woman, announcing my pregnancy to one and all by fainting. We could not keep our news to ourselves for long and soon afterwards we told my parents and our friends, but they had already guessed.

We booked our passage to Sydney on a P&O liner, due to depart from Southampton in August 1958. We stayed with my parents for the last few days before our departure. They tried to be positive, but they both looked so old and unhappy. I had looked after them for so long and they had exerted such an influence on my life that I felt guilty for abandoning them. When it was time for us to leave to catch the train to Southampton I felt torn. We hugged and kissed and as Mama clung to me she whispered, 'Promise me that you will look after Kurt.' I gave her my promise, though I found it rather odd that after all these years she still worried about her son Kurt and expected me, who was four years his junior, to look after him. Finally we had to disentangle ourselves and set off for the station.

As we turned the corner I had a chilling premonition that I would never see Mama again. I burst into tears and Bill tried to comfort me, reminding me that we were embarking on our new life together and before too long there would be three of us. My mood changed as soon as we reached the station as a host of our friends had come to see us off. We clambered on to the train amidst their cheers and best wishes, and as the train pulled out of the station my excitement overtook me. It felt wonderful to be off on my travels again, but this time I wasn't alone. I had the man I loved beside me and I was carrying his child. My life had really turned a corner. I relaxed into Bill and he put his arm around me. I felt content in a way that I had never felt before.

We spent the journey relaxing and enjoying each other's company. It should have been like a second honeymoon, but fate decided to play a cruel trick on me. As the ship neared the Australian coast, I began to suffer terrible cramps and I knew at once that something was wrong. I was admitted to the ship's small hospital and discovered that I was haemorrhaging. Bill immediately took charge and phoned Otto to arrange for an ambulance to meet us on our arrival in Sydney. There was little the ship's doctor could do to stem the flow and I spent the remainder of the journey sobbing, while Bill sat by my bedside trying to reassure me by telling me that a high proportion of women miscarry with their first pregnancy. I desperately wanted to believe him but I kept wondering, why me?

As we docked in Sydney, instead of our anticipated joyful reunion with Otto and his family I was carried by stretcher to the waiting ambulance and rushed to hospital. Bill stayed with me as long as he could and then made his way to meet his new brother-in-law. I felt guilty leaving him to his own devices with a family he had never met before, but there was little I could do. Two days later I was discharged and feeling somewhat sad and empty was collected by Otto and Bill, who I was delighted to see had already formed a close bond. They had arranged a wonderful reunion with champagne. It felt strange to be celebrating after what I had just been through, but when Otto raised his glass and made a toast to 'the future Epstein offspring!' I managed to shake off my melancholy.

After a couple of weeks in Sydney Bill and I went on to Canberra and presented ourselves at the Australian National University (ANU). Bill already had a fellowship in the department of social anthropology and I was subsequently offered a similar position in the newly established department of economics chaired by Sir John Crawford, one of the most distinguished Australian economists. Bill and I spent hours discussing what studies we should undertake and where. We knew from the field-work experience of other married social anthropologists that joint studies can put a strain on a relationship, so we decided that we would study a different society. However, we wanted to be within easy reach of each other.

We finally drew up a proposal to conduct two complementary studies among a New Guinea tribe called the Tolai, who lived on the Gazelle Peninsula of New Britain. In line with Bill's earlier studies in central Africa, where he had focused on the politics of urban societies, he planned to study Rabaul, the only sizable town among the Tolai, while I intended to do a socio-economic study of a Tolai rural society similar to the one I carried out in South India. Our respective heads of department accepted our proposals and after overcoming some difficulties in obtaining permission from the Australian authorities we departed for Rabaul.

We were both very excited at the prospect of venturing into territory that was new to us. Bill's African experience, in which he had studied tribal societies, made it easier for him to adjust to New Guinea tribal cultures: whereas my knowledge of tribal societies was based solely on what I had read, since I had studied only South Indian caste-dominated societies, which were quite different.

Rabaul was like something out of a holiday brochure: the beautiful natural harbour was enclosed by volcanic hills covered with lush tropical vegetation and the beaches, lined with palm trees, stretched for miles. The climate was hot and humid and we made the most of the romantic tropical evenings. During the days we set about organizing our field studies. It felt good to be a research team, as we could share our thoughts and discuss our plans and arrangements. It was fairly easy for me to find a suitable rural field site. After meeting various village headmen I decided to settle in Rapitok, situated in the hilly part of the Gazelle Peninsula about 15 miles from Rabaul.

Before either of us could make any progress with our studies we needed to find assistants to interpret and help teach us the Tolai vernacular. Pidgin English was commonly spoken in the towns, but since we intended to live in the Tolai villages and understand their way of life we did not want to communicate in pidgin but rather learn the local language. We soon discovered that there were only a few Tolai who could speak English and they were employed in the public service. Bill was deeply disappointed as the shortage of assistants precluded him from studying the town of Rabaul. He therefore decided to move to Rapitok with me in order to give himself time to make alternative research plans. There we could both begin to learn the local language.

With the help of some of the villagers we pitched our tent which the ANU had given us in the centre of one Rapitok hamlet. Our Tolai neighbours thought it very strange that two white people should want to live among them. They could not understand why we were prepared to live in a tent unlike the other whites who lived in large, well-furnished homes. They used to laugh at us as we listened to their words and hastily tried to scribble down what they had been saying. Bill and I used to compare notes on what we had understood and were always cheered when we came up with the same translation. Thus we accelerated our learning and managed to make friends with the villagers, who found our attempts at speaking Tolai highly amusing.

When we first moved in I had planned to cook on the small kerosene stove we had brought with us. However, the villagers would have none of it as they considered us their guests. From our first breakfast they insisted on providing us with cooked meals. I was delighted as I did not have to worry about preparing meals and their food was so delicious. The children brought us fruit and nuts in exchange for sweets. In the evenings our tent was packed with villagers who had gathered round our pressure lamp to come and talk to us. Bill and I hesitantly tried out our new words, which were often met with much hilarity. If all else failed we resorted to sign language and it felt like an evening of charades.

The friendly reception we had received boded well for our studies, so we decided to make our dwelling more permanent. We had a house made of bamboo built on stilts with thatched roofing, just like the villagers' homes. It was fascinating for us to watch the building process and we proudly moved in once it was ready. At this point Bill realized he was getting too comfortable and needed to get on with the plans for his own field studies. He explored the area and established that there was an island called Matupit that was connected with Rabaul by a causeway, where many of the urban workforce lived. It seemed to offer the best setting for Bill's study and we set off to reconnoitre.

Our reception was very different from that at Rapitok and we were greeted by one of the Matupi elders who railed at us in pidgin for coming to exploit his people the way most other white Australians were doing. We listened to him without saying anything; only after he had stopped did Bill quietly say in the vernacular: 'We do not understand pidgin we are in the process of learning the local language. We have come all the way from England to learn about your culture; please forgive us if we are not yet fluent, but we have only been here a few weeks.'

The old man, together with the rest of the crowd that had gathered, was astounded to hear Bill speak in his language and it immediately broke the ice. He ushered us to the central meeting-place and asked us to sit down. He then proceeded to tell us how he had worked as a bank clerk under the German colonial rule before World War I and that he knew German. He could not believe it when I started to speak to him in German and his whole demeanour changed. Soon afterwards Bill moved to Matupit having managed to rent a house on the island.

The first night on my own in Rapitok made me feel very lonely, and I wished that we could have worked closer together. We agreed that we would try to get together at least one night each week, but even that proved quite difficult. We each had a car, but the state of the roads was such that it usually took me at least an hour to travel the 20 miles from Rapitok to Matupit. I tended to visit Bill on Saturdays when I went with my Rapitok friends to Rabaul market and then stayed the night with him before returning to my village home the following evening. We would often meet during the week as well, when accompanying our respective village friends to one or other Tolai function. We were amused how Bill's Matupi friends considered my Rapitok friends ignorant bush-dwellers, while my friends considered the Matupi islanders as arrogant urbanites.

Bill soon earned the respect of the Tolai for his knowledge of their language and understanding of their customs. His quiet ways won him a place in the hearts of the Tolai, which continues until this day. My reputation, however, was based on the fact that I was the first white woman ever to join in a dance with local women. I was accepted on a very different level. We often discussed the different treatment received from our interaction with the Tolai and were both proud and amused by the way we had established a Tolai-wide reputation.

Among the Tolai there exists a male secret society which is central to their culture and into which most young Tolai men aspire to be initiated. Bill's research interests made him keen to find out what this initiation involved, but the Matupi were reluctant to enlighten him. However, my Rapitok friends were more open and agreed to let me pass through the first stage of the initiation as long as I promised the organizers of this male secret society not to divulge their secret to the village women. Bill and I looked forward to the ceremony with great excitement.

About a month before the date of my initiation I found out that I was pregnant. Bill and I were ecstatic about becoming parents after all and began to make plans for the event. We decided that this time we would wait before we announced our news and that I should continue my research for another few months before we returned to Australia. I tried not to think about my previous experience and imagined the day I would hold my baby in my arms. However, on the day of my initiation I discovered I was haemorrhaging again. It was dreadful. I had to send my village headman in his car to Bill with a note telling him what had happened and to fetch me in an ambulance. I lay down on my mattress, crying softly to myself. I was desperately hoping that they would be able to save this baby, but I knew inside that I had already lost it. I began to think I would never be able to have a child and Bill would stop loving me. It seemed so unfair that not only had I lost my second child but it had happened on a day that I had been so looking forward to and had strived so hard to achieve.

After three days in a private hospital in Rabaul I was ready to return to Rapitok. Pale and still somewhat shaky, I slowly climbed out of the car. My village friends rushed to welcome me home. I had not told them why I had been rushed to hospital, but the women guessed what had been the problem. They also knew that I had arranged with some of their menfolk to be allowed to join the male secret society, though I never found out how. That evening, sitting with them round my pressure lamp, they explained why I had miscarried. They told me that the *Dukduk*, the spirit of the male secret society, was punishing me for having tried to join the secret male cult and had made me lose the baby as a stark reminder that I was a woman.

A few months later we returned to Australia, where I consulted a gynaecologist. He recommended that I underwent a fibroid operation, which we hoped would put things right. A couple of days after the operation, just as I was beginning to recover, Bill and Otto visited me in hospital with the news that Mama had died in England. I had been so wrapped up in my own life that I had spent little time thinking about my parents and the news came as a great shock. I remembered her drained face and sad expression as I had said my last farewell to her before departing for Australia. I could not help but feel that my departure had caused her death. I could not believe I would never see her again. I could not stop crying: death was all around me. My baby, my mother; what was next? Bill tried to calm me, but to no avail. Eventually he and Otto had to leave.

Shortly after they had gone, the patient with whom I shared the room asked me why I was so upset. When I told her of my mother's death she turned to me and in a firm voice said: 'Don't cry, it will only upset your mother who is now in heaven watching over you.' As I listened to her words I began to think how wonderful it would be if I could have shared her belief in a God and an afterlife; it would have made it so much easier. But try as I might I could not make myself belief that my mother was floating on a cloud somewhere and was still part of my life. To me death seemed so final.

After Mama's death Otto and I decided that it would be best if Papa came to live in Sydney. He seemed pleased at the prospect of staying with Otto since he had not seen him since 1953. It seemed so strange to greet him without Mama and it made my grief all the more real. It had been a long time since I felt I had needed her and just when a daughter should have her mother around to help and guide her, she was no more. I was bereft.

# 13 • *The Balancing Act*

Our life settled into a routine in Canberra and after a few years we were ready to move on. In 1961 we received a letter from Max Gluckman offering us a lectureship at Manchester University. We laughed as we imagined ourselves joined at the hip, lecturing together. We debated who should take the position, Bill felt I should take the secure academic position, whereas I insisted that I had a wider variety of skills and would therefore find it easier to obtain another job. So Bill accepted the position, and we prepared for our departure. Before we left, Sir John Crawford, vice-chancellor of the Australian National University, called me into his office and said: 'Scarlett, I want you to know that I have been so impressed with your study that if you ever decide to return to Australia there will always be a position open for you.' Finally, I felt I was receiving the recognition I so desperately craved.

The return flight was quite pleasant as we stopped off in Hawaii, but I could not help thinking about the baby I had lost as we had sailed out to Australia. Life seemed so different now, I still half expected Mama and Papa to be waiting for us in Manchester, with outstretched arms. However, Kurt was waiting at the airport by himself when we arrived. He had conveniently arranged for us to rent the first floor of his mother-in-law's terraced house in Manchester. As soon as we had settled in I contacted a number of my old friends asking if they knew where I could find a job. One of them said that the Salford College of Advanced Technology had recently advertised for a senior lecturer in their liberal studies department, but unfortunately the closing date for applications had already passed. On hearing this I immediately decided to find out more about the vacancy. I phoned the college principal and having impressed him with my academic qualifications and research experience I managed to convince him to make an exception for me. I rushed over with my cv and he agreed to include my name on the shortlist of candidates.

I was very excited at the prospect of becoming a senior lecturer and was bubbling over when Bill came home that evening. Bill was always much more prudent than I and brought me down to earth with a bump, trying to protect me from possible disappointment. But I would not listen; I was determined to get the job. The next day I was invited for an interview and as I left Bill hugged me and made me promise that I wouldn't be too upset if I didn't get the job. I was infuriated and retorted: 'Don't worry. I'll get it!'

On arriving at the college I was ushered into a room in which there were two other candidates waiting to be interviewed. I soon discovered that they were currently lecturers in the liberal studies department and that they had applied for promotion. Both seemed confident that they would succeed. As I watched them emerge separately from the interview room they still seemed confident. They nodded at me and said that the principal had told them they would be informed of his decision by the end of the day. I tried not to let their confidence worry me and reassured myself that with my doctorate, research experience and forthcoming publication I was better qualified than either of them. When my name was called I collected myself and prepared to do battle.

The interview panel consisted of three men who seemed intent on testing my knowledge and suitability for the position to the nth degree. This only made me rise to the challenge and we sparred for the next half hour or so. Finally, the principal broke in and the interview changed style. All of a sudden I was being asked whether I would be able to cope with classes of junior managers, many of whom were so sure of themselves that they were often very difficult to control. I replied cockily, 'Sir, I have just spent a year living with and studying a New Guinean tribe that until not so long ago were cannibals and I managed to make many friends among them. Therefore, I am sure I shall be able to tame even the most difficult junior managers!' The men chuckled when they heard my response and I was offered the senior lectureship right away. I was thrilled and felt triumphant after the battle. I thanked the panel for the enjoyable interview and tried to walk calmly out of the hall, but I really wanted to jump and shout. As I walked into the waiting room I saw the other two candidates presumably discussing their chances. I couldn't help but admit gleefully that I had just been offered the job. I should have realized that this was not the way to win myself friends in the department, but I was like the cat that had got the cream and wasn't really thinking.

I sped over to the university to tell Bill. He was delighted with my success and so were our academic colleagues. I wondered whether he would be concerned that I had now secured a senior lectureship whereas he only had a lectureship, but I should have known that it would never have occurred to him to have been jealous. That evening Bill took me out for dinner and we celebrated my appointment with a bottle of champagne, toasting our successful future together.

To complete the happy picture I found out I was pregnant again and since I had had the fibroid operation we were fairly confident that things should go to plan. However, after a few weeks we both confessed how worried we were that I would lose another baby, so once again I turned to Beccie. Following her advice I consulted one of the top gynaecologists in Manchester, who examined me and said he thought that there was nothing to worry about. This made us feel confident again and we spent hours in the different baby shops planning our nursery. We had just started to let ourselves believe that we would finally become parents when I was rushed to hospital in the middle of the night with yet another threatened miscarriage. I was distraught and could not stop crying. I was angry with myself for believing that my life could ever be so simple. I felt like an emotional ball, constantly bouncing up and down.

I was admitted as a private patient of my gynaecologist and given a sedative to make me sleep. In the morning, when the specialist examined me, he assured me that all was not lost: there was still a good chance that the pregnancy would go to term. I immediately cheered up and we continued to talk about 'our baby'. I lay in bed for five days, bored but relieved. I was feeling so much better that the specialist told me that I could go home again. I was jubilant and so was Bill. The following day he came to collect me, but as I began to get dressed I realized immediately that I was miscarrying. I became hysterical and when the specialist arrived I shouted at him: 'Why did you lie to me? How could you let me believe my baby was all right when you knew all along that there was something wrong with my pregnancy?' He looked upset and assured me that he could not have predicted this. I hated myself, and felt such a failure that I could not produce the child we both so desperately wanted. I turned away from Bill, as I could not bear to see his pain. I wanted to die and kept crying that my life was no longer worth living, at which point they posted a nurse by my bedside to watch over me. She tried to comfort me and told me how there was no justice in the world: there I was desperate for a child and yet every night she attended to young women who had tried in all sorts of ways to abort their own pregnancies.

The next morning the specialist arrived. In order to make the necessary curettage easier he prescribed a strong laxative to facilitate the expulsion of the foetus. He had not thought that I would therefore see the foetus of my unborn child. I had been four months' pregnant, so the embryo was tiny but fully formed. It would have been a boy. I had to be prised away from my child. I did not want to leave my little boy and I knew I would never forget the sight of my first baby, with his tiny limbs. I so much wanted to hold him, but I knew he was gone.

That night, as I lay awake, I decided that I could not go through another miscarriage and Bill would therefore have to find another wife to bear him a child. I even wrote him a letter explaining that, much as I loved him, I was prepared to grant him a divorce so that he could find a better, more productive wife. I was preparing myself for a life alone: without Bill, without a baby, I was dying inside.

Two days later, when I was on my way back home with Bill, I told him of my decision. He turned to look at me, his eyes brimming with tears. Angrily he said, 'Surely you must be joking. I married you because I love you and though I very much want a child I only want a child by you and not by any other woman. So please stop talking such nonsense. Somehow we will manage to solve this problem, but please get it into your head that you are the only woman I have ever loved and shall ever love!' I so much wanted to believe him.

During the subsequent two years I had two more miscarriages, which left me listless and resigned to the fact that we could not have our own child. Outwardly our lives seemed well settled. We each had an interesting and satisfying academic position with a reasonable income and a promising future; we had bought a lovely large, old Victorian house in one of Manchester's nicest suburbs. Yet inwardly we were both grieving. Thus it was that Bill and I began to consider adoption. Bill insisted that we should adopt only a fully Jewish child. He wanted to ensure that a child carrying his name would have a strong Jewish identity and he did not think it would be fair to impose this on a non-Jewish child. We consulted numerous agencies and soon learned that the chance of a Jewish child coming up for adoption was very remote.

Then one evening in January 1963 Jack, Beccie's doctor brother, phoned asking whether we still wanted a Jewish baby. I remained silent, thinking perhaps it was some hoax, but he then went on to explain that one of his young female Jewish patients had been to see him and confided that she was seven months pregnant. Jack told me that she was a law student at Manchester University and had attended a Jewish camp the previous summer where she had met a young solicitor who had been keen to marry her. She quickly realized that she was not in love with him and when she found out she was pregnant couldn't bring herself to marry him just because of the baby. Instead she had decided to put the baby up for adoption so that she could continue with her own life. She seemed determined, so Jack did nothing to try to persuade her to rethink her plans and he thought of us immediately when she asked whether he could help her find a nice Jewish couple who would love and care for her baby.

My heart started to pound and my mind raced. I wanted to hug Jack then and there as he continued to reassure me what a lovely, intelligent girl she was and how confident he was that she would produce a beautiful, healthy baby. Jack finally paused for breath and asked if we are interested, I wanted to scream at him, 'Of course we were interested. This is our dream come true! But all I said was, 'Thank you. Thank you so much.' Jack could tell by my reaction how dumbstruck I was and gently told me to discuss it with Bill and call him back later. I came off the phone shaking. Seeing me like that Bill rushed over and asked what had happened. I simply put my arms around his neck and as if in a trance, whispered, 'We have found our baby.' Thinking I had gone crazy he told me to sit down and tell him what was going on. As soon as I told him about Jack's phone call he jumped up and shouted, 'who said that miracles don't happen?' We knew there was nothing to discuss; this was what we had both been dreaming of but had never thought we would get. Within minutes we phoned Jack back and told him we wanted the baby.

That night neither Bill or I could sleep. Just as one of us was about to drop off we would start to muse whether we would have a boy or girl; what names we liked; what the baby would look like; and how we would have to adjust our lives to accommodate our first child. Most parents have months to deliberate over such things, but we only had a matter of weeks. We started what we termed 'Operation Child' with a host of lists that we diligently ticked every time we bought an item. We read numerous books on how to treat a newborn, and I was delighted that Bill wanted to take such a proactive role with the baby. The unborn baby had already become 'our child' and we were determined that nothing was too good for it. The days passed in a flurry of shopping sprees and preparing the house. Those were happy days for us. We put all the miseries of my miscarriages behind us and concentrated on the fact that at last we were going to start a family.

On 7 February 1963 Jack phoned to congratulate us on the birth of our baby daughter. He told us that she was a beautiful baby. I was immediately worried that there might be something wrong with her, but he reassured me that she was perfect. I was amazed at how maternal I felt. He advised us to take on a nurse for the first four weeks to help us learn all the things one has to know about looking after babies, and offered to help us find someone. Having arranged dates and times to collect our daughter we put the phone down and danced around the room. After we had calmed down a little we cracked open a bottle of champagne and drank a toast 'to our little Micky'.

The next five days dragged. I was desperate to hold my baby in my arms, but finally the day arrived and we set out to collect her. Having seen lots of photos of newborn babies I was prepared to find a little red, crumpled face, but when Jack handed me the little bundle all I could see were these huge eyes staring at me. She was beautiful and I could not take my eyes off her. I was relieved that she seemed quite content to be held by us and didn't cry as we took turns in holding her. We had decided to give her the name of 'Michelle' and call her Micky while she was little As I watched Bill cradling her in his arms I knew we had made the right decision: he looked the perfect happy father. We didn't stay long, as we were keen to introduce Micky to her new home and having thanked Jack over and over again we left with our daughter and her nurse.

Micky settled in quickly and was such a bundle of joy. We had had no idea how she would enrich our lives. She behaved like the perfect baby; she hardly ever cried and took her bottle hungrily. I started to work with Micky beside me, enjoying the gurgles and squeals she made. Although friends had told me that babies of that age can't smile I was convinced that her wind was definitely a smile and was happy in the belief that she was as content with me as I was with her. Bill was just as besotted with Micky as I was, and invested in a movie camera so that we could capture every step in her development. It became increasingly obvious that Papa shared our excitement and longed to meet Micky. We therefore arranged for him to sail back to England and to stay with us. I fetched him from Southampton and drove him straight back to Manchester, eager to introduce him to his new granddaughter. Although it was late at night when we arrived home he was desperate to see her and I picked her up, trying not to wake her. However, she opened her eyes and instead of screaming held out her arms to her Opapa and he melted. I knew what he was thinking and we hugged quietly, wishing that Mama could have been there to share the moment with us.

Micky's arrival made me forget about trying to get pregnant and I was therefore surprised to find myself pregnant soon after we had celebrated her first birthday. Bill was thrilled when I told him, but I refused to allow myself to get too excited. I already had Micky, and if I miscarried I would still have my lovely daughter. We discussed at length whom we should consult and decided that we should contact the gynaecological department at the university to see if they could offer any advice. Having examined me, Dr Morris, the professor of gynaecology, diagnosed a lazy muscle in the uterus around which he tied a ring. He told me this would stop me from miscarrying, which I found hard to believe, but I soon felt the baby's first movements inside me. I could not quite accept that I was going to have a baby, but my growing belly bore witness to the fact.

On 26 November 1964 Debbie was born by Caesarean section. Professor Morris was understandably proud of having helped us to have our own baby after my numerous miscarriages. Debbie's birth thus became a case in medical history, and medical students watched her birth while Bill paced the corridors waiting for news. When I woke up from the anaesthetic and saw my baby sleeping in a little cot by my bedside I thought it was all a dream; it was simply too wonderful to be true. She was tiny, with dark hair and a lovely little face. She looked just like a little doll, and I loved her with all my heart.

It seemed as if Micky had arrived with a clean bill of health, but with Debbie I became anxious that everything was a danger sign. When she cried I was convinced she was dying and when she slept I thought she had stopped breathing. When Bill first saw her he joked that she looked like the Chinese leader, Mao Tse-Tung. If only he knew what that did to me: throughout the pregnancy I had been petrified that she would be a Down's Syndrome baby. I was 42 when I had Debbie and well aware that the incidence of Down's increases with age. However, Professor Morris and the nursing staff reassured me that Debbie was a normal baby and when on Bill's next visit he pronounced that she now looked like Mussolini I realized that my worries were unfounded.

At first Micky treated her baby sister like a new doll to play with, but became increasingly frustrated when Debbie did not respond as she wished. Micky was such an easy baby in comparison to Debbie and I constantly wondered what was wrong with her. She cried a great deal of the time and I became exhausted trying to comfort her. Night after night she lay beside me howling and I began to fear that I was too old to look after a baby or that she was terribly ill. I couldn't understand why my own baby should prove too much for me while Micky had been such a joy. It was only when the nurse at the local clinic advised me to try bottle-feeding Debbie that I realized I had not been producing enough milk and that she must have been permanently hungry. I felt such a failure. I wanted to be the perfect mother and already my age was working against me. However, when I saw the change in Debbie I knew I had done the right thing.

Claude, our French au pair girl who moved in with us shortly after Micky's nurse left, was wonderful with the children and since Bill and I felt that we were fairly old parents we thought it would be good to have a younger person around. We decided to divide our responsibilities: I concentrated on the baby, while Bill took care of Micky. This meant that Micky became a daddy's girl, whereas a closer bond developed between Debbie and me.

Bill's parents had never been to visit us, but as soon as they heard I had produced their long-awaited grandchild they made plans to come over from Belfast. Bill's mother never really accepted Micky, as in her mind she would rather believe that I had failed as a wife and daughter-in-law. However, once Debbie was born she knew she would have to change her attitude if she wanted to visit us. She was almost amicable during the visit, and as most of our time together was taken up with baby talk it went off quite smoothly. Bill's father was gentle and loving and had a way with Micky, preferring to spend time with a toddler rather than a newborn. I wished he could spend more time with us and as he left I urged him to come back soon. It was a prescient plea as only days after we received a phone call late at night telling us that he had had a serious heart attack. Bill immediately flew to Belfast and was at his father's bedside when he died. Bill had been very close to his father and found it difficult to cope with the grief. He shut himself away for days trying to bury himself in books and it was only Micky that managed to break through his grief.

My three months' maternity leave was soon up and I had to return to my teaching duties at the college. My priorities had changed and I found it difficult adjusting to the new demands placed on me. I no longer wanted to stay late and miss bedtime and I no longer had limitless hours to prepare for lectures. I found I was constantly torn and frustrated that I could not seem to give 100 per cent to anything anymore. Everything became a compromise. I tried to remember what Mama would have done, but our circumstances were entirely different and I had to find my own way. I tried to set aside the weekends for the girls and on Sundays we always had family cuddles in bed. I used to make up stories for the children and found it a great way to introduce different concepts. I built my stories round two characters: Micky-ticky-tooks and her adopted sister Dibbie-debbie-dabbie. At one level the girls simply saw these two characters and their adventures as imaginary, but at another they realized that they also represented them. Debbie would often ask 'Am I adopted, Mummy?' and Micky would then ask the same question, to which I jokingly replied, 'Both of you are adopted!' and left it at that. Bill and I debated when we should tell Micky that she was adopted and decided to wait until she was a little older. We feared the sibling rivalry it might cause. We loved the girls equally, but we were worried that Micky might find it difficult to accept so we kept putting off the moment of truth.

Life soon settled into a pattern, but once I had overcome the challenge of balancing work and home life I began to long for something new. The last few years had been taken up with teaching and child-rearing and I now longed to get back to a research job. Someone must have been listening, for just as I confided my wanderlust to Bill he received an invitation to take up a professorial fellowship in the department of social anthropology at the Australian National University. I was so excited, but Bill was worried about me giving up my senior lectureship with no specific job to go to in Canberra. I shrugged off his concern feeling confident that I would easily find something, having been given a personal assurance by the vice-chancellor that there would always be a position open for me. Bill was happy to be persuaded, and we started to prepare for our departure. We couldn't believe how our lives had changed since our last journey. We were no longer travelling empty-handed but had two children in tow and all our household belongings. We were a family.

In February 1966 we set sail for Sydney. I laughed how I had gone up in the world, as this time we had the best cabin on board ship. I looked out of the porthole and across the sea, thinking how lucky I was. I thought back to the days in Vienna and that teacher's scathing prediction. How I wished I could show him how far I was from the gutter! Bill asked who I was thinking about and I just shrugged and said no one of any importance. He put his arms round me and I felt nothing could ever harm me again.

Shortly before we were due to dock at Sydney, I woke one morning and wondered why Debbie was still in bed. (Normally the girls were up and bouncing around long before we wanted to surface.) I went to her bunk and found her soaked in sweat and her brow feverish. She was pale and listless and her eyes were glazed over. I yelled for Bill and kicked myself for having allowed myself a moment to reflect on my contentment. Bill ran off to get the ship's doctor, who promptly dismissed me as an hysterical mother and told me that it was just a cold or possibly flu. I tried to keep Debbie cool with a wet flannel, but her temperature refused to come down. I tried everything I could think of. Bill and I took turns sitting by her bedside and watched her over the next 24 hours, as she became weaker. Bill tried his best to reassure me that high temperatures occur frequently among small children and that most of them recover pretty quickly. However, Debbie showed no signs of improvement. She began to hallucinate and started to vomit, and I began to scream at Bill that we were going to lose her if we didn't do something. I cursed our decision to take such a long sea voyage when our two children were still so small.

By the time we were nearing Sydney, Debbie had not taken food or water for five days except for the teaspoons of milk that I forced down her which simply came straight back up. We called the doctor several times and pleaded for some medication, but he was adamant that Debbie was just suffering from flu and that she would get better quickly. I felt like throttling this doctor, but of course had to control myself. All the life had gone out of our little Debbie, and Bill and I were grief-stricken. We managed to forewarn Otto that we needed a doctor and he arranged for us to see one as soon as we arrived. I had lost a baby the last time we arrived and I could not believe that fate would play such a cruel trick again.

When we arrived in Sydney, the doctor whom Otto had called examined Debbie. He immediately diagnosed pneumonia and prescribed a course of antibiotics. It was amazing watching her come back to life. It made me realize how precarious the balance is between life and death.

After the strain of the journey it felt good to set up home again and see our children running around in the sunshine. Just as I had predicted, the vice-chancellor offered me a visiting fellowship at the Australian National University and I had quickly to hire a live-in help to look after the girls while I pursued my career.

Life was full and we soon became active members of the small Jewish community in Canberra, the majority of which were fellow academics. There were so few of us that we had to remain committed or the community would have collapsed. We held our services in a rented hall, as there was not a single synagogue in the whole of Canberra. Bill took on the responsibility for ensuring that there would be the required minimum number of men present at the shabbat services, and much to my amusement I became the chairperson of the Canberra branch of the Australian Council of Jewish Women and spent many weekends fundraising for various functions.

After some months in Canberra in suburban bliss we decided we wanted to return to New Guinea to conduct further studies among the Tolai. By this time the university had acquired houses in Rabaul so we were able to stay together. I was so excited as we drove out to Rapitok and I proudly showed off my girls. I was pleased to hear that I would no longer be referred to as a 'dried-up betel nut' now that I had fulfilled my responsibilities as a woman.

Feeling like seasoned researchers we quickly chose our subjects. Bill decided to focus his study on the forthcoming first parliamentary elections in New Guinea, while I chose to concentrate on the dynamics of the open markets. I discovered that all the local growers (they could hardly be termed farmers) brought their own produce for sale rather than using a middleman, yet there seemed to be a set price for all the different fruits and vegetables, regardless of who was selling them. It seemed amazing to me that there appeared to be a monopolistic pricing mechanism and I set about trying to establish how it operated. For this I had to be at the marketplace by 6 a.m., when the sellers arrived and could only leave as they were packing up, at about 5 p.m.

At first this did not create too much of a problem with Bill's schedule. However, soon after moving to Rabaul Bill was recalled to Canberra to take on the job of acting head of the department of social anthropology. (Initially he was reluctant to accept the position as he did not want to leave the children and me, but we jointly decided that he had to prepare to become a professor sooner or later.) I had not really bargained for the additional workload. Not only did I have my own studies but I had also offered to take over Bill's research project for him. It also came as a shock as to how I was meant to cope with the demands of the children and my own daily schedule. I found I was constantly running from dropping Micky at school and Debbie at the care centre to the market to supervise my research assistants – of which there were over a hundred – and then back to pick the girls up. It was not ideal as I was always late for everything. In order to get to the girls on time I had to leave the market early and therefore could not collate my assistants' data on market transaction details. If I stayed on the girls would be kept waiting and I knew that this would also have repercussions. I tried to make it up to the children, as I knew that it was a difficult time for all of us and after a hard day's work as a research supervisor I was usually glad to spend quality time with them. I so wanted them to know that although I spent the days working and away from them I still loved them. However, I would be lying if I didn't sometimes just want to walk away from it all and leave all the demands behind, even for just a moment.

I was delighted when Bill and I and the children were reunited. Although I missed Rabaul, I was relieved to be able to share the burden of parenthood once more. I had thought we would relax back into our old ways, but soon after our return to Canberra we were already preparing for our sabbatical. We planned a round-the-world trip which would take us to Hong Kong, Israel, Austria, England and America with a last stop in Japan.

The time flew by and the girls soon became seasoned travellers. They each had a little shoulder-bag into which they were allowed to squeeze as many toys as they could. They quickly learned how to create a familiar environment in the various strange hotels in which we stayed. As soon as they entered their hotel room they would quickly empty their bags and drape their toys around their beds. Bill and I were proud to see how well our little girls managed to adapt to the many strange places in which we stayed and the many strange people whom we met on our travels. In Kyoto we were the only guests in a small typical Japanese inn. Though none of us could speak any Japanese and the kind elderly lady running the inn could speak no English we managed to communicate. She made us understand that we could leave our girls safely with her while we could go sightseeing. Micky and Debbie stayed happily with her, endlessly fishing for goldfish in her pond. They even learned to call her 'Obasan' (Granny).

During our stay in England Bill was invited to apply for the professorship in social anthropology both at the London School of Economics and Sussex University. He made it clear that he would only accept the chair of either if I too were offered a position. By this time we had decided that we wanted our girls to grow up in England in a Jewish community. We could not believe that on our return to Canberra we would find that we had both been offered professorships at Sussex University: Bill as the professor of social anthropology and I as a research professor at the Institute of Development Studies (IDS). I had thought that two doctors in one family was a lot to hope for but two professors?

We planned to return to England in the summer of 1972. To my surprise the IDS invited me to participate in one of their study seminars three months earlier. This visit to England, though it lasted only three weeks, enabled me to make all the necessary domestic arrangements before we would arrive as a family. I had always dreamed of living by the sea and was excited at the prospect of buying a house on the seafront in Brighton. However, it was the time of property gazumping, and every time I saw a house that I liked I found I had been outbid. Each day, after my various commitments at the university, I would spend time looking for a house. I was getting increasingly despondent until finally I was shown a reasonably priced Victorian house of the size we needed situated on a quiet road in Hassocks, a village near Brighton. Though it was in a poor state of repair I was drawn to it as it reminded me of our house in Altrincham. After getting Bill's consent over the phone I bought it. I felt triumphant when I returned to Canberra to help pack up the family.

When Papa heard that we were going back to England he insisted on coming with us, and so in June 1972 we all sailed back together and within a few months it felt as if we had never been away. The girls were enrolled in the local junior school and we found a lovely French au pair to look after them. It was the first time I had really settled anywhere for any length of time and I enjoyed the time spent with the family and on the house.

Work at the Institute of Development continued to be stimulating and fulfilling and I really felt I had found my niche. I was beginning to get recognition for my developmental work from organizations around the world and the invitations to visit satisfied my wanderlust. The New York-based Agricultural Development Council (ADC) invited me to join their board of trustees. I was their first female member. I felt I was becoming a pioneer in my field and developed a new research model whereby I selected the focus, secured the funding and recruited a team of Third World doctoral students to conduct action-oriented microsociety studies in their respective home countries. I thus began our 'Cross-Cultural Study of Population Growth and Rural Poverty' in 1973 with five Asian and three African Ph.D students. It was not easy to supervise eight doctoral students simultaneously, but ultimately it gave me the ability to compare and contrast the many different cultural aspects of the various societies my students had studied. My band of students became like family and I rather enjoyed the maternal role which I assumed towards them. We used to have curry evenings at our house where we would sample the food from their different countries of origin. My children soon got used to our house being full of strange people from around the world and developed quite an appetite for spicy food.

I was sad when my first study programme drew to a close and the joint studies were published. I was at a loss as to know how to maximize them. However, I managed to get funding for a documentary film based on the findings of one of my African students, and I was so proud when *Maragoli* was made. It was the first documentary to result from IDS research and it received excellent reviews from around the world. I felt that I had finally made it. I had become used to Bill's academic brilliance leading the way, but I was now gaining my own professional recognition.

In 1974 Bill and I were each offered a one-year fellowship at the Stanford Center for Advanced Study in the Behavioral Sciences, which was a great honour. It gave us both the opportunity to take time out and write up material for subsequent publication. We didn't think it would be too unsettling to take the children out of school for a year and felt sure they would enjoy the experience of going to an American school. We found a beautiful house in a lovely area and the year sped by. At the end of our stay at the Center we arranged with my cousin Paul, who lived on the east coast of America, to have our girls while we went on a tour of the Mexican archaeological sites, which was a wonderful experience.

We were glad to return to England, but it took the girls a little while to adjust: their American accents made them stand out at school and we had not predicted that the different subjects and methods of teaching would create such a hurdle for them.

They were growing up fast. Micky had turned 13 and wanted to be called Michelle rather than Micky. Boyfriends appeared on the scene and suddenly we had teenage daughters. We had tried to instil a sense of Jewish identity and taken them every weekend to Sunday school, but it was difficult living in a town where we were the only Jewish family. I worried that we had failed when Michelle became seriously involved with a boy from the next village, but there was little we could do.

It was difficult for me to identify with them, as at their age I was already facing the hardships of anti-Semitism and fitting in was a very different ballgame. I wished I had Mama around to offer her words of wisdom. It was strange how as a young adult I had taken charge, but now that I had children of my own I desperately needed her to turn to. I couldn't consult Papa as he had moved into an old people's home in Manchester while we had been in America. Being a working mother had precluded me from joining in all the school activities and I had no female friends other than colleagues with whom to discuss the trials and tribulations of being a mother. I felt very alone.

In 1976 Papa died in his sleep and I mourned his death deeply. When Mama had died I had been caught up in my own struggles, but now that both my parents were dead it brought home to me how much I had loved them and how much I wanted them around for my own children to know and love.

# 14 • *Hard Times*

I found it hard adjusting to life without Papa. I had thought I was such a strong person and surprised myself by my constant tears and sentimentality. It was exacerbated by the arrival of Bill's mother, who had come to live with us. Belfast was no longer safe and the unrest was growing. Bill had been worried about her for some time, but it wasn't until a couple of young hooligans forced their way into her house, locked her in the kitchen and ransacked the place that we made the decision that she should live with us. Fortunately we had a disused stable-block which we converted into a granny bungalow for her. I had not been enthusiastic about having her so close by, but I knew she could not stay in Belfast. I cheered myself by thinking that it would be nice for the girls to have a grandparent around since after Papa's death she was the only one they had left. However, I had not expected that she would be such an unloving grandmother who was more concerned about the state of her lounge floor than her two granddaughters. Michelle and Debbie had been eager to rush to Grandma's after to school to watch her colour television, but they soon became aware that they were not welcome. She was obsessed with cleanliness and left nobody in any doubt at how she felt about having children in her home. Having picked this up, Debbie once said to me: 'I know why Daddy did not grow any taller. Grandma washed him too much when he was a little boy.'

Grandma was an astute woman and quickly realized that she was now dependent on me. She became very pleasant towards me and whenever she met any of our friends she always told them how she had liked me from the moment she had met me. She even went on to say how she considered me as one of her sisters. I wanted to believe her, but I couldn't help thinking that she was just trying to annoy me. I have often wondered had I confronted her with the true account of how she had treated me she would have called me a liar. However, I did not want to upset the relatively peaceful status quo and therefore went along with the façade until she died. She never knew what I really felt about her.

At the same time as adjusting to the loss of Papa and the arrival of Ethel I was planning the next phase of my cross-cultural project. This time it was to be a four-year study of the role of rural women in Asian rural development and I dubbed it ACT/WOM. I aimed to recruit ten Asian students from at least five Asian countries and felt confident that I could once again produce important results. However, when I presented the proposal to the IDS research committee I found that a number of my colleagues considered I was taking on too large a research venture. They also had grave doubts about my being able to find young female Asian doctoral students prepared to live on their own for a lengthy period of time in villages to collect primary field data. I was shocked as I thought they would be pleased not only with the renown I was bringing to the institute but also the funding. I was fuming when I left the room and determined to get the project off the ground.

I began the lengthy process of completing funding applications and sent them to the various donor agencies recommending that they might consider funding a single country study rather than committing themselves to funding the project as a whole. I had figured that agencies might be more open to funding to the tune of 200,000 rather than a million US dollars. My colleagues were scathing about my chances of raising the money and I became increasingly anxious as I opened my post every morning. They watched triumphantly as I received rejection after rejection, but I refused to give up. I was determined to show them.

While on a brief visit to Washington DC I had been fortunate enough to meet a high-ranking US aid official. We got talking about my proposal and my recent rejections, and with a twinkle in her eye she said that she would teach me the tricks of the trade. The next day she met me at the World Bank cafeteria and I showed her my applications. She laughed and told me outright that I had fallen into the first trap. I had assumed that someone who actually understood what I was talking about would read my application. She explained that most academic funding applications are too longwinded and too theoretical and are read by administrators rather than fellow academics. She went on to tell me about the hilarious comments that she could hear coming from the team examining them and proceeded to teach me how to prepare proposals that would have a much better chance of being favourably received. By the time we parted in the late afternoon I came away with a revised draft of my project which was much shorter and more to the point than my original version. I thanked her profusely and came home optimistic.

I sent out a second round of applications and within a couple of weeks I had secured my first donation of $200,000 for the Sri Lankan component of ACT/WOM. I was ecstatic and felt sure I would be able to raise the remaining $800,000. I buried myself in my fundraising activities, never noticing the distance developing between my colleagues and me. Therefore, I was surprised one morning when I was summoned to vice-chancellor's office. I still remember that I was humming as I went in, having put together a brief update of where I was with the fundraising. However, I never got the chance to tell him, for as soon as I had sat down he launched into his obviously rehearsed speech. He coldly told me that my five-year contract had recently been reviewed since it expired the following year and it had been decided that it would only be extended for a further three years since the committee felt that my publication record was below the expected standard. He finished with a sarcastic little jibe, saying that of course they would be forced to reconsider if I happened to have a manuscript hidden in my bottom drawer.

At first I thought he had been joking, but as I looked into his steely eyes I knew he was deadly serious. Trying to stem the shaking in my voice I replied politely that I had never been fortunate enough to have a bottom drawer and therefore had no hidden manuscripts to offer. I then thanked him for conveying the message from the chairman of the IDS appointment committee and commented that I found it hard to understand why he could not deliver it himself. As a final riposte I said that I supposed that it must have been due to the fact that my colleagues had objected to the way I put my students' achievements before my own. Unlike most of my IDS colleagues, who usually acknowledged only in a footnote the contribution of their Third World research assistants, I had chosen to publish their essays in their names rather than passing them off as my own work. As I got up to leave I turned back and advised the vice-chancellor that since they were only prepared to offer me a three-year contract when I was just about to start a four-year project he would have my written resignation later that day.

I shut the door firmly and gulped. I refused to let anyone see me cry, but my throat hurt as I tried to swallow back the tears. I had worked so hard to get to where I now was and I felt as if the last half hour had wiped it out completely. In my despair I had visions of having to return to machining or becoming a clerk again. I reluctantly made my way to Bill's office. I desperately needed his comfort, but felt so ashamed that I had been told my performance was below professorial standard. I knew that his work had been well received and his career seemed to go from strength to strength, and I felt such a failure in comparison to him.

I soon found myself outside his door. I was glad to find that he was alone and as soon as I entered he took one look at me and said 'What's up, darling? You look thunderstruck!' (He could obviously read me like a book.) I immediately burst out telling him what had happened and finally gave vent to the hurt I had just suffered. In his usual gentle way he took me in his arms and tried to calm me down, just as he did with Debbie or Michelle when they had lost a precious toy. I kept repeating that my career was over and that I wanted to tell the director of the IDS what he could do with his three-year contract.

Bill then sat me down and began to weigh up the situation. As I had just secured the first $200,000 towards my women's project he felt sure that there would be numerous academic institutions that would welcome somebody with my fundraising abilities. He even thought that AFRAS, the School of African and Asian Studies, where he worked, might offer me a research professorship if I could transfer the funds from the IDS. This immediately appealed and the next few days I was on tenterhooks while Bill sorted out the details. Within a few days he managed to get the dean of AFRAS to offer me a research professorship on condition that I came with research funds. I was petrified that the donor agency might consider the IDS more important than I was and therefore prefer to leave their funding with them rather than allow me to transfer it to AFRAS. However, I thought it was at least worth a try. The following day I wrote to the donors explaining that I was about to leave the IDS for a post at AFRAS and asked their permission to transfer the funds they had already committed to my women's project.

The next few weeks were horribly stressful for me as all I could do was sit and wait. I checked the post every morning, hurriedly searching for the donor agency's reply. In the meantime I had to carry on my duties at the IDS, not knowing how long I could endure it. I began to hate the place and felt all eyes were upon me. I had a succession of visits from my IDS friends, who all advised that I should accept the three-year extension offered since at the end of that period I would be certain to get a further extension. As each of them tried to persuade me I shook my head and tried to explain that I did not want to work somewhere where my performance was considered substandard, to which they were at a loss to respond.

Finally, one morning I discovered among my mail the long-awaited letter. At first I did not want to open it because I was afraid of what it might contain. I played with the letter-opener, trying to put off the fateful moment, but I knew that I had to find out. I glanced quickly through the letter, searching for the answer I was hoping for, and was so relieved to read that they had decided to commit the sum of $200,000 to the project and not to the IDS. It all seemed so simple; they just asked that I advise them where the money should be redirected. I grabbed the letter, ran across to Bill's office and burst through his door shouting: 'It worked. Your suggestion worked!' Bill was obviously also delighted and we toasted ourselves over a celebratory lunch that day.

AFRAS honoured their promise of a research professorship and allocated offices to me and my secretary right opposite Bill's. My IDS colleagues seemed rather surprised about my being able to transfer the donor funding to AFRAS, and I revelled in their dismay. Before I left I was given a farewell party by IDS that seemed the height of hypocrisy, but I went along and listened to the various speeches about how sad they were to see me go. I wondered at their apparent ease in glossing over the real sequence of events and how two-faced many of my colleagues were. I couldn't let it go without saying something and when I was asked to say a few words I slowly got up and looking straight at the director of the IDS, said: 'I must admit that I was greatly surprised to hear such regret expressed about my resignation as it had come about as a result of being told by the vice-chancellor that my publication record was below professorial standards.' I then went on to say that only time would tell whether I had been right to cite my students' achievements rather than take the credit for their studies, but I felt I had done what I needed to do to ensure their future professional careers. I could feel an uncomfortable silence fall on the party and within minutes of finishing the room was virtually empty except for my loyal friends.

The move from the IDS to AFRAS required a lot of adjustment on my part, for it meant that I had to direct a research unit almost entirely on my own without the institutional support I had enjoyed at the IDS. I had nightmares that I would not be able to cope with it all and I had still to raise a further $800,000, recruit Asian female research students and prepare the study. I was lucky that my two secretaries, both deeply committed, worked with me to ensure that the project got off the ground. I managed to recruit a group of highly intelligent female Asian students (two each from Bangladesh, India, Pakistan, Sri Lanka and Indonesia, plus the husband of one of our Indonesian researchers) and the project got off to a good start. I was still worried that something might go wrong, but after a couple of months I began to relax and enjoy my second research project as much as the first.

The roller-coaster existence of the last few months settled down and life took on a new routine. I was even getting used to the strain of having Bill's mother living with us. I told myself that we had entered a new phase of contentment, but I knew that something was looming on the horizon.

For some months I had become aware of a lump in my right breast, but had tried to ignore it. By the time Bill had noticed it I was beginning to get somewhat worried. We rationalized that it was just a result of my skin graft all that time ago, and I put it to the back of my mind. However, once I was settled at AFRAS it began to worry me more and more, and I could no longer ignore it. I casually asked my doctor's opinion when I was having some routine travel inoculations, and without even examining me he reassured me that it was probably due to the skin graft. Though I wanted to believe him I pressed him further, at which point he agreed to refer me to a specialist.

A few weeks later Bill and I turned up for the appointment. I was nervous. The specialist examined me and immediately arranged for me to have a chest X-ray. I was scared, as I knew that this meant he was considering the possibility of breast cancer. Bill watched me as I came out of the examination room and rushed to put his arms round me. My eyes filled with tears and he told me not to assume anything until I had the results. (The specialist had told me that I should call the following day to find out the results.) I spent the remainder of the day agitated and tense, unable to concentrate on anything and unable to relax. I kept wondering what I would do if I was told that I had a malignant growth. How would Bill cope? What about the girls?

The next morning I watched the minutes tick by as I waited for his office to open. At 9.30 precisely the telephone rang. It was the specialist. I then knew that it wasn't good news. I listened, as if in a trance, as he told me that my X-ray indicated that I had a cancerous growth and that I needed to have it removed right away. He seemed so matter-of-fact, and went on to tell me that I should call his receptionist to make the necessary arrangements. I wanted to shout at him that it was my life he was so coldly referring to, but simply thanked him and put the phone down.

I had often thought of myself as one of the luckiest women in the world, in spite of, or possibly because of, the many hurdles I had had to overcome. I was then a woman in her mid-fifties, happily married with two lovely teenage daughters and an exciting professional career. Being diagnosed with cancer simply did not fit in with my plans. I had always been a firm believer in the power of mind over matter and suddenly I felt terribly vulnerable and no longer in control. I cursed myself for having been such a fool to believe that my body was invincible.

I began to feel pain in different parts of my body and became convinced that the cancer had spread. I reasoned that the proposed mastectomy would therefore only provide temporary relief, simply delaying my agonizing death. I decided that I did not want my family to suffer the anguish of watching me die and that I would take an overdose, never to wake up. Bill was by my side while all these thoughts were racing through my mind. He knew me so well that I did not have to tell him my thoughts. He tried his best to console me and to reason with me, and he gently talked me into giving life another chance. I agreed reluctantly on the understanding that if during the operation further spread of the cancer was discovered (which I knew happened in many cases) he would bring me home, however sick, so that I could make a quick end to myself. I knew from experience that patients in hospitals have no control over their own destinies and I had watched too many friends with cancer die slow and painful deaths.

I never did call the receptionist as I decided that if I was going to go through with the surgery then I would rather be treated by someone with a more sympathetic approach. Through personal contacts Bill arranged for me to see Mr H., a surgeon at Guy's Hospital in London, at short notice. We hardly said a word to each other as we drove up to London. From time to time Bill reached out for my hand and gave me a gentle squeeze as if to say 'I know what you are going through, but we are in this together.' As soon as we arrived we were ushered into an examination room and Mr H. joined us shortly afterwards.

I was immediately put at my ease as his manner reminded me of Otto and since he was one of the leading British breast cancer experts I trusted him implicitly. After examining me he confirmed the diagnosis of breast cancer and made it clear to me that it was a matter of urgency that my right breast be removed. However, he managed to convey this dreadful message in such a gentle way that I felt not only his mind but also his heart reaching out to me. Although he bore no physical resemblance to Otto, I saw through my tears my loving brother rather than a strange surgeon. This made me more prepared to ask questions and discuss possible outcomes of my forthcoming operation. He told me that if I did not agree to the operation my chances of surviving more than one year would be very slim. He said: 'The chances that you will survive the operation are pretty good. Statistics show that the death rate reduces with the number of years the patient survives after the operation; the first three years take the highest toll.' I realized I had no option and therefore agreed to check in for the mastectomy the following week.

The days before I went into hospital were difficult for us all. Bill, who I had always looked upon as a lovable absent-minded professor type, displayed tremendous inner strength – much more than I would have credited him with. Perhaps special circumstances necessitate special responses. Still, I admired him for it greatly. While I suffered bouts of deep depression he kept reminding me that Mr H. was one of the top breast cancer specialists in the country, but it did not make things any easier for me.

As I lay on the hospital bed I began to wonder whether I would come out of the operation and if I survived would I ever be able to lead a normal life again? What would I look like? How disfigured would I be? How do husbands respond when their wives have had such drastic surgery? Admittedly Mr H. had tried to explain to me most of the implications of the operation, but at the time I had been so overwhelmed that I had been too dazed to take it all in. At one level I was convinced that I would either die during the operation or shortly afterwards, while at another I was desperately hoping that things would turn out well and was determined to make a come-back provided my body would not let me down. I argued with myself that I had been through so much that I could not let it all end here. I went through in my mind the days of Nazi persecution, my accident, my first marriage, the men who had let me down, the miscarriages and the many joyful times that bound them all together. I tried to reassure myself that I would continue to live after the operation, but at the same time a nagging voice kept insisting that my time was up; and so I continued arguing with myself.

I had brought with me my hand dictaphone because I had decided to leave a message for Michelle to tell her about her adoption. Convinced that I did not have much longer to live, I wanted to spare Bill the additional burden of having to break the news to Michelle, who was then 17 years old, without me around to soften the blow. I reasoned that if I couldn't be there in person to tell her how I felt, then at least she would hear my voice. I imagined how eerie it would be for Bill and Michelle to hear me speak after I had been buried and thought it strange how life would go on for them even though I was no longer part of it. I pressed the record button and began to speak into the microphone. I kept having to choke back the tears as I tried to piece my words together.

> Darling Michelle,
>
> I don't know whether you will ever have to hear this tape. I would much rather have you sit on my lap and talk to you and put the honest truth to you after all these years that we have been hiding it from you. I know you may think we have done wrong in not telling you that we adopted you. But believe me it was simply because we loved you so much; we regarded you as our firstborn – as our first child. You have brought us so much happiness that we felt we could not and did not want to distinguish between you and Debbie, who is our biological child, particularly as both daddy and myself were fully aware of the usual sisterly rivalry and jealousies. We feared that had we told you, you would have attributed any little sign, which to you would have meant that we preferred Debbie simply because we adopted you while she is our own child.
>
> Now that you are mature enough I hope you appreciate that we never, never in our lives distinguished between you and Debbie or discriminated against you because you were adopted. Quite the contrary: in a sense, although it may sound strange, you mean a lot more to me and I think also to Daddy because we chose you; you came to us when you were only a few days old and we counted our blessings because we had wanted to adopt a Jewish child and Jewish children are very hard to come by for adoption. But we were very fortunate: Uncle Jack, Auntie Beccie's brother, our doctor friend, rang us one day after he knew that we had decided to try to adopt a child. He told us that a young Jewish undergraduate who was pregnant had

turned up in his surgery. The father of her baby was a young Jewish lawyer. The girl's parents were keen to have her baby adopted by a Jewish couple. So it all seemed the answer to our prayers. We never knew your biological mother, nor of course your real father. But in our own minds we regard ourselves as your parents. As I have been telling you so often you were a wonderful baby; not only were you goodlooking but you were also goodtempered. You were our pride and joy. We could show you off to all our friends...

You have often quizzed me on what I remember about the time when I gave birth to you, and I think you were intelligent and shrewd enough to realize that I was stalling. I did not want to lie to you. On the other hand, I felt that I could not tell you the truth at the time; particularly, you may remember that the night before I went into hospital you asked me about the anaesthetic I had before you were born and when the moment was that I first saw you. And again my answers were evasive, as I felt you realized at the time. I very much wanted to tell you the truth at that moment, because I did not want to go into hospital and possibly never come out and leave to Daddy the difficult task of telling you the truth about your adoption. Yet I realized that I was already putting such a heavy burden on your very young shoulders and that it was unfair of me to make it even more difficult for you.

Please forgive us if you feel that we did wrong in letting you grow up believing that you were our own flesh and blood. But believe me, as far as we are concerned there just was and never will be a difference between you as our adopted daughter and Debbie who came out of my womb. I don't think you will ever be able to appreciate how much getting you and bringing you up has meant to Daddy and even more so to me. It is very important for a woman to have a child; possibly much more so for a woman than for a man. I had had all these miscarriages and I felt that I was a complete failure as a woman. In particular because I knew that Daddy wanted children and I was desperately trying to give him the child he wanted. When you came along and you were fully Jewish we could not believe our good fortune, particularly when we watched you grow up into such a lovely little girl and now into a beautiful, intelligent and gifted young woman. I wish I could know for certain that I'll be around many more years to guide you and help you if you need me. But right now things don't look too hopeful. So please sweetheart, if I am no more around to give you advice and help then always listen to Daddy and perhaps also talk with or write to Uncle Otto, or even visit him in Australia to seek his advice. Also, of course I very much hope that the bond that already exists between you and your younger sister will grow stronger as you get older. Always remember that family ties are very important and that you are a member of a closely knit family.

How I wish I wasn't lying here in bed and talking into this impersonal dictaphone. I would much prefer to have you sit on my lap – or maybe I would sit on your lap since you are now so big – and we could hug each other and I could talk to you in person and tell you all this. I know it will be difficult for you to absorb the news of your adoption. I know only too well how difficult it was for me to accept the fact that I was suffering from this dreadful disease. Though I realize that being told that you are adopted is quite a different thing, but I expect it will also hit you hard.

I wish I could be there to soften the blow for you. How I now wish I could believe in God and pray that my operation will be a success and that you will never have to listen to this tape and that instead I will be able to tell you everything in person. Should things go wrong for me – and I think you will appreciate that at this point in my life when I am practically at death's door one doesn't say things lightly – I want you to know that I have loved you with all my heart from the first moment when I held you in my arms, and that I will love you until my dying moment. Daddy, who has been the most wonderful husband any woman could wish for, will need yours and Debbie's support if I don't come out of this operation. Please give it to him; please help him over what I expect will be a very difficult period for him.

Debbie of course does not know that you were adopted, and I assume it will come not only as a surprise but also as a shock to her, because although you may not have realized it, she has been and still is jealous of you

> because she, from her point of view, thinks that you have been receiving preferential treatment and that you have got all the advantages of beauty, brains and skill which she, wrongly, assumes she is lacking. I know it is asking a lot of you to show understanding and continue to treat her as your little sister, who in spite of all the quarrels and fights you have been having – which after all are normal between sisters – also loves and admires you a lot.
>
> Believe me, it's not been easy for me to talk into this dictaphone, particularly since I know that I shall shortly be wheeled into the operating theatre where I guess my fate will be decided. Whatever it is, whether I am going to live or die, you must believe that as far as I am concerned you are my daughter and I dearly love the little girl who was such a happy child and who I was fortunate enough to be able to watch grow into a lovely young woman. My love will always be with you. Please continue to be happy. That is all I want for you and that you should always remember me as your Mummy!

Shortly before I came to the end of my dictation the ward sister arrived to give me my pre-operation sedative. Suddenly, as I had finished my message to Michelle, it struck me that these might be the last words I would ever utter to any member of my family. There was so much more that I wanted to tell them. In particular I wanted Bill to know how much I loved him; how I still marvelled that a man of his mental calibre had chosen me as his partner; and how grateful I had been for the way he always put up with my idiosyncrasies. But the sedative began to take effect and I knew I did not have time for another message. All I could do was hope that he would know what I had wanted to tell him. I sadly realized that we seldom told each other what we really felt and how much we meant to each other. Our love was only rarely discussed between us. Throughout our 23 years of marriage we had had few disputes. Our love and mutual admiration was expressed through touches and glances and I longed for the opportunity to tell him how I felt. Warm tears trickled down my cheeks at the thought of never seeing Bill's twinkly eyes again and the way they lit up when he saw me.

My eyes began to close and my head started to swim. The next thing I knew was when I heard voices calling me: 'Scarlett, wake up, wake up!' The nurses were trying to revive me from the anaesthetic. I felt something on my head and slowly opened my eyes. It was Bill gently kissing and stroking my hair. I wept. He gently took my hand and I had a chance to look around me and found that I was back in my hospital bed with a drip in my left arm and a drain coming out of where my right breast had been and which was now heavily bandaged. Bill kept whispering into my ear: 'Darling, you've made it, you've made it – I knew you would!' I looked at him, searching for the twinkle in his eyes, but all I saw were tears. I tried to squeeze his hand, but the pain overwhelmed me and I was given another sedative to put me back to sleep. During the following days Mr H. came to see me regularly and assured me that my mastectomy had been a great success as he had been able to remove all the cancerous growth, which augured well for my survival. For a while I was too weak to take it all in. Bill came to see me daily and said that he would bring the girls to see me on Sunday, though Debbie had in the meantime been diagnosed with glandular fever. I wondered how he was coping.

By the time the girls came I was able to walk around, though I had to carry with me the bottle that contained the drain from my wound. It was a great boost to my morale to have my family with me. However, as I watched Bill I noticed that the left part of his face was drooping, and I began to fear that he was having a stroke. I did not want to alarm him or the girls, but when we said our fond farewells I made them promise that they would phone me immediately after they had got back so that I would know that they had arrived home safely. I calculated that it should take them a maximum of two hours, so when three hours had passed and there had been no phone call I rang home, but got no reply. I was convinced that Bill had suffered a serious stroke while driving and they had all been involved in a fatal accident. I kept hearing the sirens of the many ambulances bringing casualties in and I wondered whether my family was among them. The irony struck me how I had gone through a near-death experience only to lose my own family. The sound of the phone broke my thoughts, and I was so relieved to hear Bill's voice. They had stopped off to get something to eat and consequently were a bit late home. A few days later, when Bill came to fetch me home from hospital, I tackled him about his face. He admitted that he had been suffering from slight facial palsy but did not know what was causing it. I kept thinking that at least it wasn't a stroke.

It was good to be home again, but I still felt pretty weak and had great psychological problems in adjusting to the mutilation my body had suffered. Being left now with only one breast I felt I was no longer a proper woman and I could not expect Bill to remain my husband. I therefore told him as we were lying in bed next to each other that I would quite understand if he wanted to leave me and that I would not stand in his way. He smiled at me shyly and told me he married me because he loved me, not because of the fact that I had two breasts. He held me tight and whispered that he would always love me regardless of whether I had only one eye, one arm or one leg, and he took me gently into his arms and made love to me.

Bill was attentive and very loving, which greatly restored my self-confidence. However, I still felt my days were numbered and that I wanted to cram in as much as possible. I told Bill about how I had planned to reveal Michelle's adoption to her and since I had made it through the operation I felt I wanted to tell her myself, now that I could be with her to comfort her and show her how much I loved her. Bill thought I was still too weak for such an emotional exercise, but I argued that I was strong enough to dictate the message so I was strong enough to deliver it. I wanted to make sure Michelle heard the news in the least distressing way possible, and that, I felt sure, was for me to tell her in person.

Otto and Marian were visiting from Sydney while I was recuperating. I sent them off with Debbie for a long walk. She was excited at the prospect of having her favourite uncle to herself, and of course Michelle had no idea why we had kept her back.

I was nervous when Bill asked Michelle to come and sit with us in the lounge. I drew her close to me and switched on the tape, telling her that I had recorded a message for her before my operation and felt it was right that she should hear it now. I stroked her hair and cheeks as she listened in silence. She hardly moved during the whole time and I was scared what her response might be. When the tape had finished Bill said gently: 'We wish we could tell you more, but legally we were not allowed to know the details of your biological mother. However, if you wish to find out more we will do everything that we can to help you.' Whereupon Michelle put her arms round me and said emphatically: 'As far as I am concerned you are the only mother and father I have ever known and I will always think of you as my parents.' I was relieved at her initial reaction and marvelled at her mature and loving response. It made me appreciate her all the more.

# 15 • *Fighting the Fire*

I had assumed that once the operation was over and I had regained my strength I would be back to normal – or as normal as I could be expected to feel after having a breast removed. However, I had to undergo extensive radiotherapy treatment, which though not painful was physically exhausting. It took me quite some time to adjust to my changed appearance. I felt physically mutilated and psychologically indignant and resentful. I kept asking 'Why me?' I felt I had gone through enough, but the challenges continued to present themselves. I fell into a pool of deep self-pity that no one seemed to be able to pull me out of. Bill and the girls had to watch as I crumpled before their eyes. I felt guilty. They had always seen me strong, fighting on all fronts and suddenly I was reduced to a morose and melancholic mass.

Some weeks later I was watching a documentary on the Holocaust, which was a watershed in my recovery. As I watched the victims of the concentration camps and what they had had to suffer I quickly became ashamed of my self-pity and told myself that it could have been a lot worse. With Bill's loving support I began to accept my mutilated body and adjusted to life with it.

Soon after my change in spirits Bill was invited to spend the academic year 1980/81 in Holland at NIAS (Netherlands Institute for Advanced Studies). Trying to be strong I urged him to accept it, while inwardly I was wondering how I would cope without him. Michelle and Debbie both had important exams that year and needed a lot of support and encouragement, but I knew he desperately wanted to go and I did not want to stand in his way. In September we drove over together to settle him into a flat in Wassenar and sort out his domestic situation. As we left him in his new home I wondered who was going to help me.

The next few months flew by. I was back at work, the girls had mock exams and we were all absorbed in our own lives. I so much wanted to be there for the girls, but in January, at my routine medical check-up, Mr H. discovered three nodules in the area where he had thought he had removed all the cancerous growth. He explained that a minor operation was necessary to extract one nodule so that he could determine whether or not it was malignant. Since he was leaving very shortly for Japan he wanted to perform the operation the next day.

His words went round and round in my head and I could not speak. I wanted to run away from him, from the reality, from life; but instead I simply got up, put on my coat and told him that I would see him the next day. I spent the whole train journey home contemplating giving up altogether, I had had enough and had nothing left to fight with, but when I saw Michelle's face when I walked through the door I realized I couldn't leave them. I told them what Mr H. had said and they put their arms round me and kissed and cuddled me. That night I tried to block out thoughts of the following day and after swallowing four sleeping tablets I finally managed to reach a state of oblivion.

The following day dawned and in a daze I made my way to the hospital. The staff was surprised that I was on my own. I tried to laugh it off, but inside I felt so alone. As I lay waiting to be wheeled into the operating theatre I decided that I needed to write to Bill. I was crying out for him. I desperately wanted him with me and felt so hurt that he wasn't there. I wanted to hurt him as I was hurting, but I knew inside that it wasn't fair. I just had to lash out at someone, and who but Bill could I hurt?

The operation itself was very quick and required only a local anaesthetic, which meant that I could return home the same day. Before leaving, Mr H. told me that he would phone me in a few days with the results of the test. Michelle and Debbie met me with anxious faces and Debbie climbed on to my lap. They desperately wanted to behave like adults, but they were so scared, particularly since only a few days earlier the mother of one of Debbie's best friends had died of breast cancer. When they saw the state I was in they wanted me to phone Bill and let him know what had been happening to me, but I refused. Somewhat childishly I wanted to sort it all out by myself. Since he had left me on my own, I was going to show him that I could manage. How stupid of me!

The next few days passed so slowly. I felt I was caught in a time warp. I could not concentrate and kept debating with myself the possible outcomes. I suspected the worst yet hoped for the best. Mr H. finally telephoned and told me the results. He was so calm about it all and went through the various arrangements he had made for further tests. All I wanted to do was scream 'You butcher. You removed my breast only to let me suffer more cancer.' When I first met Mr H. I hero-worshipped him; now I had discovered my idol had feet of clay.

Debbie was already home from school and had gathered that the news was not good. She put her arms round me and I sobbed into her hair. Soon we were both crying. When Michelle found us she took charge and threatened that if I did not phone Bill then she would. She was true to her word and called her father in Holland. He was obviously dreadfully upset and insisted on talking to me. I tried to pretend that I was coping because I did not want to admit to him how much I longed to have him with me. When he said that he would catch the next flight the relief flooded through me, but instead of just saying thank you I persuaded him to stick to his original plan and return the following week. My pride would not allow me to admit to him how much I needed him. The next day I stupidly watched out of the window wondering whether I would see him walking up the drive. I kept hoping that he would have decided to come home even though I had dissuaded him from doing so.

When Bill ultimately returned he looked so exhausted and worried that I wanted to reach out and hold him and comfort him. However, I was so hurt and angry that I could not forgive him for having gone away and left me to cope on my own. I felt so mixed up. When we finally got to bed that night and he tried to embrace me I turned my back on him and cruelly said that I thought he had stopped caring for me since my mastectomy. I felt him wince and immediately regretted my words as I realized how much I had hurt him.

In the morning I gave Bill the note I had written to him while lying on the hospital stretcher. It had the desired effect: he was overcome and I felt glad that I had hurt him as much as he had hurt me. He took me in his arms and kept saying he was sorry over and over again. I crumpled into his arms, relieved that he was finally here to take some of the strain. However, I don't think he ever realized how much I needed and loved him, otherwise he would not have returned to the Netherlands. When I drove him to the airport a few days later I felt as if a part of me was saying goodbye to him forever.

I tried to be positive, but I was in a lot of pain. I suffered persistent discomfort along the scar on my chest and I felt as if I had a knife cutting between my shoulder-blades. I assumed, pessimistically, that it was the cancer spreading through my body. I was still awaiting the results of all the tests I had recently undergone and imagined that the lengthy wait was due to the fact that the doctors did not want to tell me the awful truth. I kept having nightmares. I dreamed that I discovered a big black mark on my left breast and while I was looking at it, it kept growing and growing until it swallowed up my whole being. It was one of those dreams that I could not shake off even after I had woken up. I became increasingly dependent on my sleeping pills to drug me into a deep sleep.

I found it hard to drag myself out of bed in the mornings. I would always hope for a letter from Bill to cheer me up a little. His letters were so warm and loving and gave me the strength to carry on. He often wrote how he thought that he would shrivel up inside himself if I were to die. It made me realize that it is a lot harder to see someone you love suffer than to suffer the pain yourself.

Finally the results came through. I was assured that another course of radiotherapy would put me right. I was relieved that no more surgery was involved and tried to be as optimistic as the doctor. After six weeks I decided to return to work. When I got to my office I started to wade through the post that had accumulated. I found my pain disappeared whilst I was absorbed in my work and when I discovered a letter from a donor agency keen to fund another project of mine, I felt better than I had in months. I threw myself back into my work and once more tried to live by my philosophy of mind over matter.

As soon as I had regained control over my body and focused my mind on my work the rewards paid off. The two books I had published on my Indian village studies appeared in a local translation and were used as texts in South Indian high schools. I considered this one of my proudest achievements. As my 'Women's Project' had come to an end and almost all the participating researchers had managed to get their doctorates I tried to follow this with a project that would involve less travel. I thus secured funding for a 'Women, Work and Family' project which involved collaborating with the German Youth Institute at Munich. It involved numerous trips to Germany where I made good friends among the young researchers at the institute. I found it quite easy to relate to young postwar Germans; it was only when I met older Germans who had lived through World War II that I felt uneasy and wondered what part they might have played in the atrocities of that war.

One evening we were all taken out for a pub dinner. As I entered the smoky room I saw a long table round which the institute's staff members were sitting with pints of beer in front of them, chatting noisily. The scene reminded me of the pictures I had seen portraying Hitler's pub meetings in the early 1930s when he was plotting the Nazi takeover of Germany. I felt very uncomfortable and it was made worse by the fact that I was placed at the head of the table next to the director who was an elderly German. His English was poor so I volunteered to converse with him in German. I couldn't believe it when he asked me the incredibly naïve question: 'How is it that a professor from an English university can speak German as well as you?' I hesitated a few moments before answering that German was my mother tongue. I went on to explain to him that I had been born in Vienna and had left in 1938. It never occurred to me that he would not realize I was a Jewish refugee. When he asked me why I had left I was somewhat surprised. I didn't know quite what to say and was rather nervous when I quietly replied: 'Because I am Jewish and it is highly unlikely that I would have survived had I not managed to escape.' A deathly hush descended on the table and my heart began to pound. I was sure I was going to be frog-marched off somewhere. Then suddenly every one started speaking at once and questions were hurled at me from all sides. They were fascinated by my experiences and eager to know how I felt about coming to Germany. It was not easy for me to answer many of their questions as my hatred for what they had done boiled so close to the surface. I had thought that the memories had faded, but faced with the barrage of questions I suddenly realized it was no longer just something that had happened to me but had become in a sense part of who I was.

While in the Netherlands Bill had decided to take early retirement at the end of the academic year 1981/82, so that he could concentrate on research and writing. At the conclusion of the 'Women, Work and Family' project I decided to follow suit. Ever since I had left the IDS I had managed to establish a reputation for my research work in my own right, which made me confident that I would be able to continue my career without the constraints of formal employment. Thankfully, I was right and soon began to receive requests to give lectures and act as a development consultant. I enjoyed the newfound freedom and felt that life was beginning to fall back into place again.

I had just accepted another invitation to lecture at Oldenburg

University in Germany, when Bill asked me to join him in his study. I wondered why he looked so sombre. He quietly told me that he had been having some heart problems and had consulted our doctor who had immediately arranged for him to have an angiogram at the Cromwell Hospital in London. I wanted to shake him. Why had he not told me? But I already knew the answer: he had not wanted to worry me. I cancelled my trip to Germany and instead went with Bill for his angiogram. I couldn't believe our sudden role reversal. Only months before he had sat holding my hand, trying to comfort me, and now it was my turn to sit by his bedside, comforting him while we waited to hear the results of the angiogram. I squeezed his hand as we saw his consultant returning and he turned to me and said: 'Do you know what marriage is all about? It is about sitting by each other's hospital bed and offering each other support.' I just hoped I was strong enough to give him the support he needed.

The consultant casually informed us that Bill needed a triple heart bypass and opened his diary to fix a date for the operation. I felt as if he was arranging to have us round for dinner rather than organizing a life-threatening (or life-saving) event. I was shocked at the seriousness of Bill's complaint and struggled to keep my composure. Bill absorbed the consultant's words without saying a thing. Then, after a moment or two, he calmly thanked him for his time and tried to decide when would be the best time for the operation. I could see he was trying to keep a tight control on his emotions to hide his true fear from me. We were quiet in the car, each of us trying to come to terms with the news. The only thing Bill mentioned was how sorry he was that I had missed my trip to Germany. I didn't know what to say: how could he think that under the circumstances I would have wanted to go? He never truly believed my love for him and he never took it for granted that I would be prepared to go through the worst with him. His modesty made me smile. I took his hand and squeezing it gently, told him I would never be anywhere but by his side.

During the weeks before the operation Bill said little, and I wondered at his calm. I always asked 'Why me?' But Bill seemed to accept his fate in a way that I never could. Before my mastectomy I had been obsessed about the possibility that I might not survive the operation and kept talking in morbid tones about what he should do if I died. Bill never mentioned such a possibility and I didn't want to be the first to broach it.

Instead we concentrated on the practicalities of his operation and illness. I had planned to stay in Michelle's flat in London, as by this time she had finished her degree and was working in central London. Debbie had arranged to be with me on the day of the operation.

When the day came I stayed with Bill as long as I could. I did not want to let him go, but I did not want him to see my distress. I gave him a last hug, and trying to sound optimistic, left saying that everything would be all right and that I would be in to see him later. As I left the ward I burst into tears and wondered what I had done that was so bad to warrant such punishment.

Debbie and I sat by the phone for most of the day, not knowing what else to do with ourselves. As the minutes ticked by I became increasingly anxious. The operation was due to start at 10 a.m. and by 2 p.m. I assumed the worst. Debbie tried to calm me down, but by 5 p.m. we were both frantic. Michelle arrived home and the three of us huddled together as I tried to get through to the surgeon. I was kept hanging on and transferred numerous times which just added to my tension. Did no one know what was going on? Finally they located a nurse who reported that Bill had been transferred to intensive care and was as well as could be expected. She advised me that I could visit the next morning and that they would call me if there were any change in his condition. I didn't know whether to laugh or cry: he had made it through the first round, we just had to get through the night.

Debbie accompanied me to the hospital the next morning. She tried to lighten the atmosphere by joking how we looked as if we were going to take a walk on the moon, as we had to put on gowns, overslippers and headgear. However, I almost collapsed when I saw Bill lying there. I could hardly see him for the tubes attached to him with various fluids going in and out. He was ashen and still and looked as if he had grown old overnight. He didn't seem to notice us and I was worried that he was unconscious, which frightened me. Debbie took my hand and I could feel her trying to keep me together. At that moment his eyes flickered open and he smiled wanly at me. It was difficult for him to talk with all the tubes so I just stroked his cheek.

I could hardly believe that within a matter of days Bill was back home with me. It took him a long time to regain some of his strength, but I was just so happy to have him home. He had lost a lot of his former energy and would frequently get frustrated as he watched me fetching and carrying. However, I never complained as the surgeon had warned me that Bill would need a lot of care, particularly with the added complication of his being diabetic.

Once Bill's recuperation period was over we fell into an easy pattern at home. We spent most of our days in our studies reading or writing and got together in the evenings. We often debated long into the evening and I could see us growing old gracefully in our academic haven. We were both enjoying our work and each other's company. However, I should have known that it was not to be.

On Yom Kippur I discovered I was haemorrhaging. I immediately thought the worst and, following a thorough examination by a gynaecologist, my fears were confirmed. On hearing that I had a growth that needed to be removed I was convinced that the cancer had spread. I decided then and there that I was not prepared to undergo another operation or radiotherapy or chemotherapy. If I was dying then I wanted to go quickly, rather than prolonging the agony. The specialist, having let me finish my melodramatics, assured me that the growth was benign, at which I agreed to have the operation.

By now the hospital routine was becoming pretty familiar but the big difference was that Bill could no longer offer me the same support. He was still weak and unable to drive and I had to get myself to and from the hospital. I didn't blame him but I was saddened by this new phase in our relationship. I couldn't talk to him about my fears as I did not want to worry him unnecessarily and instead of planning how we would cope when I came home I had to consider how he would cope on his own.

The operation was more radical than they had first thought and the surgeon reluctantly admitted that he had removed a growth the size of a tennis ball from my uterus. They tried to keep up the pretence that the growth had been benign, but when they started mentioning chemotherapy I knew that I had been suffering from ovarian cancer. I was furious. I had been lied to. I called for my consultant and when he came in somewhat sheepishly, I shouted at him: 'You lied to me. You knew all along that I had cancer. I shall never, never forgive you for this!' He sat on my bed and took hold of my shoulders firmly, explaining that he had lied because he had known, that otherwise I would have refused the operation. His next words shook me to the core. He said that without the operation I would have died within a matter of months. He got up to leave, and as he did so he quietly said that in a few years' time he hoped I would appreciate his decision. However, at that moment a quick death seemed more appealing and I sobbed into my pillow.

Bill tried his best to be supportive and cheerful, but I noticed that he had started to look grey and positively unwell. However, at the time I could only concentrate on getting through the chemotherapy that I had heard such dreadful things about. I became depressed and felt such a failure: my mind had let me down again and had given into the cancer and I felt I had no strength left to fight it.

The chemotherapy made me nauseous and took every ounce out of me. It was as much as I could do to get through the day. Most of the time I just wanted to curl up and die, but I somehow managed to adjust just in time to find Bill at the edge of the next precipice.

One morning, finding that he no longer had the strength to carry his burden alone, he confided in me that he had started coughing up blood. I looked at him and wondered why we found it so difficult to lean on one another: why did we always need to try to be so strong? I hugged him and quickly realized that he was burning up. I immediately tried to get our doctor to come and see him, but it was difficult to get medical help over the festive season (it was New Year's Eve) and we only managed to see a young locum who did not grasp the severity of the situation. Ever since we were married we had always seen in the New Year with a drink at midnight, and though Bill was feeling very shaky he insisted on staying up. But shortly before midnight he started shivering and I helped him upstairs to bed.

He made it through the night, but the next day we started the round of doctors and specialists, and Bill was diagnosed with lung cancer. We both knew that there was no real treatment for lung cancer unless it was operable and I felt it was the beginning of the end. The hardest part was trying to hide my despair from Bill. I tried so hard to be strong for him. For the first time we discussed our deaths openly, as we feared that we had to make plans for the girls. We had of course made our wills and provided for them as best we could, but except for my brother Otto, who was ten years older than me and who lived in Australia, we did not have any relative to whose care we would be happy to entrust them.

As a last hope Bill was sent to see a surgeon who specialized in lung cancer operations. As I waited outside while the surgeon examined Bill I started to pray for the first time in my life. I wanted to believe that there was someone up there who could help. When the surgeon asked me to join them he obviously saw the strain in my face and kindly told me to sit down and try to relax: he was going to operate. I let out a huge sigh of relief and made a silent pact with God. He told us that, depending on the state of the growth, he might have to remove one of the lungs, which would leave Bill considerably weaker, particularly since he had already had a heart bypass, but that it should give him at least another few years of life.

To try to relieve the tension I reminded Bill of his definition of marriage and told him that had I known that it would be exclusively about sitting at each other's hospital bedside then I would have reconsidered the whole thing. He tried to laugh but at that stage could only manage a cough.

A few days later he went into Guy's Hospital. Debbie was again by my side as we waited anxiously for Bill to come out of the operating theatre. I was almost at breaking point, but having her with me helped me through those long hours. Finally, Bill was wheeled out, still anaesthetized, with a plethora of tubes coming out of his body. A nurse continually monitored his progress. A little later the surgeon came in and explained to me that he had had to remove Bill's affected lung. 'I'm afraid he is now left with only one lung, which will severely affect his breathing capacity, but if he takes life easy he should be able to cope all right. I suggest you and your daughter go home now because your husband is not going to wake up for a few hours yet and both of you look as if you could do with a rest. You can phone in the morning to find out how your husband is progressing'.

Bill looked pretty awful when we left him, but I thanked my lucky stars that he was still alive. I could not sleep at all that night and at 7 a.m. the following day I phoned the ward where the sister told me that Bill was doing very well and if I wanted she would put me through to him. I could not believe that after what he had looked like only a few hours earlier he was now able to speak on the phone. Then I heard his voice: 'Darling, relax, I'm feeling fine.' I could hardly speak as I tried to hold back the tears.

The next few months were some of our worst. I was still having my chemotherapy and Bill was recuperating slowly. His lung operation had adversely affected his heart condition, which brought on angina attacks in the middle of the night. I soon became used to the drill of phoning for the ambulance, waiting anxiously for them to arrive to rush him to intensive care and then waiting anxiously again for them to return him a few days later. Bill now became increasingly difficult to live with, and my once loving and caring husband became a distant memory. He was constantly frustrated by his disabilities and deeply resentful of having become dependent on me. I felt guilty that I was failing him, but also resentful that I had to cope with everything on my own.

We quickly realized that we would have to change our lifestyle dramatically if we were to survive. So we sold our house in the country and moved to a flat on the seafront. Our house in Hassocks had been my only really permanent home, and I found it traumatic to pull up our roots and move on. I once more felt like a nomad, particularly as we had to spend the winters abroad to escape the cold and damp of the British winter. Neither of us really adjusted to our new circumstances and the strain on our relationship was almost palpable. We couldn't live with each other, but neither could we live without each other. Both of us felt a degree of imprisonment. I could no longer accept travel invitations, as I did not dare leave Bill, and he was trapped by the constraints of his condition. I became short-tempered and we quarrelled in a way that we had not done before. However, as soon as we argued we made up as our love and mutual respect was still as strong as ever. I often cuddled up in Bill's arms remembering the happy times we had spent together when we were both young and healthy. I could not believe where the years had gone and how our lives had changed.

# 16 • *Life and Death*

Bill and I continued with our professional work as best we could. He managed to complete a further two books and several articles, while I spent a lot of my time researching and writing and involving myself in different projects to keep me stimulated. I missed my overseas consultancies as they had provided me with a welcome change of scenery and had always been such a boost to my morale. Each time I was invited somewhere I could never really believe that they actually wanted me and I was nervous that I would not produce the desired results. I was always wrong on both counts and returned from these trips in a buoyant frame of mind. However, it became increasingly hard to leave Bill, as before I left he would often suffer a severe angina attack and I would feel so guilty. It was difficult trying to balance my own needs against his and sometimes I felt I would go crazy in our flat day after day. I did not want to sacrifice my own life, but I knew that our days together were numbered and I wanted to be with him as much as possible.

Although the years seem to revolve around hospitals, operations and recuperation they were thankfully punctuated by normal family events. Whilst Michelle was studying at Keele University she met Neil. We were delighted that he was Jewish and wondered whether he was her Mr Right. After they had been together for some years they announced that they wanted to get married. We were overjoyed as we got on well with him and his family and thought he would make a warm and loving father should they ever decide to have children.

Michelle's wedding was a joyous occasion. Bill was so proud and looked so happy as he accompanied Michelle up the aisle. As we all stood under the *chuppah* (the Jewish wedding canopy) he squeezed my hand and whispered into my ear: 'Darling, we never thought we would live long enough to see Michelle married. We can count this as one of the happiest days of our lives!' which brought tears to my eyes.

As we stood in the reception line greeting our guests it was a stark reminder of the devastating effect the Holocaust had had on my family. Our guest list had been short, Kurt and his family were the only ones representing our side of the family. However, Neil's large family had come from far and wide to enjoy the family gathering. I tried not to let this mar the occasion for me and watched as Michelle was lifted high on a chair and carried round by the men, in the traditional Jewish fashion.

Michelle seemed to adjust to being a wife much more quickly than I did. Before long she announced that she was pregnant. I dearly hoped that she would not have to go through the ordeal that I went through. So when she gave birth to a bonny, bouncing baby nine months later we were over the moon. Rebecca was a beautiful baby, with huge eyes and a solemn expression. We quickly discovered the advantage that grandparents enjoy of being able to love and cuddle our granddaughter without having to face any of the responsibilities of looking after her or disciplining her as she grew up. Michelle was a doting mother and seemed totally fulfilled in this role in a way that I had never been.

When Michelle was expecting her second child she asked me to stay with Rebecca when she went into hospital. Shortly after midnight on 19 January 1993 she summoned me. I got there as quickly as I could and arrived to the sound of Rebecca's screams. I picked her up and took her into bed with me, as I rocked her she continued to scream, but finally she fell asleep in my arms. I held her close and remembered when my two girls were little and I used to rock them back to sleep in the middle of the night. I had just started to fall asleep myself when the phone rang and Neil announced that Michelle had given birth to Benjamin. I was desperate to phone Bill as I knew how thrilled he would be at the thought of having a grandson to pass the family traditions on to. He was deeply moved when he saw Ben for the first time, but as I offered to pass the baby to him he sadly shook his head. He confessed he was simply too frail. The fact that he could not even hold his first grandson brought me back to the harsh reality of just how ill he was.

I myself had a different confession and was once again torn between my professional and family commitments. I had accepted an invitation to deliver a paper at a conference in New Delhi long before I knew Michelle was pregnant and I felt I could not possibly cancel it. As it got closer to Michelle's due date I became increasingly worried that I would have to leave before she had had the baby. Fortunately Benjamin arrived in good time, but I still had to leave a few days after his birth which meant that I missed my grandson's *brith* (circumcision). I was very upset and felt guilty about not fulfilling my grandmotherly duties, but I felt there was nothing else I could do. I called Michelle on the day and at the time I knew the circumcision would take place and tried to show that I was there in spirit if not in person, but I knew it wasn't the same.

Bill and I spent many happy hours watching our grandchildren develop from babies into young children. Bill used to love sitting with Rebecca in his lap as they read story after story. Being with the children made him come alive again and he used to summon up all his strength for their visits, only to be drained after they had gone. Sometimes they stayed with us, and after I had managed to put them to bed Bill and I would sit smiling silently at each other in happy mutual understanding that this was what life was all about. Since we both felt we were living to some degree on borrowed time we treasured every moment we could spend with them.

Debbie's life was somewhat more complicated. She found it difficult to settle and spent a year trying to rid herself of the travel bug. She had numerous jobs and numerous boyfriends and seemed to have no inclination to put roots down with anyone anywhere. Bill and I discussed this many times, particularly since he was concerned that most of her boyfriends were not Jewish. Though I obviously would have preferred her to choose a Jewish partner she knew that I had a much more liberal approach and just wanted her to be happy.

Having just returned from a skiing trip, Debbie came to visit us one day and confessed that she had just met someone she could imagine spending the rest of her life with. I teased her, asking what he had that all the others didn't, but I soon realized that she was serious. I was rather taken aback at the depth of her feelings after such a short time, but I did not want to dampen her spirits. She went on to describe him and his family and then stopped. She took a deep breath and said, 'He's not Jewish. I know that Daddy will never approve and I don't know what to do.' I knew how devastated Bill would be if Debbie 'married out', for we had often talked about the possibility. I was torn: I wanted to share in my daughter's happiness but knew that if I did so it would upset Bill even more. The last thing I wanted was for something to happen that would shorten his life. I felt as if I were being forced to choose between my love for my husband and my love for my daughter.

Before I worked out how to break the news I decided to meet James and vet him for myself. Debbie brought him round when I knew Bill would be out and he struck me as a solid, well-balanced young man who would make Debbie a good partner. However, I was plagued by stories of how Jews had been betrayed by their non-Jewish partner and I desperately wanted to protect my daughter from such an experience. When I put the question to James about how he would act under these circumstances he gallantly told me that he would always stand by Debbie and protect her to the best of his abilities. I had nothing left to test him with and I decided it was time to tell Bill about James.

Bill's immediate response was that Debbie was helping to finish off the job that Hitler never managed to complete. He was angry and confused at how such a thing could have happened. Over and over again he asked the question: 'Where did we go wrong with Debbie?' Debbie tried to talk to him, but Bill was not prepared to surrender what he considered his right and moral stance and Debbie was reluctant to give up the man she loved just because he did not share her religious background. I could see that Debbie was torn: she loved her father deeply and she could see how unhappy she was making him. I tried my best to build a bridge between them, but Bill kept repeating: 'Debbie is of age and therefore can make her own decisions, but she cannot expect me to like them!' Remembering the trouble we had in producing our offspring and how happy we had been when Debbie was born, it broke my heart to see the distance developing between father and daughter. I was thus greatly relieved when Debbie announced that the strain was too much for her and that she had broken off her relationship with James. Bill was delighted with this news, whereas I could see what a difficult decision this had been for her. She became sullen and withdrawn and while I longed to take her in my arms and cuddle her as I had done when she was a little girl, she insisted on keeping her distance.

I had thought our field research days were long over but in 1993 Bill decided that he needed to return to the Tolai once more to collect some more data. I could not quite believe it as I prepared for our trip. We were to stay for four months, so I had to take all the necessary medications and make sure that Bill would have the medical assistance he might require. I was rather nervous but also excited as we boarded the plane. As I sat holding Bill's hand during take-off, I was overcome with grief: there we were, both in our seventies, setting out on what I knew would be our last adventure together.

The climate suited Bill's condition and he became more animated than he had been for years. He was invited to take part in the final stages of initiation into the Tolai male secret society, which was an ambition of a lifetime. We were offered some land as a gift and I started to dream of having a house here and bringing the girls over to visit. I began to think there might still be a future. However, when we received a call from Debbie saying that James had just proposed to her a shadow fell across Bill's face. I knew it was not to be. I congratulated her immediately, but Bill just walked away from the phone, his shoulders slumped and his feet kicking the ground.

On our return there followed another difficult period when relations were strained between Debbie and her father and I was caught in the middle. Debbie had found a rabbi willing to conduct the ceremony. Bill spent many hours on the phone to him trying to reconcile himself to the event, but he remained adamant that even if he agreed to attend the ceremony he would certainly not make a speech at the reception. He kept reminding Debbie that she was old enough to make her own decisions but that she couldn't expect him to approve of them. Debbie tried to hide her disappointment, but I could see how much it was hurting her. When Debbie and James fixed their wedding day Bill suffered several serious angina attacks, and for the first time I felt I could no longer cope. I shut myself off from Debbie and the wedding plans and concentrated on my life with Bill. I was trying to get our precarious balance back and I knew that any mention of the forthcoming wedding would tip the balance. Debbie seemed somewhat confused by my lack of interest, but I could not explain to her that I had chosen her father's health over her plans.

The wedding turned out to be a wonderful occasion and Bill, after much persuasion, made a moving and sensitive speech. I saw Debbie draw a deep breath as he got to his feet, obviously wondering what he was going to say, and as he sat down she hugged him and I could see the tears in her eyes.

After the wedding Bill established a reasonably friendly relationship with his new son-in-law, which relieved us both. The link between Bill and James was finally sealed when Debbie gave birth to Eleanor in Minneapolis. Debbie phoned us minutes after the birth, eager to share the news with us. We were overjoyed to have another granddaughter and immediately arranged to fly out and visit. I could not believe that I would live long enough to hold

Debbie's baby in my arms. I had never thought that I would see her married, let alone see her first child. Eleanor was a beautiful baby and reminded me so much of Debbie. I guessed Bill felt the same as he held her close and gazed into her eyes. We spent a quiet week with them, during which time Bill and Debbie were able to rebuild some of their former closeness.

We returned to England and Bill seemed more settled: so much so that when I was invited to India to attend the launch of the documentary *Village Voices – Forty Years of Rural Transformation in South India* (which was based on my own studies all those years ago) he encouraged me to accept. I was so excited, but at the same time was anxious as to whether Bill would be able to survive the nine days without me. I tried to shrug it off and let myself get caught up in the trip of a lifetime. I received VIP treatment wherever I went and was feted by federal ministers, senior administrators and the governor of Karnataka State. They all congratulated me on my groundbreaking work and claimed that it had made a significant contribution to India's development. I had to pinch myself to make sure that it was not just a dream. This was the pinnacle of my career and I was determined to enjoy it.

I had phoned Bill frequently while I was in India and he had assured me that he was fine. However, I started to worry when he kept asking me to promise him that I would continue my work without him. I tried to shrug it off, but when I returned home I could understand his words. He looked grey and shrivelled and I knew that my trip had taken it out of him. He suffered another serious angina attack and I went through my routine of phoning for the ambulance and waiting with him until it arrived.

It was exactly eleven days before we were due to fly to Australia for the winter and Bill insisted that I tell the doctors to get him well enough for the journey. I immediately had serious doubts about whether he would be well enough to travel. Having treated Bill on previous occasions the doctors reassured me that he should be all right again within a few days. Yet this time I didn't believe them: something seemed different, but I wasn't quite sure what. I refused to leave his bedside even when the doctors insisted that I went home to rest.

The next couple of days he seemed to stabilize and I started to wonder whether I had been wrong. I phoned Otto and told him we would be there as planned and began to pack in earnest. On the third day I turned up at the ward, confident that I would be taking him home that day. However, as soon as I entered the ward a nurse stopped me and put her arm round my shoulders. I could hardly speak and as she saw me struggle she quickly interjected and told me that Bill had suffered a major heart attack and the doctors were trying to save him.

I didn't know what to feel now that my worst nightmare was finally coming true. I thought I had had time to prepare myself for that moment, but I quickly realized that nothing I could have done would have made it any easier. The sister gently guided me into a private room where a doctor came soon after to ask me to sign a consent form for Bill to be given beta-blockers, which he explained could cause a stroke. I couldn't make a decision. I felt completely helpless and so alone. I needed to talk it over with Bill, but of course that was impossible. All I could think of was that my love, my husband, was now at death's door and that I wanted to die with him rather than to continue living without him. The doctor looked at me, waiting patiently for an answer, and the sister, seeing my inability to think or act, asked if I would like to call anyone. At first I could not think who to call – my brain felt like jelly – but then I remembered our GP, who had been a tower of strength over the last few years. Luckily I was put through immediately. He told me I had no choice: it was Bill's only chance. I signed the consent form and sat down heavily with my head in my hands.

I sat for what seemed like hours before I was allowed to see Bill. He was unconscious and breathing with the help of an oxygen mask. There were tubes attached to him in several places. I wanted to touch him and hold him, but I was scared to upset all the paraphernalia surrounding him. I willed him to wake up and could not believe that I might never hear his voice again, who would I confide in? Who would I share my triumphs with? Who would encourage me when everything seemed to be against me? I so needed him with me and could not imagine a life without him.

I followed the trolley as they transferred him to intensive care. At that moment Michelle arrived and I could finally let out the grief that I was feeling. We spent the next four days and nights at his bedside, leaving only to get something to eat. We both tried to talk to him, hoping that he could hear and understand us, but there was no response. During the long nights I lay with my head beside his and whispered all the things I should have said to him when he was well enough to hear me. I told him that I had always loved him and would never, never stop loving him. I told him how lucky I was to have shared my life with him and I thanked him for always having been my star, my guide. I repeated it over and over again, hoping at some level he would hear and understand.

I hoped against hope that our words would give him the strength he needed to fight back, but the doctors were pessimistic and said it was only a matter of days. I phoned Debbie daily, and when she heard the prognosis she decided to catch the next flight back. That afternoon Michelle and I had finally been persuaded by the doctors to take a break. We agreed that Michelle should go home to her family and when she returned I would go home for a shower and a rest. Neil drove me home and went shopping with the intention of collecting me later. As I turned the key in the lock I could hear the phone ringing. Fumbling anxiously, I managed to get into the flat in time to hear Michelle's voice on the answer-phone telling me to come back as quickly as possible, as Bill's condition had suddenly worsened. I had left my car at the hospital since Neil had driven me home and when I phoned the local taxi company they told me I would have to wait at least half an hour. I dashed outside in the hope of hailing a taxi and bumped into one of my neighbours who, when he saw how distraught I was, immediately offered me a lift. Michelle grabbed me as I raced into the ward and said that Bill had settled down again. I was relieved, but I wondered how long I would be able to survive this roller-coaster existence. I decided to phone Debbie before she boarded the plane to let her know Bill's present state. As I broke the news to her she sobbed that I must keep him alive for her: she had to see him again. I promised to do what I could, though I knew that it was not in my hands.

Michelle and I spent another long night by Bill's bedside, constantly checking to see if he was still breathing. We kept willing him to last the night and told him how Debbie would be arriving in the morning, which would do him the world of good, but there was no sign of acknowledgement. Neil had agreed with his children to fetch Debbie and family from the airport and to bring them all straight to the hospital. After the agonizing endurance-test on the flight, she arrived the next day, early on Sunday morning, desperate to know whether her father was still alive. I was very worried how Debbie would respond seeing her father at death's door, but as she entered the ward and Bill heard her voice he opened his eyes. I felt as if I was witnessing a miracle and Michelle and I looked at each other in utter amazement. The medical staff on duty rushed over to check him, but quickly moved away when they saw what was going on.

Debbie walked over to his bed and took his hand and he simply said, 'Debbie, my darling.' I could see her start to cry and I quickly brought little Eleanor round to present her to her grandfather. She sat on his bed and tried to play with the tubes, and he pronounced that she was a 'smasher'. He then asked for his grandchildren to gather round him and blessed each one of them before blessing the rest of us. Finally he reached for James's hand and squeezed it with whatever strength he had left, as if asking his forgiveness for all the pain he had caused him. He then pulled his mask off, shut his eyes and started to say *Kaddish* (the Jewish prayer for the dead) for himself. I knew that he was telling me that he had had enough and I ran out of the ward so that he could not see my distress.

It was so like Bill to think of everyone before himself and it must have taken every ounce in him to claw his way back to consciousness. I admired him then more than I had ever done before, for his strength of character and his unselfish love.

As Bill slipped back into his unconscious state the doctors arranged to move him into a single room to give us a chance to be together with him undisturbed during the last hours of his life. We made our way across the hospital and it felt like a funeral march. It was strange being in the side-room. In the bustling intensive care unit there had been a degree of hope, but now it was just a matter of waiting. The only break in the sombre atmosphere were the little gurgles from Eleanor as she played quietly in the corner. I could not help but think how close life and death were. And at that moment I knew that I needed to let go and let Bill die with the dignity he so deserved. The cardiologist arranged for all the various tubes and drips to be removed, and once Bill was propped up in bed he looked as if he were just sleeping. The rabbi arrived and sat with us and it was not long before his breathing eased and we heard him draw his last breath. A silence fell, as none of us knew what to say. I bent over him and told him once more: 'I love you with all my heart and I don't know how I shall be able to carry on living without you.'

As I sat there, I could not quite believe that he was no more. His death marked the end not only of 42 years of a happy and exciting marriage but also of a successful working partnership. I sat there completely numb.

Bill was buried on the day we were meant to fly to Australia. Instead he was setting out on a journey into the unknown, while I was left behind to mourn him. I was just grateful that he had left me the legacy of our children. We were united in our grief and leaned heavily upon each other as we prepared for the funeral and life beyond. I had no idea how much Bill had come to mean to both Neil and James, and was struck by their concern and need to be involved. I was particularly grateful for the concern both Neil and James showed for my distress.

After a few days Debbie and James had to return to America which made me feel more alone than ever. I found it extremely difficult to sleep in the bed that I had shared for so many years with Bill and kept waking reaching for him, only to remember that he was not there. This prompted Neil give me a spare key to their house saying: 'This is now your home too. Come and stay with us whenever you feel like it.' I was so touched and wished Bill could witness the goodness of the close and loving family he had left behind.

Slowly I began to adjust to life on my own, I had to adjust to shopping for myself and no longer had the routine of preparing Bill's meals. Often I found myself thinking I had to get back to him only to remember that he would not be waiting for me when I got home. I hated the evenings when I would sit in silence next to his empty chair and found myself rearranging the furniture at 3 a.m. to try to ease the pain. Friends whose husbands had been dead for many years tried to initiate me into the life of a widow, but I refused to consider myself as such, Bill was still with me and always would be.

# 17 • *Life after Death*

I tried to continue with my work, as I had promised Bill, but he had been so much part of the process that I found it almost impossible to go on without him. He had frequently been the inspiration behind my ideas and had always been the sounding-board for my plans. I desperately needed his advice and the benefit of his wisdom. I realized I had never told him all this when he was alive and was angry that the words came only after his death. I wanted to turn back the clock so that I could tell him how much I loved and appreciated him and how he had been my mentor.

I was not the only one who wanted to tell Bill how they felt about him: messages of condolence came flooding in, and a number of obituaries were published. I was surrounded by people wanting to share in my grief, but I did not want their company. I just wanted Bill back. I received many kind invitations from our colleagues, none of which I accepted simply because I felt I could not face them without losing my composure. I even received calls from one of my South Indian village friends who considered me as his 'mother'. When he heard that I now lived on my own he insisted that I should come to India and join his family where they would give me the loving care he considered I needed and deserved.

For the first time in my life I did not know how to fill my time and felt aimless. My work had lost its purpose and I spent my days reading and rereading the condolence messages, as if it would bring me closer to the man I had lost. I tried to talk to him but his silence only made it worse. I no longer had the energy to swim upstream, particularly if it meant doing it on my own.

My salvation came in the form of Ruby, Debbie's second and very difficult baby. I found someone who needed me unconditionally and who I could hold through the night. I sang to her and fed her and I recaptured some of the precious times I had had when Michelle and Debbie were babies. I managed to lose myself for the first time in months. However, when I returned home to my flat the emptiness was tangible and the need to escape overwhelming.

From then on I accepted every invitation and returned to the life of an academic nomad, giving lectures and seminars around the globe. I found that it was easier to spend time in hotels or staying with various people rather than being on my own in the flat. As long as I was away I could pretend that Bill would be waiting for me back in England. Each time I turned the key in the lock I let myself believe that he would be sitting in his chair waiting for me with a bouquet of flowers on the table.

In a single year I spent time in the Netherlands and Berlin, and taught a full term at the University of Papua New Guinea. I went to China and Laos for the first time, conducting consultancies, as well as Bulgaria and Nigeria. Each time I encountered the challenges that the different cultures posed I used to try to think what Bill would have suggested and I thanked my now silent mentor.

I found the project in Bulgaria particularly challenging, as I had been asked to conduct a training workshop that focused on 'Culturally Adapted Market Research and Social Marketing' for the Sofia Voluntary Centre for Independent Living. The centre had been established to help the disabled by providing them with a facility which would allow them to be as self sufficient and independent as possible. It was unlike any project I had undertaken before, and involved meeting young people with different kinds of disabilities, many of whom were confined to wheelchairs. Having been there for a few days I could not help but admire their tremendous courage and zest for life. It gave me a new sense of purpose and I realized how lucky I was. I had led a full life, with a loving husband and I therefore really had no reason to feel sorry for myself. I came away, my resolve strengthened and determined to continue devoting my expertise and efforts to helping improve the lives of at least some of the underprivileged of this world. I felt Bill smiling down on me and I felt better than I had done in ages.

One morning some months later, as I was sifting through my post I discovered a letter from the Jewish Welcome Service in Vienna inviting me to return to Vienna. I had vaguely heard of the organization and how they invited groups of refugees back to Austria, wanting to give them the opportunity to visit their birthplace once more. I had mixed feelings about the offer, but I was in desperate need of a break and at least I would not be on my own.

I flew to Vienna, wondering if I would know anyone in the group, but found that although all 40 refugees originated from Vienna, I did not recognize a single name. We were a strange bunch: a group of people with nothing more in common than a shared history, but it did not take us long to feel as if we had known each other for years. Everyone had a story to tell, many of which gave me nightmares as I was transported back to the days in Vienna when every knock at the door made us jump and every time we went out in the streets we were scared of being rounded up by the Nazis. I so much missed not having Bill's arms around me when I needed comforting.

On the first evening back in Vienna I wandered through the inner city expecting little to have changed. However, except for the major landmarks, I would have hardly recognized the city as my own. The *Kaffeehaus* (coffee shop) where Papa used to play cards was now a large clothes shop. All the traditional *Kaffeehäuser* seemed to have disappeared only to be replaced by the universal fast-food restaurants. I had expected to feel at home, but I could find nothing familiar in this new Vienna and I felt a stranger in a strange land. It was as if my time in Vienna was from an entirely different life and I had been reborn into a different existence altogether. I had hoped to find a sense of my roots, but I had great difficulty in establishing a link between my early years in Vienna and my subsequent life. I wanted to ask the man in the street where he had been and what he had been doing since the Anschluss, as there was no evidence that it had ever happened. I needed to know that it had been as traumatic for them as it had been for me, but I saw no signs.

I went to the Karl Marx Hof and the couple who lived in it allowed me to revisit our old apartment. It was now a smart flat restored to a glory it had never had. As I walked through the rooms I could see my mother at the kitchen sink and my brothers sitting reading at the table. The couple followed me around, obviously wondering why the place meant so much to me. I tried to explain that the flat had been my safe house and my prison, and our family home, all those years ago.

Before I had made the trip to Vienna I decided to reread my old journal in which I had recorded the hopes and fears of a 16-year-old girl. The entry for 23 July 1938, the day I left Vienna, read:

> Departure from Vienna into the Unknown. On the one hand I am really happy to have succeeded in securing our visas for Yugoslavia and that we can finally get out

> of Austria; on the other hand I am terribly upset about leaving Vienna under the present circumstances. Whatever happens to me I know I shall never, never want to return to this country where I have seen people discard their humanity completely and be ready to commit incredibly horrible atrocities.
>
> Last summer when I went with a group of young people to Paris and fell in love with Willie, I never thought for a moment that our lives would turn out like this. I would never have imagined then that the Austrian people could turn as nasty as they have done. Well, now I know better; I shall never be prepared to trust people again unless I know them personally very well. I wonder what happened to Willie? Yet I must stop myself from thinking about him, for I must continue to try to be alert and strong so as to be able to find a place for us where we can start a new and hopefully better life.

In the taxi, on the way to the railway station that fateful day, I looked for the last time at the city in which I had up until now spent my whole life and whispered: 'Farewell, Vienna. I shall never see you again!'

Yet here I was again, 65 years later. While I was in Vienna I was invited to give a lecture at the university: a place I had always considered as a holy shrine but had never gained entrance to. As I stood looking over the lectern I noted the irony that here I was being introduced as a professor and authority in my field to a student body that I had been denied from joining. I was glad that my lecture was warmly received and I left feeling that I had laid a ghost to rest.

The remainder of the week was packed with various outings and functions arranged by the Jewish Welcome Service. For most of them I felt like a tourist being shown round as if I had never been there before. But one evening we were taken to a *Heurigen* (wine bar) which immediately made me feel uncomfortable. They had laid on entertainers who soon had the whole bar singing and waving their tankards in time to the music. I felt the atmosphere closing in on me and I had to get out. As I pushed my way out I was suddenly overcome by fear, half expecting to see soldiers in Nazi uniforms. I felt physically sick. I wanted to shout: 'Has everyone gone mad? Has everyone forgotten what took place here?' I couldn't breathe and I made my way back to the hotel on my own; only in the peace of my room did I begin to calm down.

The next day a reception was being held in our honour at the Vienna town hall. I wondered what the deputy mayor would say and was feeling angry and frustrated. However, I was relieved to hear him apologize on behalf of the Austrian people for what we had gone through and thank us for having agreed to return to Vienna to give them the opportunity to demonstrate their remorse. He went on to say that they were doing everything possible to ensure that a Holocaust would never be allowed to happen again in Austria. I wanted to tell him that it was much too late for us. In a brief interview I made it clear to him that I may be able to forgive but I could never forget.

I often wondered what my life would have been like had I not been catapulted into adulthood by Hitler's arrival. Would I have become the medical doctor I dreamed of becoming? Would I have married Willie, my first love? But I am now 80 years old and I am trying to stop this endless questioning and concentrate on what has been and what will continue to be.

I celebrated my 80th birthday surrounded by friends and family from the many different stages and places in my life: from Ruskin College, India, Africa, Papua New Guinea, Manchester and Sussex. My two brothers, my two daughters and my four grandchildren all came to share the day with me. Messages came in from all over the world and I felt cherished and loved.

But now autumn has arrived and I sit and watch the leaves fall from the trees, heralding the decline of the year. It is symbolic of my own decline and I long for the spring and the renewed energy and growth. I think of death and its finality and I fear its closeness. I envy those with strong religious faith who have the comforting thought of an afterlife. But because God had forsaken me many years before, and because the prayers of so many were not answered, I feel religion can offer me no solace. So instead I stave off death by being ever busier. Friends and family think I am crazy as I work out at the gym every day. The staff welcome me warmly as one of their oldest members and it feels good that I am still breaking new ground. I continue to take on new projects. Everyone asks why don't I just put my feet up and enjoy myself. But they do not realize that swimming upstream is the only way I know.